Briefcase on Employment Law

Second Edition

Cavendish
Publishing
Limited

London • Sydney

Titles in the series:

Commercial Law
Company Law
Constitutional and Administrative Law
Contract Law
Criminal Law
Employment Law
Equity and Trusts
European Community Law
Evidence
Family Law
Land Law
Tort Law

Briefcase on Employment Law

Second Edition

Charles Barrow, BSc, LLM, Cert Ed, Barrister,
Senior Lecturer in Law, University of North London

John Duddington, LLB, Barrister,
Director of Legal Studies, Worcester Law School,
Worcester College of Technology

Cavendish
Publishing
Limited

London • Sydney

Second edition first published in Great Britain 2000 by Cavendish Publishing Limited, The Glass House, Wharton Street, London WC1X 9PX, United Kingdom

Telephone: +44 (0) 20 7278 8000   Facsimile: +44 (0) 20 7278 8080

E-mail: info@cavendishpublishing.com

Visit our Home Page on http://www.cavendishpublishing.com

© Barrow, C and Duddington, JG 2000

First edition   1998

Second edition   2000

British Library Cataloguing in Publication Data

Barrow, Charles
Briefcase on employment law – 2nd ed
1 Labour laws and legislation – Great Britain
I Title II Duddington, John G III Employment law
344.4'1'01

ISBN 1 85941 544 X

Printed and bound in Great Britain

Preface

The success of the Briefcase Series has shown that there is a need for books which give greater detail about cases than are found in textbooks, yet, at the same time, are more succinct than casebooks. We hope that we have achieved this aim with this particular addition to the Briefcase Series.

Employment law is very largely a creation of both statute and, increasingly, EC legislation; accordingly, it has been necessary to give greater extracts from legislative provisions than are found in some other books in this series. A collection of cases on employment law with nothing more would give a very misleading picture. We have also included some questions at various points, which are designed to stimulate thought and discussion.

Every preface to a book on employment law points out how quickly the subject is changing and we must do so here, both to protect ourselves against any charge of being dated and also to stimulate students into keeping up to date with new developments. For example, the preface to the first edition referred to the imminent publication of the White Paper, *Fairness at Work*, which has now resulted in the Employment Relations Act 1999. In addition, since the publication of the first edition in 1998, employment case law has developed considerably in virtually all of the areas covered by this book.

The great joy when writing a preface is the opportunity it gives to thank those without whose help a book would never have been written. John Duddington would like to thank his two children, Mary and Christopher, who have provided constant stimulation and necessary distraction and, above all, his wife, Anne, for her help and encouragement in this as well as in so many other projects over many years. Charles Barrow would like to thank Alan Robertshaw for his assistance in compiling Chapter 5.

It is finally necessary to add that, as is the case with all books written by co-authors, although we have each been responsible for separate chapters, we accept liability for the whole.

Charles Barrow
John Duddington
1 March 2000

Preface

Contents

Preface   v
Table of Cases   xi
Table of Statutes   xxxiii
Table of Statutory Instruments   xxxvii
Table of European Legislation   xxxix

1 Employee Status
   1.1   Statutory definitions   1
   1.2   Tests applied by the courts to determine
           whether a person is an employee or an
           independent contractor   4
   1.3   Rights of employees to be provided with a
           statement of initial employment particulars   11

2 Terms of the Contract of Employment
   2.1   Express terms   17
   2.2   Implied terms   17
   2.3   Duties of the employer and the employee   23
   2.4   Duty of mutual trust and confidence   39
   2.5   Doctrine of restraint of trade   42
   2.6   Changing the contract of employment   47
   2.7   Payment of wages   48

3 Health and Safety at Work
   3.1   Liability of the employer under the tort of negligence   53
   3.2   Health and Safety at Work Act 1974   59
   3.3   Working Time Regulations 1998   65

4 Terminating the Contract
   4.1   Termination not involving dismissal   67
   4.2   Termination by dismissal   78

5 Unfair Dismissal
   5.1   Establishing the reasons for dismissal   93
   5.2   Fairness of the dismissal   97
   5.3   Time limits   114

6   Redundancy

6.1	Definition of redundancy	119
6.2	Right to claim a redundancy payment	127
6.3	Offer of alternative employment	129
6.4	Redundancy procedures	131

7   Continuity of Employment and Transfer of Undertakings

7.1	Continuity of employment	137
7.2	Transfer of undertakings	143
7.3	The Transfer of Undertakings Regulations and 'contracting-out'	153
7.4	Transfers of undertakings and consultation	158

8   Equal Pay

8.1	Equal Pay Act 1970	161
8.2	European Community law	163
8.3	Meaning of 'like work', 'work rated as equivalent' and 'work of equal value'	165
8.4	Genuine material differences	170
8.5	Area of comparison	178
8.6	Meaning of 'pay' for the purpose of the Equal Pay Act 1970	180
8.7	Remedies	181

9   Discrimination

9.1	Direct discrimination	183
9.2	Indirect discrimination	187
9.3	Discrimination in employment	192
9.4	Exceptions	193
9.5	Vicarious liability and liability for the actions of a third party	195
9.6	Procedure and proof	197
9.7	Remedies	200
9.8	Discrimination and European Community law	202
9.9	Discrimination on grounds of sexual orientation	207
9.10	Disability Discrimination Act 1995	209

10   Trade Unions and their Members

10.1	Members' rights and the common law doctrines	215
10.2	Members' rights and the rule book	217
10.3	Members' rights and statutory control over discipline	224

11 Industrial Action
11.1 Civil liability – the economic torts   229
11.2 Inducing breach of contract   229
11.3 Interference with contract, trade or business   233
11.4 Intimidation   235
11.5 Conspiracy   236
11.6 Inducing breach of a statutory duty   238
11.7 Economic duress   240
11.8 Inducing breach of an equitable obligation   241
11.9 Trade union immunities – the Trade Union
      and Labour Relations (Consolidation) Act 1992   241
11.10 Loss of immunity – the Trade Union and
      Labour Relations (Consolidation) Act 1992   246

Glossary   257

Index   277

Table of Cases

ABP v TGWU [1989] IRLR 291 251
AM v WC and SPV [1999] IRLR 410...184
APAC v Kirvin Ltd [1978] IRLR 318 135
Abbey National v Formoso [1999] IRLR 222...206
Abdoulaye and Others v Regie Nationale
   des Usines Renault (1999) unreported 181
Abernethy v Matt, Hay and
   Anderson [1974] ICR 323 97
Adams v Derby City Council [1986] IRLR 163 96
Addis v Gramophone Co [1909] AC 488 ....40, 41
Alboni v Ind Coope Retail Ltd [1998] IRLR 131 95
Alcan Extrusions v Yates [1996] IRLR 327 81
Ali v Christian Salvesen Food Services Ltd
   [1997] 1 All ER 721; [1997] ICR 25 18
Allcock v Chief Constable of South Yorkshire Police
   [1992] AC 310 54
Allen v Flood [1898] AC 1 234
Allen and Others v Amalgamated
   Construction Co Ltd (1999) The Times, 10 December, ECJ 149
Amber Size and Chemical Co v Menzel [1913] 2 Ch 239 34
Anderson v Pringle of Scotland Ltd [1998] IRLR 64 21
Aparau v Iceland Frozen Foods plc [1996] IRLR 119................................87
Arnold v Beecham Group Limited [1982] IRLR 307................................167
Askew v Governing Body of Clifton Middle
   School and Others [1999] IRLR 708 149
Associated British Ports
   v TGWU [1989] IRLR 291; [1989] IRLR 399 ....240, 245
Associated Newspapers Group Ltd v Wade [1979] IRLR 201 239
Atkinson (Octavius) & Sons v Morris [1989] 111

BBC v Hearn [1977] IRLR 273 243
BBC v Ioannou [1975] ICR 267 82
BBC v Kelly-Phillips [1998] ICR 1; [1998] IRLR 294 82
BSG Property Services v Tuck [1996] IRLR 134......................................155
Baker v Cornwall County Council [1990] IRLR 194................................200
Balgobin v London Borough of Tower
   Hamlets [1987] IRLR 401 197

Bank of Credit and Commerce International
  v Ali (No 3) [1999] IRLR 508...40, 87, 88
Barber v Guardian Royal Exchange
  Assurance Group [1990] IRLR 240...180, 181
Barber v RJB Mining (UK) Ltd [1998] IRLR 308 65
Barclay v City of Glasgow
  District Council [1983] IRLR 313 69
Barretts and Baird v IPCS [1987] IRLR 3 239
Barry v Midland Bank plc
  [1999] 3 All ER 974; [1999] IRLR 581 177
Bartholomew v London Borough of
  Hackney [1999] IRLR 246 28
Bass Leisure Ltd v Thomas [1994] IRLR 104 121
Baynton v Saurus General Engineers [1999] IRLR 604 212
Bell v Lever Bros Ltd [1932] AC 161 31
Bentley Engineering Co Ltd v Crown [1976] IRLR 146 140
Bents Brewery Co Ltd v Hogan [1945] 2 All ER 570 243
Benveniste v University of Southampton [1989] IRLR 122 178
Bernadone v Pall Mall Services Group
  Ltd and Others [1999] IRLR 617...149
Berriman v Delabole Slate Ltd [1985] IRLR 305 151
Berwick Salmon Fisheries Co Ltd
  v Rutherford [1991] IRLR 203 140
Bhatt v Chelsea and Westminster
  Health Care Trust [1997] IRLR 660..82
Bilka-Kaufhaus GmbH v Weber von Hartz
  [1986] IRLR 317 ....172, 173, 177
Birmingham Midshires Building Society
  v Horton [1991] ICR 648 118
Blackall v National Union of Foundary
  Workers (1923) 39 TLR 431 218
Blyth v The Scottish Liberal Club [1983] IRLR 245..89
Bodha v Hampshire Area Health Authority [1982] ICR 200...........................115
Bonsor v Musicians' Union [1956] AC 104 217
Booth and Others v United States of
  America [1999] IRLR 16..141
Bork (P) International (In Liquidation) v Foreningen
  of Arbejdsledere [1989] IRLR 41...144, 150
Botzen v Rotterdamsche Droogdok
  Maatschappij BV [1985] ECR 519..148
Bowater v Rowley Regis Borough
  Council [1944] 1 All ER 465..59
Bracebridge Engineering Ltd v Darby [1990] IRLR 3 ....85, 184

Bradley v NALGO [1991] IRLR 159 226
Breach v Epsylon Industries Ltd [1976] IRLR 180 24
Breen v AEU [1971] 2 QB 175; 1 All ER 1148..216
Brimelow v Casson [1924] 1 Ch 302 233
British Coal Corp v Smith [1996] IRLR 404 179
British Fuels Ltd v Meade and Baxendale
    [1999] 2 AC 252; [1998] 4 All ER 609; [1998] IRLR 706 158
British Gas plc v McCarrick [1991] IRLR 305 99
British Home Stores Ltd v Burchell [1978] IRLR 379............................98, 99
British Labour Pump Co Ltd v Byrne [1979] IRLR 94 110
British Leyland (UK) Ltd v Ashraf [1978] IRLR 330 71
British Railways Board v Jackson [1994] IRLR 236 103
British Railways Board v NUR [1989] IRLR 349.....................................252
Bromley and Others
    v H & J Quick Ltd [1988] IRLR 249 167
Brooke Lane Finance Co v Bradley [1988] IRLR 283 150
Brown v Knowsley Borough Council [1986] IRLR 102 83
Brown v Merchant Ferries Ltd [1998] IRLR 682 ....41, 86
Brown v Rentokill Ltd [1998] IRLR 445 ....205, 206
Browning v Crumlin Valley
    Collieries Ltd [1926] 1 KB 522...23
Budgen & Co v Thomson [1976] IRLR 174 106
Burrett v West Birmingham
    Health Authority [1994] IRLR 7 185
Burroughs Machines Ltd
    v Timmoney [1977] IRLR 404 84
Burton v De Vere Hotels [1996] IRLR 596 196
Burton, Allton & Johnson Ltd
    v Peck [1975] IRLR 87; [1975] ICR 193...72
Buxton v Equinox Design Ltd [1999] IRLR 158.....................................209
Byrne v BOC Ltd [1992] IRLR 505..105

CBS Songs Ltd v Amstrad Electronics [1988] Ch 61 239
CRE v Dutton [1989] IRLR 8 186
Cadoux v Central Regional Council [1986] IRLR 131 21
Cain v Leeds Health Authority [1990] IRLR 168 102
Calder and Another v Rowntree Mackintosh
    Confectionery Ltd [1993] IRLR 212 ....167, 170
Calendonia Bureau Investment and Property
    v Caffrey [1998] ICR 603; [1998] IRLR 110 206
Caledonian Mining Co Ltd v Bassett [1987] IRLR 165.........................68
Camden and Islington Community Services
    NHS Trust v Kennedy [1996] IRLR 387...118

Campbell v Secretary of State
for Scotland [1992] IRLR 264 99
Capital Foods Retail Ltd v Corrigan [1993] IRLR 430 117
Capper Pass v Lawton [1976] IRLR 366 165
Carmichael v National Power plc [1999] 1 WLR 2042 8
Caruana v Manchester Airport plc [1996] IRLR 379 205
Cassidy v Minister of Health [1951] 2 KB 343...4, 5
Catamaran Cruisers Ltd v Williams [1994] IRLR 386...114
Chakki v United Yeast Co [1982] ICR 141 77
Chapman v Goonvean and Rostowrack
China Clay Co Ltd [1973] ICR 310 123
Chapman v Simon [1994] IRLR 124 200
Charles Early and Marriott (Witney) Ltd
v Smith and Ball [1977] IRLR 123 178
Chattopadhyay v Headmaster of
Holloway School [1981] IRLR 487 200
Cheall v APEX [1983] IRLR 213...216, 217
Chessington World of Adventures v Reed
[1997] IRLR 556 208
Chief Constable of Lincolnshire v Stubbs [1999] IRLR 81...195
Chubb Fire Security Ltd v Harper [1983] IRLR 311 ....112, 113
Clark v Civil Aviation Authority [1991] IRLR 412 105
Clark v Oxfordshire Health Authority [1998] IRLR 125 8
Clark v TDG Ltd [1999] IRLR 318 211
Clarke Chapman-John Thompson Ltd
v Walters [1972] ICR 83 142
Clarke v Chadburn [1984] IRLR 350...222
Clarke v Trimco Group Ltd [1993] IRLR 148...97, 106
Clarkes of Hove Ltd v Bakers Union [1978] ICR 1077 136
Clay Cross (Quarry Services) Ltd
v Fletcher [1979] IRLR 361...175
Clifford v Union of Democratic Mineworkers
[1991] IRLR 518 11
Coker and Osamor v Lord Chancellor [1999] IRLR 396 190
Collier v Sunday Referee Publishing Co Ltd [1940] 2 KB 647 23
Collison v BBC [1998] IRLR 238...141
Coltman v Bibby Tankers Ltd [1987] 3 All ER 1068 58
Commission of the European Communities
v United Kingdom [1982] IRLR 333 ....168, 169
Condor v Barron Knights Ltd [1966] 1 WLR 87 73
Connex South Eastern Ltd v RMT [1999] IRLR 249 251
Construction Industry Training Board
v Leighton [1978] IRLR 60...16

Cook v Thomas Linnell & Sons [1977] IRLR 132 108
Courtaulds Ltd v Andrew [1979] IRLR 84...84
Courtaulds Northern Spinning Ltd
  v Sibson and TGWU [1988] IRLR 305 17
Cowell v Quilter Goodison Co Ltd and QC
  Management Services Ltd [1989] IRLR 392 147
Cowen v Haden Ltd [1983] ICR 1 125–27
Crawford v Swinton Insurance Brokers Ltd [1990] IRLR 42 152
Credit Suisse First Boston (Europe) Ltd
  v Lister (1998) unreported...151
Cress v Royal London Insurance [1998] IRLR 245 ....81, 83
Cresswell v Board of Inland Revenue [1984] ICR 508 30
Crofter Handwoven Harris Tweed v Veitch [1942] AC 435 236
Cunard Co Ltd v Stacey [1955] 2 LR 247 238
Cuthbertson v AML Distributors [1975] IRLR 228...16

Davis Contractors Ltd v Fareham Urban
  District Council [1956] AC 696 74
Davies v Presbyterian Church of Wales [1986] IRLR 194 10
Davis v New England College of Arundel [1977] ICR 6 9
Dawkins v Department of the Environment
  [1993] IRLR 284 186
Day v T Pickles Farms Ltd [1999] IRLR 217 88
De Souza v Automobile Association [1986] ICR 514 192
De Souza v London Borough of Lambeth
  [1997] IRLR 677 202
Dedman v British Building and Engineering
  Appliances Ltd [1974] ICR 53 117
Dekker v VJV Centrum [1991] IRLR 27 204
Delaney v Staples [1992] IRLR 191 49
Denco v Joinson [1991] IRLR 63 ....90, 106
Devis (W) & Sons Ltd v Atkins [1977] AC 931 93–95
Devonald v Rosser & Sons [1906] 2 KB 728 23
Dimbleby & Sons v NUJ [1984] IRLR 67 233
Dimskal Shipping Co v ITWF [1990] IRLR 102..240
Dines and Others v Initial Health Care Services
  and Another [1994] IRLR 336 ....154, 157
Diocese of Hallam v Connaughton [1996] IRLR 505 165
Dixon v BBC [1979] IRLR 114..82
Dobie v Burns International Security
  Services (UK) Ltd [1984] IRLR 329 114
Doble v Firestone Tyre Co Ltd [1981] IRLR 300 80
Dryden v Greater Glasgow Health Board [1992] IRLR 469....................................18
Duffy v Yeomans & Partners [1994] IRLR 642..110

Dugdale v Krafts Foods Ltd [1976] IRLR 368 166
Duncan Web Offset (Maidstone) Ltd
    v Cooper [1995] IRLR 633 149

ECM (Vehicle Delivery Service) Ltd
    v Cox and Others [1999] IRLR 559..157
East Berkshire Health Authority
    v Matadeen [1992] IRLR 336 103
East Lindsey District Council
    v Daubney [1977] ICR 556; [1977] IRLR 187..107
East Sussex County Council v Walker [1972] ITR 280 67
Eaton Ltd v Nuttall [1977] IRLR 71..167
Eclipse Blinds Ltd v Wright [1992] IRLR 133 107
Edwards v National Coal Board [1949] 1 KB 704 60
Edwards v SOGAT [1971] Ch 354 ....215, 217
Edwards v Surrey Police [1999] IRLR 456 88
Egg Stores Ltd v Leibovici [1976] IRLR 376 ....74, 76
Eke v Commissioners of Customs
    and Excise [1981] IRLR 334 192
Ely v YKK Fasteners Ltd [1994] ICR 164 70
Emerald Construction Co Ltd
    v Lowthian [1966] 1 WLR 691...230
Enderby v Frenchay Health Authority [1993] IRLR 591 ....174, 176
Esterman v NALGO [1974] ICR 625 ....220, 221
Etam plc v Rowan [1989] IRLR 150 195
Evans v Elementa Holdings Ltd [1982] IRLR 143..113
Evesham v North Hertfordshire Health Authority
    and Secretary of State for Health [1999] IRLR 155 174
Express & Echo Publications Ltd v Tanton
    [1999] ICR 693; IRLR 369 6
Express Newspapers Ltd v Keys [1980] IRLR 247 244
Express Newspapers Ltd v MacShane [1979] ICR 210...242

FDR v Holloway [1995] IRLR 400 111
Faccenda Chicken Ltd v Fowler [1986] IRLR 69 33
Fairfield Ltd v Skinner [1992] IRLR 4 50
Falconer v ASLEF and NUR [1986] IRLR 331 231
Ferguson and Others v Prestwick Circuits Ltd
    [1992] IRLR 267 110
Ferguson v John Dawson and Partners
    (Contractors) Ltd [1976] 3 All ER 817 8
Fitzgerald v Hall Russell & Co Ltd [1969] 3 All ER 1140 139
Flack v Kodak Ltd [1986] IRLR 258...140

Ford v Warwickshire County Council [1983] IRLR 126 139–41
Foreningen af Arbejdsledere i Danmark
   v Daddy's Dance Hall [1998] IRLR 315..151
Forster v Suggett (1918) 35 TLR 87 42
Foster v British Gas [1990] IRLR 354; [1991] IRLR 268 204
Foss v Harbottle [1843] 69 ER 89..221, 222
Frames Snooker Centre v Boyce [1992] IRLR 472...102
Fransisco Hernandez Vidal SA
   v Gomez Perez and Others [1999] IRLR 132 157
French v Barclays Bank plc [1999] IRLR 4 41
Fuller v Lloyds Bank [1991] IRLR 336 106
Futty v D & D Brekkes Ltd [1974] IRLR 130 79

Gair v Bevan Harris Ltd [1983] IRLR 386 108
Garland v British Rail Engineering [1982] IRLR 111 181
Gascol Conversions v Mercer [1974] IRLR I55 15
General Billposting v Atkinson [1909] AC 118 47
General of the Salvation Army
   v Dewsbury [1984] ICR 498...138
Gibson v East Riding of Yorkshire Council
   [1999] ICR 622; IRLR 358 65
Gillespie v Northern Health and
   Social Services Board [1996] IRLR 214..181
Glasgow City Council v Smith [1987] IRLR 326 97
Glasgow City Council v Zafar [1998] IRLR 36 200
Goodwin v The Patent Office [1999] IRLR 4 209
Goring v British Actors Equity
   Association [1987] IRLR 122 216
Gouriet v UPW [1978] AC 435..238, 239
Governing Body of the Northern Ireland Hotel and
   Catering College v NATFHE [1995] IRLR 83 136
Grant v South West Trains Ltd [1998] IRLR 206 208
Greenaway Harrison Ltd v Wiles [1994] IRLR 380...87
Greenhall Whitley plc v Carr [1985] IRLR 290 95
Greenwood v British Airways plc [1999] IRLR 600 210
Greer v Sketchleys Ltd [1979] IRLR 445...44, 45
Grieg v Insole [1978] 1 WLR 302 216
Griffin v London Pension Fund
   Authority [1993] IRLR 248 180
Griffin v South West Water Services Ltd [1995] IRLR 15.......................................135
Grootcon (UK) Ltd v Keld [1984] IRLR 302 97
Gwynedd County Council v Jones [1986] ICR 833...186

HM Prison Service v Johnson [1997] ICR 275 201

Haddon v Van Den Bergh [1999] IRLR 672 ....99, 100, 101, 114

Hadjioannou v Coral Casinos Ltd [1981] IRLR 352 102

Hadmor Productions Ltd v Hamilton [1981] ICR 690 235

Halfpenny v Ige Medical Systems Ltd [1999] IRLR 177 ....80, 206

Hall (Inspector of Taxes) v Lorimer [1994] IRLR 171 ....5, 6

Hampson v Department of Education
    and Science [1989] ICR 179 190

Handels v Dansk Handel [1997] IRLR 643 ....

Handels-OG Kontorfunktionaerernes
    Foribund i Danmark v Dansk Arbejdsgiverforening
    (acting for Danfoss) [1989] IRLR 532..172

Hanley v Pease and Partners Ltd [1915] 1 KB 698 23

Hare v Murphy Brothers [1974] ICR 603 76–78

Harman v Flexible Lamps Ltd [1980] IRLR 418 75

Harrington v Kent County Council [1980] IRLR 353 77

Harvey v RG O'Dell Ltd [1958] 1 All ER 657 31

Haseltine Lake & Co v Dowler [1981] IRLR 25......................................80

Hayes v Malleable Working
    Men's Club [1985] IRLR 367 204

Hayward v Cammell Laird
    Shipbuilders Ltd [1988] IRLR 257 168

Hedley Byrne v Heller [1964] AC 465 28

Hellyer Brothers v Atkinson
    and Dickinson [1994] IRLR 88 68

Herbert Morris v Saxelby [1916] 1 AC 688 42

Heron v Citylink-Nottingham [1993] IRLR 372 110

Hertz v Aldi Marked K/S [1991] IRLR 31 ....204, 206

Hicking v Basford Group [1999] IRLR 764 182

High Table Ltd v Horst [1997] IRLR 513 121

Hill Ltd v Mooney [1981] IRLR 258 87

Hilton Hotels (UK) Ltd v Protopapa [1990] IRLR 316 86

Hilton Hotels Ltd v Kaissi [1994] IRLR 270...81

Hindes v Supersine Ltd [1979] ICR 517 130

Hindle v Percival Boats Ltd
    [1969] 1 WLR 174; [1969] 1 All ER 836 121

Hivac Ltd v Park Royal Scientific
    Instruments Ltd [1946] ICR 169 32

Hogg v Dover College [1990] ICR 39 81

Hollister v NFU [1979] ICR 542 114

Home Counties Dairies v Skilton [1970] 1 WLR 526 ....42, 44

Home Office v Holmes [1984] IRLR 299 188

Hong Kong Fir Shipping Co v Kawasaki
    Kischen Kaisha [1962] 2 QB 26 78

Hopkins v NUS [1985] IRLR 157 222
Horsey v Dyfed County Council [1982] IRLR 395 185
Hotson v Wisbech Conservative Club [1984] IRLR 422.............................96
Housing Services v Cragg [1997] IRLR 380 82
Hudson v Ridge Manufacturing Co Ltd [1957] 2 QB 348 54
Humber and Birch v University of Liverpool
    [1985] IRLR 165 72
Huntley v Thornton [1957] 1 WLR 321...237
Hurley v Mustoe [1981] ICR 490 185
Hussain v Elonex plc [1999] IRLR 417 106
Hussman Manufacturing v Weir [1998] IRLR 288 51

Iceland Frozen Foods v Jones [1982] IRLR 439 ....100, 101
Igbo v Johnson Matthey Ltd [1986] IRLR 215 71–73
Imperial Chemical Industries
    v Shatwell [1964] 2 All ER 999 59
Insitu Cleaning Co Ltd v Heads [1995] IRLR 4.......................................184
International Sports Ltd
    v Thomson [1980] IRLR 340 108
Ironmonger v Movefield Ltd [1988] IRLR 461 83
Irving v Post Office [1987] IRLR 289..195
Isle of Wight Tourist Board
    v Coombes [1976] IRLR 413 ....25, 87

J and J Stern v Simpson [1983] IRLR 52 79
Jack Allen (Sales and Services) Ltd
    v Smith [1999] IRLR 22 47
James v Eastleigh Borough Council [1990] IRLR 288..............................183
James v Hepworth & Grandage Ltd [1968] 1 QB 94 58
Jean Sorelle Ltd v Rybak [1991] IRLR 153 116
Jenkins v Kingsgate (Clothing Productions)
    Limited [1981] IRLR 228 171
John Brown Engineering Ltd v Brown [1997] IRLR 90............................111
Johnson v Nottinghamshire Combined Police
    Authority 1974] ICR 170 ....123, 124
Johnson v Peabody Trust [1996] IRLR 387..125
Johnson v Unisys Ltd [1999] ICR 809 41
Johnstone v Bloomsbury Area Health
    Authority [1991] IRLR 118 ....26, 30, 55
Jones v Associated Tunnelling Co Ltd [1981] IRLR 477...........................16
Jones v Mid Glamorgan County Council [1997] IRLR 685 68
Jones v Tower Boot Co Ltd
    [1997] IRLR 168; [1997] 2 All ER 406 195
Jones v University of Manchester [1993] IRLR 218 189

Katsikas v Konstantinidis [1993] IRLR 179 147
Kelman v Oram [1983] IRLR 432 114
Kenny v Hampshire Constabulary [1999] IRLR 76 213
Kenny v South London Manchester
    College [1993] IRLR 265...156, 157
Kent County Council v Gilham [1985] IRLR 18 114
Kent Management Services Ltd
    v Butterfield [1992] IRLR 394 50
King v Eaton Ltd [1996] IRLR 116 111
King v Great Britain China Centre [1991] IRLR 513................................198
Kuickly Shrive [1999] IRLR 55 207
Kwik Fit (GB) Ltd v Lineham [1992] IRLR 156 69

Langston v Amalgamated Union of Engineering
    Workers (No 1) [1974] 1 All ER 980 24
Langston v Amalgamated Union of Engineering
    Workers (No 2) [1974] IRLR 182...24
Lasertop Ltd v Webster [1997] IRLR 498 195
Lassman and Others v Secretary of State for
    Trade and Industry (1999) unreported 141
Latimer v AEC Ltd [1953] 2 All ER 449 ....55, 61
Law Debenture Trust Corp v Ural Caspian Oil
    Corp Ltd [1993] 1 WLR 138...241
Lawrence and Others v Regent Office Care Ltd
    and Others [1999] ICR 654; IRLR 148 180
Laws v London Chronicle [1959] 1 WLR 698 88
Ledernes Hovedorganisation (acting for Rygaard)
    v Dansk Arbejdsgiverforening (acting for Stro
    Molle Akustik A/S) [1996] IRLR 51 ....155, 156
Lee v Chung and Shun Sing Construction and
    Engineering Co Ltd [1990] IRLR 236...9, 10
Lee v Showmen's Guild [1952] 2 QB 329 219
Leicester University v A [1999] IRLR 352 184
Leicester University Students' Union
    v Mahomed [1995] ICR 270...200
Leigh v NUR [1970] Ch 326 219
Lesney Products & Co Ltd v Nolan [1977] IRLR 77.........................123, 124
Leverton v Clwyd County Council [1989] IRLR 28 ....178, 179
Levez v TH Jennings (Harlow Pools) Ltd [1999] IRLR 36....................182
Lewis v Motorworld Garages Ltd [1985] IRLR 465 85
Lewis Woolf Ltd v Corfield [1997] IRLR 432 206
Links (A) & Co v Rose Ltd [1991] IRLR 353 108
Lister v Romford Ice and Cold Storage Co Ltd
    [1957] 1 All ER 125 30

Litster v Forth Dry Dock and Engineering Co Ltd
  [1989] IRLR 161 ....149, 150, 205
Littlewoods v Harris [1977] 1 WLR 1472 ....43, 45
Lloyd v Brassey [1969] 1 All ER 382 143
Lloyd v Taylor Woodrow Construction [1999] IRLR 782 111
Lloyds Bank v Secretary of State for Employment
  [1979] IRLR 41 ....140, 141
Lock v Cardiff Railway Co Ltd [1998] IRLR 358..103, 106
Logan Saltan v Durham County Council [1989] IRLR 99 72
London Borough of Lambeth v CRE [1990] IRLR 231 194
London Fire and Civil Defence Authority
  v Betty [1994] IRLR 384 108
London International College v Sen [1992] IRLR 292 116
London Transport Executive v Clarke [1981] IRLR 166.....................................70, 81
London Underground Ltd v Edwards [1998] IRLR 364 189
London Underground v Noel [1999] IRLR 621 118
London Underground Ltd v NUR [1989] IRLR 341 251
London Underground v RMT [1995] IRLR 636...252
Longley v NUJ [1987] IRLR 109..221
Lonhro Ltd v Shell [1982] AC 173 239
Lonhro v Fayed [1991] 3 All ER 303 237
Loughran and Kelly v Northern Ireland Housing
  Executive [1998] IRLR 593...2
Lovie Ltd v Anderson [1999] IRLR 164 99
Lynock v Cereal Packaging Ltd [1988] IRLR 510 108

McMeechan v Secretary of State for Employment
  [1995] IRLR 461 10
McAlwane v Boughton Estates [1973] ICR 470..71
Macari v Celtic Football and Athletic Co Ltd
  [1999] IRLR 787 41
Macarthys Ltd v Smith [1980] ICR 672..164
McCory v Magee [1983] IRLR 414...97
McGrath v Rank Leisure Ltd [1985] IRLR 323 152
McInnes v Onslow Fare [1978] 1 WLR 1520 216
MacLelland v NUJ [1975] ICR 116...219
McNeil v Charles Grimm Ltd [1984] IRLR 179 87
McVitae v Unison [1996] IRLR 33 219
Machine Tool Industry Association
  v Simpson [1988] IRLR 212 115
Maidment v Cooper Co (Birmingham) Ltd
  [1978] IRLR 462 167
Malik v Bank of Credit and Commerce International
  SA (In Liquidation) [1997] 3 All ER 1 39–41

Mandla v Lee [1983] IRLR 209 186
Market Investigations v Minister of Social
   Security [1969] 2 QB 173 ....5, 9
Marleasing SA v La Comercial Internacional de
   Alimentacion [1992] 1 CLMR 305 205
Marley (UK) Ltd v Anderson [1994] IRLR 152 115
Marley v Forward Trust Group Ltd [1986] IRLR 369 21
Marriot v Oxford Co-op Society [1970] 1 QB 186 84
Marshall v Harland Woolf [1972] ICR 101 74
Marshall v Southampton and South West Hampshire
   Area Health Authority [1986] 1 IRLR 140 ....164, 203
Marshall v Southampton and South West Hampshire
   Health Authority (No 2) [1994] IRLR 445 202
Martin v MBS Fastening Ltd [1983] IRLR 198 68
Mason v Provident Clothing and
   Supply Co Ltd [1913] AC 724 42
Massey v Crown Life Assurance Co [1978] 1 WLR 676 9
Meade v Haringey Borough Council [1979] 2 All ER 1016 239
Meade-Hill v British Council [1995] IRLR 478 190
Medhurst v NALGO [1990] ICR 687 226
Meer v London Borough of Tower Hamlets [1988] IRLR 399 189
Melon v Hector Powe Ltd [1980] IRLR 477 143
Merckx and Neuhuys v Ford Motor Co Belgium
   [1996] IRLR 467 156
Merckx v Ford [1996] IRLR 499 ....
Mercury Communications
   v Scott-Garner [1983] IRLR 494 244
Merkur Island Shipping Corp
   v Laughton [1983] IRLR 218 ....230, 234
Metall und Rohstoff AG
   v Donaldson Inc [1989] 3 All ER 14 241
Michael Peters Ltd v Farnfield [1995] IRLR 190 148
Miles v Wakefield Metropolitan District Council
   [1987] IRLR 193 22
Millbrook Ltd v McIntosh [1981] IRLR 309 87
Ministry of Defence v Cannock [1994] IRLR 509 202
Mitchell v Arkwood Plastics (Engineering) Ltd
   [1993] IRLR 471 108
Mogul Steamship Co v McGregor, Gow & Co
   [1898] QB 598 236
Monie v Coral Racing Ltd [1981] ICR 109 94
Monsanto plc v TGWU [1986] IRLR 406 253
Moon v Homeworthy Furniture
   (Northern) Ltd [1977] ICR 177 119

Morley v CT Morley Ltd [1985] ICR 499 72
Morris Angel Ltd v Hollande [1993] IRLR 169 150
Morrish v Henlys (Folkestone) Ltd
    [1973] ICR 482; [1973] 2 All ER 137 29
Morse v Wiltshire County Council [1998] IRLR 352 213
Mugford v Midland Bank plc [1997] IRLR 208 111
Murray and Another v Foyle Meats Ltd [1999] ICR 827 ....126, 127

NAAFI v Varley [1977] 1 WLR 149 171
NACODS v Gluchowski [1996] IRLR 252 228
NALGO v Killorn [1990] IRLR 462 226
Nagle v Fielden [1966] 2 QB 633 ....215, 216
Nagarajan v London Regional Transport [1999] IRLR 572 198
National Coal Board v Galley [1958] 1 WLR 16 20
National Coal Board v Sherwin [1978] IRLR 122 166
National Vulcan Engineering Group Ltd
    v Wade [1978] ICR 800; [1978] IRLR 25..171, 172
Neary v Dean of Westminster [1999] IRLR 288...91
Nelson v BBC [1977] ICR 649; [1979] IRLR 346..126
Nethermere (St Neots) Ltd v Taverna and
    Gardiner [1984] IRLR 240 7
Newham Borough Council v NALGO [1993] ICR 189 252
Nimz v Freie und Hansestadt Hamburge
    [1991] IRLR 222..172
Nokes v Doncaster Amalgamated Colleries Ltd
    [1940] AC 1014 143
Noone v North West Thames Regional Health
    Authority [1988] IRLR 195 200
Nordenfelt v Maxim Nordenfelt Guns and
    Ammunition Co Ltd [1894] AC 535..42
Norris v Southampton City
    Council [1982] IRLR 141 77
North Riding Garages Ltd v Butterwick [1967] 2 QB 56 122
Northern Joint Police Board v Power [1997] IRLR 610 186
Notcutt v Universal Equipment Co [1986] IRLR 218 75

O'Brien v Associated Fire Alarms Ltd
    [1968] 1 WLR 1916; [1969] 1 All ER 93 120
O'Kelly and Others v Trusthouse
    Forte plc [1983] IRLR 369 7
O'Neill v Governors of St Thomas More
    School [1996] IRLR 372 197
O'Neill v Simm & Co Ltd [1998] IRLR 233 209

Oakley v Labour Party [1988] IRLR 34 114
Orlando v Didcot Power Station Sports and
    Social Club [1996] IRLR 262 202
Ottoman Bank v Chakarian [1930] AC 277 29
Owen and Briggs v James [1982] IRLR 502 187

P v Nottinghamshire County Council [1992] IRLR 362 99
P v S and Cornwall County Council [1996] IRLR 347 ....207, 208
Palmer and Another v Southend-on-Sea
    Borough Council [1984] IRLR 119 115
Pape v Cumbria County Council [1991] IRLR 463 ....56, 57
Paris v Stepney Borough Council [1951] 1 All ER 42 56
Parr v Whitbread plc [1990] IRLR 39 103
Partington v NALGO [1981] IRLR 537 221
Paton Calvert and Co Ltd
    v Westerside [1979] IRLR 108 130
Paul v East Surrey District Health
    Authority [1995] IRLR 305 102
Pearse v Bradford Metropolitan
    Council [1988] IRLR 379 188
Pepper v Webb [1969] 2 All ER 216 ....84, 89
Perera v Civil Service Commission [1982] IRLR 147 191
Philip Hodges Ltd v Kell [1994] IRLR 568 97
Pickford v ICI plc [1998] IRLR 435 57
Pickstone and Others v Freemans plc [1988] IRLR 357 169
Piggott Brothers & Co v Jackson [1991] IRLR 309 103
Polkey v AE Dayton Services Ltd
    [1987] IRLR 503; [1988] ICR 142 ....110, 132
Porcelli v Strathclyde Regional Council [1986] ICR 564 184
Porter v NUJ [1980] IRLR 404 221
Post Office v Fennell [1981] IRLR 221 102
Post Office v Mughal [1977] IRLR 178 108
Post Office v Roberts [1980] ICR 347 ....25, 87
Post Office v UCW [1990] IRLR 143 ....251, 253
Poussard v Spiers [1876] 1 QB 410 73
Premier Motors (Medway) Limited v Total Oil Great
    Britain Limited [1984] 1 WLR 377 145
Price v Civil Service Commission [1978] IRLR 3 188
Proctor v British Gypsum Ltd [1992] IRLR 7 102
Prudential Assurance Co v Lorenz (1971) 11 KIR 78 241
Pulmanor Ltd v Cedron [1978] IRLR 303 87

Quinn v Leathem [1901] AC 495 236
Qureshi v London Borough of
    Newham [1991] IRLR 264 199

R v Associated Octel Co Ltd [1996] 4 All ER 846 61
R v Attorney General for Northern Ireland ex p
    Burns [1999] IRLR 315 65
R v Birmingham City Council ex p
    EOC [1989] IRLR 173 197
R v British Coal Corp ex p Vardy [1993] IRLR 103.................................135
R v British Steel plc [1995] IRLR 311..62
R v Board of Trustees of the Science
    Museum [1993] IRLR 853 62
R v F Howe & Son (Engineers) Ltd [1999] IRLR 434 64
R v Jockey Club ex p Ram Racecourses
    Ltd [1993] 2 All ER 225 216
R v Ministry of Defence ex p Smith [1996] IRLR 100..............................207
R v Secretary of State for Defence ex p
    Perkins [1997] IRLR 297..208
R v Secretary of State for Employment ex p Equal
    Opportunities Commission and Another
    [1994] IRLR 176 173
R v Secretary of State for Employment ex p Seymour
    Smith [1995] IRLR 465 ....173, 189
RMC Roadstone Products Ltd v Jester [1994] IRLR 330 61
RS Components Ltd v RE Irwin [1973] IRLR 239 112
RSPCA v Cruden [1986] IRLR 83 106
Radford v NATSOPA [1972] ICR 484 ....220, 223
Rainey v Greater Glasgow Health
    Board [1987] IRLR 26 ....175, 176
Rask v Christensen v ISS Kantineservice A/S
    [1993] IRLR 133 153
Ratcliffe v North Yorkshire County
    Council [1995] IRLR 439 ....177, 180
Reading v Attorney General [1951] 1 All ER 517 35
Ready Mixed Concrete (South East) Ltd v Minister
    of Pensions and National Insurance [1968] 2 QB 497 ....6, 9
Redmond Stichting (Dr Sophie) v Bartol [1992] IRLR 366 ....144, 154
Reed & Bull Information Systems Ltd
    v Stedman [1999] IRLR 299 184
Rees v Apollo Watch Repairs [1996] ICR 466 206
Reid and Sigrist Ltd v Moss and
    Mechanism Ltd [1932] 49 RPC 461 34
Reid v Camphill Engravers [1990] IRLR 268 87

Reid v Rush and Tomkins Group plc [1989] IRLR 265 58

Reiss Engineering Co Ltd v Harris [1988] IRLR 232 39

Retarded Children's Society Ltd v Day [1978] IRLR 128 106

Richmond Precision Engineering Ltd
v Pearce [1985] IRLR 179 ....113, 114

Riley v Tesco Stores Ltd [1980] IRLR 103 116

Robb v Green [1895] 2 QB 315 33

Roberts v Birds Eye Walls Ltd [1994] IRLR 29 181

Robertson v British Gas Corp [1983] IRLR 302 16

Robson v Commissioners of Inland
Revenue [1998] IRLR 186...200

Robinson v British Island Airways Ltd
[1977] IRLR 477; [1978] ICR 304 ....124, 125

Robinson v Crompton Parkinson Ltd [1978] ICR 401 ....25, 87

Robinson v Ulster Carpets [1991] IRLR 348 111

Rock Refrigeration Ltd v Jones and
Another [1997] 1 All ER 1 47

Roebuck v NUM (Yorkshire Area) (No 2)
[1978] ICR 678 223

Rolls Royce Motor Cars Ltd v Price [1993] IRLR 203 111

Rookes v Barnard [1964] AC 1129 ....235, 237

Royal Naval School v Hughes [1979] IRLR 383 106

Royal Society for the Protection of Birds
v Croucher [1984] IRLR 423 98

Ryan v Shipboard Maintenance Ltd [1980] IRLR 16 83

ST v North Yorkshire County Council [1999] IRLR 98 195

Safeway Stores plc v Burrell [1997] IRLR 200 127

Sagar v Ridehalgh & Son Ltd [1931] 1 Ch 310 18

St Basil's Centre v McCrossan [1991] IRLR 455...117

St John of God (Care Service) Ltd v Brooks [1992] IRLR 346 114

Sanchez Hidalgo and Others v Asociacion de
Servicios Aser and Sociedad Cooperativa
Minerva [1999] IRLR 136..157

Sanders v Ernest A Neale Ltd [1974] ICR 565...128

Sartar v P & O European Ferries [1992] IRLR 211 104

Saunders v Richmond Upon Thames Borough
Council [1977] IRLR 362 193

Scally and Others v Southern Health and Social
Services Board [1991] IRLR 522 ....25, 39

Schmidt v Austicks Bookshop [1978] ICR 85 185

Schmidt v Spar- und Leihkasse der früheren Ämter
Bordesholm [1994] IRLR 302...154–58

Schroeder (A) Music Publishing Co Ltd
   v Macaulay [1974] 3 All ER 616 46
Schultz v Esso Petroleum Co Ltd [1999] IRLR 488 118
Scorer v Seymour-Johns [1966] 3 All ER 347 46
Scott v Avery (1856) 5 HL Cas 811 219
Scott v Coalite Fuels Ltd [1988] IRLR 131 72
Scott v Formica Ltd [1975] IRLR 104...67
Scottish Midland Co-op Society Ltd
   v Cullion (1991) IRLR 26 99
Scully UK Ltd v Lee [1998] IRLR 259 44
Secretary of State for Employment
   v ASLEF (No 2) [1972] 2 QB 455 ....18, 32
Secretary of State for Employment
   v Cohen [1987] IRLR 169 138
Secretary of State for Employment
   v Spence [1986] IRLR 248 150
Seide v Gillette Industries [1980] IRLR 427 186
Sen v International College [1993] IRLR 7 116
Shawkat v Nottingham City Hospitals
   NHS Trust [1999] IRLR 340 127
Sheffield v Oxford Controls Co Ltd [1979] IRLR 133................................67
Shepherd (FC) & Co Ltd v Jerrom [1986] IRLR 358 78
Sheriff v Klyne Tugs [1999] IRLR 481 57
Sherrard v AUEW [1973] ICR 421 243
Shields v E Coomes Holdings Ltd [1978] IRLR 263 165
Shirlaw v Southern Foundries [1939] 2 KB 206..17
Sidhu v Aerospace Composite Technology Ltd
   [1999] IRLR 683 197
Silvester v National Union of Printing, Bookbinding
   and Paper Workers [1966] 1 KIR 679 218
Simmons v Hoover Ltd [1977] ICR 61 129
Sinclair v Neighbour [1967] 2 QB 279...90
Sisley v Britannia Security Systems [1983] IRLR 404 195
Skyrail Oceanic Ltd v Coleman [1981] IRLR 398 185
Slater v Leicestershire Health Authority [1989] IRLR 16........................106
Smith v Safeway plc [1996] IRLR 456 185
Snowball v Gardner Merchant [1987] IRLR 397 184
Snoxell v Vauxhall Motors Ltd [1977] IRLR 123 ....176, 177
Sothern v Franks Charlesly & Co [1981] IRLR 278....................................69
South Wales Miners' Federation
   v Glamorgan Coal Co [1903] 2 KB 545 233
Sovereign House Security Services Ltd
   v Savage [1989] IRLR 115 70

Spencer v Gloucestershire County Council
[1985] IRLR 393 130
Spencer v Paragon Wallpapers Ltd [1976] IRLR 373 106
Spijkers v Gebroeders Benedik Abbatoir CV
[1986] ECR 1119 ....145, 153,
154, 157, 158
Spink v Express Food Group Ltd [1990] IRLR 320................................106
Spring v Guardian Assurance plc
[1994] 3 All ER 129; [1994] IRLR 460 ....27, 39
Square D Ltd v Cook [1992] IRLR 34 53
Square Grip Reinforcement Co Ltd
v MacDonald 1968 SLT 65..232
Staffordshire County Council
v Donovan [1981] IRLR 108 68
Standard Telephone v Yates [1981] IRLR 21 130
Stapley v Gypsum Mines Ltd [1953] 2 All ER 478 59
Stevenson Jordan and Harrison Ltd
v McDonald and Evans [1952] 1 TLR 101................................4
Stewart v Cleveland Guest (Engineering)
Ltd [1994] IRLR 440 184
Stoker v Lancashire County Council [1992] IRLR 75 106
Strathclyde Regional Council
v Wallace and Others [1998] 1 WLR 259 172
Sunley Turriff Holdings Ltd
v Thompson [1995] IRLR 184 148
Sutton and Gates v Boxall [1978] IRLR 486 108
Suzen v Zehnacker Gebaudereinigung GmbH
Krankenhausservice [1997] IRLR 255 ....156, 157
Sweeney v J & S Henderson (Concessions)
Ltd [1999] IRLR 306 141
Sybron Corp v Rochem [1983] IRLR 253 31
Systems Floors (UK) Ltd v Daniel [1981] IRLR 475 ....15, 16

TGWU v Webber [1990] IRLR 462...226
TSC Europe (UK) Ltd v Massey [1999] IRLR 22 45
Taff Vale Railway Co v ASRS [1901] AC 426..218
Tanks and Drum Ltd v TGWU [1991] IRLR 372 254
Tanner v DT Kean Ltd [1978] IRLR 110 79
Tarling v Wisdom Toothbrushes (1997) unreported................................213
Taylor and Foulstone v NUM (Yorkshire Area)
[1984] IRLR 445 222
Taylor v Alidair Ltd [1978] IRLR 82 108
Taylor v Kent County Council [1969] 2 QB 560 129

Taylor v National Union of Seamen
[1967] 1 All ER 767 223
Taylor v NUM (Derbyshire Area) (No 1) [1984] IRLR 440 221
Taylor v NUM (Derbyshire Area) (No 3) [1985] IRLR 99 221
Taylor v Secretary of State for Scotland [1999] IRLR 362 19
Thibault [1998] IRLR 399 206
Thomas v National Coal Board [1987] IRLR 451 ....166, 167
Thomas Wragg & Sons Ltd v Wood [1976] ICR 313 130
Thomson (DC) & Co Ltd v Deakin [1952] Ch 646 ....229, 232
Thomson v Alloa Motor Co Ltd
[1983] IRLR 403 97
Ticehurst v British Telecommunications plc
[1992] IRLR 219 32
Timex Corp v Thomson [1981] IRLR 522 95
Torquay Hotel Co Ltd v Cousins [1969] 2 Ch 106 ....231, 233–35
Tottenham Green Under Fives Centre
v Marshall [1989] IRLR 147 194
Tower Hamlets Health Authority
v Anthony [1988] IRLR 331 103
Treganowan v Knee & Co [1975] IRLR 113 114
Trico-Folberth Ltd v Devonshire [1989] IRLR 396 97
Tunnel Holdings Ltd v Woolf [1976] ICR 307 80
Turley v Allders Department Stores Ltd [1980] IRLR 4...204
Turner v London Transport Executive [1977] ICR 952..84

Ulsterbus Ltd v Henderson [1989] IRLR 251 106
Union Traffic Ltd v TGWU [1989] IRLR 127 232
United Bank v Akhatar [1989] IRLR 507 87
United Distillers v Conlin [1992] IRLR 503 101
United Kingdom Atomic Energy Authority
v Claydon [1974] ICR 128 120
Universe Tankships Inc of Monrovia
v ITWF [1982] IRLR 200..240
University College London NHS Trust
v Unison [1999] ICR 204; [1999] IRLR 31, CA 246
University of Nottingham v (1) Eyett (2) The
Pensions Ombudsmen
[1999] 2 All ER 437; [1999] IRLR 87 41

Vaux and Associated Breweries Ltd
v Ward [1968] 3 ITR 385..122
Vicary v British Telecommunications plc
[1999] IRLR 680 210

Villella v MFI Furniture Centres Ltd
  [1999] IRLR 469 76
Vokes Ltd v Bear [1974] ICR 1 111
Vokes Ltd v Heather [1945] 62 RPC 131...33

Wakeman v Quick Corp [1999] IRLR 424 187
Walker v Crystal Palace Football Club [1910] 1 KB 87..4, 5
Walker (JH) v Hussain [1996] IRLR 11 202
Walker v Northumberland County Council
  [1995] IRLR 35..54, 55
Wall's Meat Co v Khan [1979] ICR 52...117
Walmsley v Udec Refrigeration Ltd [1972] IRLR 80...30
Waltons and Morse v Dorrington [1997] IRLR 488 ....27, 87
Wandsworth London Borough Council
  v D'Silva and Another [1998] IRLR 193 ....19, 47
Wandsworth London Borough Council
  v NAS/UWT [1993] IRLR 344 245
Warner Holidays Ltd v Secretary of State for
  Social Services [1983] ICR 440 5
Warnes v Cheriton Oddfellows Social Club
  [1993] IRLR 58 87
Waters v Commissioner of Police of the
  Metropolis [1997] IRLR 589...195
Weathersfield v Sargent [1999] IRLR 94 ....88, 187
Webb v EMO Air Cargo (UK) Ltd
  [1994] IRLR 482 ....203, 204
Webb v EMO Air Cargo (UK) Ltd (No 2)
  [1995] ICR 1021 205
Wessex Dairies Ltd v Smith [1935] 2 KB 80 33
West Midlands Co-operative Society Ltd
  v Tipton [1986] IRLR 119 94
West Midlands Transport Executive
  v Singh [1988] IRLR 186...198
Western Excavating (ECC) Ltd
  v Sharp [1978] 1 All ER 71; [1978] QB 761 ....84, 87
Westminster County Council v Cabaj [1996] IRLR 399 106
Wetherall Ltd v Lynn [1978] 1 WLR 200 84
Whitbread & Co plc v Mills [1988] IRLR 501 ....95, 104, 105
Whitbread plc v Thomas [1988] IRLR 43 103
White v Kuzych [1951] AC 585 222–23
White v Reflecting Roadstuds Ltd [1991] IRLR 331 87
White and Others v Chief Constable of
  South Yorkshire Police and Others
  [1999] 1 All ER 1; [1999] IRLR 110 54

Whitehouse v Chas A Blatchford & Sons Ltd [1999] IRLR 492 152
Williams and Clyde Coal Co Ltd v English [1938] AC 57..53
Williams v Compair Maxam Ltd
  [1982] IRLR 83; [1982] ICR 156 ....109, 131
Williams v Watsons Coaches [1990] IRLR 164...76
Wilson v Racher [1974] ICR 428; [1974] IRLR 114..89
Wilson v Ethicon [2000] IRLR 4 ....100, 101, 114
Wilson and Others v St Helens Borough Council
  [1998] IRLR 706; [1998] 4 All ER 609 158
Wiltshire County Council v NATFHE and Guy
  [1980] IRLR 198 82
Wiluszynski v London Borough of
  Tower Hamlets [1989] IRLR 259..22
Withers v Flackwell Heath Football
  Supporters Club [1981] IRLR 307 5
Withers v Perry Chain Co Ltd
  [1961] 3 All ER 676 ....56, 57
Woodhouse v Peter Brotherhood Ltd
  [1972] 3 All ER 91 ....142, 145
Wood v William Ball Ltd [1999] IRLR 773 170
Woods v WM Car Services (Peterborough) Ltd
  [1981] IRLR 347; [1982] IRLR 413...25, 87
Wren v Eastbourne Borough Council [1993] ICR 955 ....156, 157

X (A Minor) v Bedfordshire County Council
  [1995] 3 All ER 353 239

Yewens v Noakes [1880] 6 QBD 530 4

Table of Statutes

Coal Mines Act 1911
   s 102(8) 60
Companies Act 1939
   s 129 143

Disability Discrimination
   Act 1995 ....209–11, 214
   s 1 209
   ss 2, 4 210
   s 5 211
   s 5(2) 213
   s 5(3) 212
   s 6 211–13
   s 7 213
   ss 55–58 214
   s 68 2
   Sched 1 209
   Sched 2 210
Disability Rights
   Commission Act 1999 214

Education Act 1944 239
Education Reform
   Act 1988 245
Employer's Liability
   (Defective Equipment)
   Act 1969
   s 1 58
Employment Act 1980 242
Employment
   Protection
   (Consolidation)
   Act 1978 75
   s 1 8
   s 140 71

Employment
   Relations Act 1999 ....20, 252
   s 17 20
Employment Rights
   Act 1996 ....50, 75,
                   127, 137
   s 1 ....8, 11–14
   s 1(1) 16
   s 1(3), (4) 13
   s 1(4)(e)–(j) 12
   s 1(4)(f) 30
   s 1(5) 12
   ss 2–4 14
   s 2 12
   s 2(3)–(6) 13
   s 2(4) 11
   s 3 ....13, 14
   ss 4–7 14
   ss 8, 9 48
   s 11(1) 16
   s 13 ....48, 50, 51
   s 13(3)–(7) 49
   s 14 50
   s 14(4)–(6) 51
   ss 23–26 51
   s 23 3
   s 27 49
   s 27(1)(a) 49, 50
   s 79 139
   s 95(1) 78, 81, 83
   s 95(1)(a) 81
   s 95(1)(b) 82
   s 95(1)(c) 87
   s 96(3) 139
   s 98 ....93, 97

s 98(1)....................................94, 96, 147
s 98(2)(b) 97
s 98(4) 100, 101,
                                    131, 147
s 99 ....206, 207
s 105(1)..131
s 111(1)–(3).......................................114
s 111(2)(b), (3) 115
s 138 129–31
s 139 119
s 139(1)(a) 120
s 139(1)(b) 121, 123
s 139(1)(b)(ii) 120
s 140(1)–(3) 128
s 140(2)..129
ss 142, 146 129
ss 147–54 131
s 155 ....127, 138
ss 156, 157, 159, 161 127
s 161(2)..138
s 196 14
ss 196(6), 197(3)..............................127
ss 198, 199 14
s 199(2)..127
s 203 ....71, 72, 83
ss 210–19 137
s 211 138
s 211(2)..127
s 211(3)..142
s 212 ....138, 142
s 212(3)(b) 139
s 212(3)(c)................................140, 141
s 212(4)..139
s 214 141
s 214(2)(a) 141
s 215 138
s 216 ....138, 142
s 217 138
s 218 ....24, 142, 143
s 218(2)..142
s 218(3)–(6) 143
s 230 14
s 230(1)..1, 2

s 230(2) 1
s 230(3)...1–3
s 230(3)(b) 3
s 235 141
Equal Pay Act 1970 ....164, 165,
                                    173, 180, 181,
                                    182, 187
s 1 ....161, 168,
                                    173, 178
s 1(1)...17, 168
s 1(2)(a)–(c), (4)..............162, 169, 170
s 1(3) 170, 173,
                                    175, 179
s 1(4)..165
s 1(5)..167
s 1(6)......................................2, 178–80
ss 1–3 168
s 2(5)..182
European Communities
    Act 1972
    s 2 164

Fair Employment
    (Northern Ireland)
    Act 1976..2

Health and Safety
    at Work Act 1974 ....61, 64
    ss 2–7 64
    s 2(1)..59
    s 2(2)..60
    s 3 ....61, 62
    s 6 62
    s 7 63
    s 8 ....63, 64
    ss 9, 21, 22, 24 63
    s 25 ....57, 64
    s 47 64
    s 53 2
Industrial Relations
    Act 1971 ....123, 218
    s 81(2)(b) 121, 123

Law Reform (Contributory
  Negligence) Act 1945
  s 1 58

Merchant Shipping
  Act 1894 238

National Minimum
  Wage Act 1998 ....3, 52
  s 1 52
  ss 34, 35, 41, 54 3
Nuclear Installations
  Act 1965
  s 12 64

Patents Act 1977 ....35, 38, 39
  s 39 35
  s 40 ....35, 36, 38
  s 40(1), (2), (7) 37
  s 41 ....35, 37
  s 41(4)–(6) 38
  s 42 38
  s 42(2), (3) 39
Pension Schemes
  Act 1993
  Pt III 13
Post Office Act 1953 238
Protection from
  Harassment Act 1997....................184
Public Interest
  Disclosure Act 1998 3

Race Relations Act 1976....................182,
                          186, 191–93,
                          196, 211, 214
  s 1 ....185, 191
  s 1(1)(b) 201
  s 3 ....186, 191
  s 4 ....192, 193
  s 4(1)(a), (c), (2)(b) 193
  s 4(2)(c)..196
  s 5 193
  s 5(2)(d) 194
  s 32 195

s 32(1)..197
s 32(3)..196
s 54 200
ss 56, 57 201
s 65(2)(b) 199
s 78 2
Race Relations
  (Remedies) Act 1994 202

Science and
  Technology Act 1965 37
Sex Discrimination
  Act 1975 ....187, 195,
                          203, 207,
                          208, 211, 214
  s 1 ....183, 187
  s 1(b)..188
  s 2 183
  s 3 183
  s 5(3) 204
  s 6 193
  s 7 194
  s 41 195
  s 77 190
  s 82 2
Social Security
  Contributions and
  Benefits Act 1992
  s 163 2

Trade Dispute Act 1965 236
Trade Union Act 1871 218
  s 4 218
Trade Union Act 1984
  s 11 251
Trade Union and
  Employment Rights
  Act 1993
  s 33(2)..144

Trade Union and
  Labour Relations
  Act 1974....................................36, 218
  s 13(1)..234

Trade Union and
Labour Relations
(Consolidation)
Act 1992 ....241, 246
s 10(1) 218
s 63 219
s 64 ....224, 226, 228
s 64(2) 226
s 65 224–27
s 67 226
ss 144, 145 254
s 174 ....227, 228
s 178 37
s 179 ....19, 21
s 179(3), (4) 20
ss 186, 187 255
s 188 133–35
s 188(1), (1A)(a), (b) 135
s 188(3)–(7A) 134–35
s 188(7) 136
s 188(7A), (8) 135
s 188A 135
s 188A(1) 133
ss 189–92 135
s 190 136
s 219 241
ss 222, 223 254
s 224 ....242, 255
s 225 255
s 226 246

s 226(1) 252
s 226A 247
s 226B 246, 248
s 226C 248
ss 227–31 247
ss 227, 228 248
s 229 ....248, 249
s 229(2) 247, 251
s 229(2A) 252
s 229(3) 250
s 230 ....249, 250
s 230(1)(a) 253
ss 231, 231A 250
s 231B 248, 250
s 233 ....249, 250, 254
s 233(3)(b) 250
s 234 250
s 234A 251
s 237 254
s 244 246
s 244(1) 245
s 244(2) 244
s 246 252
s 296(1) 2

Wages Act 1986
s 8 2
Workmen's
Compensation
Act 1906 4

Table of Statutory Instruments

Collective Redundancies and Transfer of Undertakings
(Protection of Employment) (Amendment) Regulations
1995 (SI 1995/2587) 133, 159
regs 9–11 159

Disability Discrimination (Meaning of Disability)
Regulations 1996 (SI 1996/1455) 209

Equal Pay (Amendment) Regulations 1983 (SI 1983/1794) 168

Industrial Tribunals (Rule of Procedure)
Regulations 1985 (SI 1985/16) 169

Sex Discrimination and Equal Pay (Miscellaneous
Amendments) Regulations 1996 (SI 1996/438) 170
Sex Discrimination and Equal Pay (Remedies)
Regulations 1993 (SI 1993/2798) 202

Transfer of Undertakings (Protection of Employment)
Regulations 1981 (SI 1981/1794) 24, 141, 144, 147,
149, 152, 153, 157
reg 2(1) 144
reg 3(1)–(4) 145
reg 5 ....147, 150
reg 5(1)–(5) 146
reg 5(1) 151
regs 5(3), 8(1) 150
reg 8(2) 147, 151, 152
reg 10 158
Transfer of Undertakings (Protection of Employment)
(Amendment) Regulations 1999 (SI 1999/2402) 133, 135, 159
reg 9 159

Working Time Regulations 1998 (SI 1998/1833) 3
regs 4(1), (2), 5 65

Table of European Legislation

Directives
Acquired Rights Directive (77/187/EEC)..4, 144, 147,
149, 154, 157
Art 4 150
Art 3(1)..148
Equal Pay Directive (75/117/EEC) 164, 169, 172, 208
Arts 1–3 163
Arts 4–6 164
Art 119 ....207, 208
Equal Treatment Directive (76/207/EEC) 181, 189, 204–08
Art 1 202
Art 2 ....202, 207
Art 2(1)..204
Arts 3, 5 203
Art 5(1)..208
Art 6 202
Health and Safety Framework Directive (89/391/EEC) 4
Pregnant Workers Directive (92/85/EEC)..207
Redundancy Consultation Directive (75/129/EEC) 135
Social Security Directive (79/7/EEC)..204
Working Time Directive (93/104/EEC) 65
Art 7 65

Recommendations
On the Protection of the Dignity of Women and
Men at Work (91/131/EEC) 184

Treaties and Conventions
EC Treaty 1957
Art 141...163–65, 169,
171–74, 180, 181
European Convention on the Protection of Human
Rights and Fundamental Freedoms 1950
Art 8 207

1 Employee Status

1.1 Statutory definitions

1.1.1 Employment Rights Act 1996

Section 230(1)

In this Act, 'employee' means an individual who has entered into or works under (or, where the employment has ceased, worked under) a contract of employment.

Section 230(2)

In this Act, 'contract of employment' means a contract of service or apprenticeship, whether express or implied, and (if it is express) whether oral or in writing.

Section 230(3)

In this Act, 'worker' (except in the phrases 'shop worker' and 'betting worker') means an individual who has entered into and works under (or where the employment has ceased, worked under):

(a) a contract of employment; or

(b) any other contract, whether express, or implied and (if it is express) whether oral or in writing, whereby the individual undertakes to do or perform personally any work or services for another party to the contract whose status is not by virtue of the contract that of a client or customer of any profession or business undertaking carried on by the individual.

Note ───

The width of the definition of a worker in s 230(3) is greater than that in s 230(1) of an employee. The essence of the definition in s 230(3) is the undertaking to personally perform work or services for another party.

───

The definition in s 230(1) is applied in the following Parts of the Employment Rights Act 1996 (ERA):

Part I   right to statements of employment particulars and itemised pay statements;

Part III   guarantee payments;

Part IV   protected shop workers and betting workers;

Part V   protection from suffering detriment in employment;

Part VI   rights to time off work;

Part VII   suspension from work;

Part VIII   maternity rights;

Part IX   termination of employment;

Part X   unfair dismissal;

Part XI   redundancy.

Section 230(3) is applied to Pt II of the ERA 1996 (deductions from pay) and it derives from s 8 of the Wages Act 1986. There is a similar definition of a worker in s 296(1) of the Trade Union and Labour Relations (Consolidation) Act 1992.

Section 1(6) of the Equal Pay Act 1970, s 82 of the Sex Discrimination Act 1975, s 78 of the Race Relations Act 1976 and s 68 of the Disability Discrimination Act 1995 all adopt a definition which incorporates the definitions in both s 230(1) and (3) of the ERA 1996.

They refer to employment 'under a contract of service or of apprenticeship or a contract personally to execute any work or labour'.

Section 53 of the Health and Safety at Work Act 1974 in effect uses the narrower definition of employee in s 230(2): 'Contract of employment means a contract of employment or apprenticeship.'

Section 163 of the Social Security Contributions and Benefits Act 1992 deals with the right to receive statutory sick pay, but here the term 'employee' includes officeholders as well. This is because the definition is based on liability to pay income tax under Sched E.

Loughran and Kelly v Northern Ireland Housing Executive (1998) HL

The House of Lords considered the phrase 'employed under a contract ... personally to execute any work or labour' and held that it not only applied to a solicitor who was a sole practitioner, but also to a partner in the firm. This case concerned a claim brought under the Fair Employment (Northern Ireland) Act 1976, where it was claimed that there had been religious discrimination against a firm of solicitors, but the decision was obviously of wider application.

1.1.2 Recent statutory developments

Statutes have been increasingly using the term 'worker' rather than 'employee', and have also extended protection to groups of workers not previously covered by employment protection legislation.

Section 54 of the National Minimum Wage Act 1998 defines an 'employee' as someone who works under a contract of employment and gives the term 'worker' the same meaning as in s 230(3)(b) of the ERA 1996 (see above). However, the Act also applies to agency workers and homeworkers. Section 34 provides that the Act applies as if there is a worker's contract between the agency worker and whichever of the client or the agency is responsible for paying the worker; if neither of them is responsible, then whichever of them actually does pay the worker. Section 35 provides that a 'homeworker' is a person who contracts to do work for the purposes of another person's business, but the work is to be done in a place not under the control or management of that other person. A homeworker is treated by the Act as a worker. Moreover, s 41 contains power to extend the scope of the Act even further.

The Public Interest Disclosure Act 1998 expressly states that the term 'worker' includes persons who are not covered by this term as defined by s 230(3) of the ERA 1996; it then goes on to specify four groups that are within the definition of the term 'worker' for the purposes of this Act: agency workers; homeworkers; NHS doctors, dentists, ophthalmologists and pharmacists; and trainees on vocational or work experience schemes. The definitions are slightly different than in the National Minimum Wage Act 1998; for instance, an agency worker is defined as someone who works for a person to whom they were introduced by a third person, and their terms of work were determined by the person for whom they work, or the third person, or by both of these persons. On the other hand, the Working Time Regulations 1998 use the same provisions in relation to agency workers as s 34 of the National Minimum Wage Act (see above).

The most significant development is contained in s 23 of the Employment Rights Act 1999, which gives the Secretary of State power to extend the scope of employment legislation to groups not already covered by it. Accordingly, orders can be made, providing that individuals can be treated as parties to workers' contracts or contracts of employment and can make provision as to who are to be regarded as the employers of individuals.

1.1.3 Definitions in European Community law

The Acquired Rights Directive refers to rights and obligations arising from a contract of employment or from an employment relationship. However, the Framework Directive of 1989 on Health and Safety refers to 'workers', who are defined as persons 'employed by the employer'.

Q   There is an obvious need for a single, clear definition of which persons are entitled to the protection of employment legislation. How should such a definition be framed?

1.2 Tests applied by the courts to determine whether a person is an employee or an independent contractor

1.2.1 Control test

Yewens v Noakes (1880)

> ... a servant is a person subject to the command of his master as to the manner in which he shall do his work [*per* Bramwell LJ].

Walker v Crystal Palace Football Club (1910) CA

The question to decide was whether a professional football player was employed for the purpose of a claim under the Workmen's Compensation Act 1906. It was argued that he was not an employee, because he was not under the control of the employers as to precisely how he should play; it was for the footballer to decide how he would exercise his skill.

Held, by the Court of Appeal, that, as he was bound to observe the general directions of the club and also directions given by the captain during the game, he was an employee, even though he was also exercising his own judgment.

1.2.2 Organisation test

Stevenson Jordan and Harrison Ltd v McDonald and Evans (1952)

> Under the contract of service, a man is employed as part of the business, whereas under a contract for services, his work, although done for the business, is not integrated into it, but only accessory to it [*per* Denning LJ].

Note ───

Although the organisation test, as with the control test, is no longer applied on its own today in order to determine employee status, it can still be useful, especially in relation to skilled employees. See, for example, *Cassidy v Minister of Health* (1951), where a resident hospital surgeon was held to be an employee. However, one problem with the organisation test is that it fails to deal with the now common situation where businesses subcontract parts of their operations.

Q   Would the surgeon in *Cassidy v Minister of Health* have been an employee under the control test as used in *Walker v Crystal Palace Football Club*?

1.2.3   The 'economic reality' test

Market Investigations v Minister of Social Security (1969) HC
A company, whose business was in market research, employed interviewers in addition to its permanent staff. The interviewers worked as and when required by the company.

Held, by the High Court (QBD), that the interviewers were employees. Cooke J said that the test to be applied was: 'Is the person who has engaged himself to perform those services performing them as a person in business on his own account?' If the answer to that question is 'yes', then the contract is a contract for services (not employment). If the answer to that question is 'no', then the contract is a contract of service (that is, employment). Cooke J then went on to mention some indicators to help in deciding this issue:

> Factors which may be of importance are such matters as whether the man performing the services provides his own equipment, whether he hires his own helpers, what degree of financial risk he takes, what degree of responsibility for investment and management he has, and whether and how far he has an opportunity of profiting from sound management in the performance of his task.

Hall (Inspector of Taxes) v Lorimer (1994) CA
A freelancer vision mixer worked for a number of television production companies.

Held, by the Court of Appeal, that he was self-employed. Mummery J disapproved of the idea that one could determine employment status simply by running through a checklist of the kind set out by Cooke J, above. Instead, he emphasised that the object of the exercise was to paint a picture from an accumulation of detail. It was a matter of evaluation of the overall effect of the detail, which was not necessarily the same as the sum of the individual situation.

Note ———————————————————————————————
See, also, *Warner Holidays Ltd v Secretary of State for Social Services* (1983) and *Withers v Flackwell Heath Football Supporters Club* (1981).

1.2.4 The multiple test

Ready Mixed Concrete (South East) Ltd v Minister of Pensions and National Insurance (1968) HC

The plaintiff company employed a driver, Latimer, under a contract where he bought the lorry from the plaintiff on hire purchase. He had to wear the plaintiff company's uniform and the lorry had to be painted in the company's colours and with its insignia. He had to drive the lorry only on the business of the company and he agreed to obey all reasonable orders 'as if he was an employee'. However, he was not required to drive the lorry personally; instead, he was allowed to use a substitute driver.

Held, by the High Court (QBD), that he was self-employed, one of the deciding factors being that he was not contracting to necessarily drive the lorry personally.

MacKenna J said:

... a contract of employment exists if these three conditions are fulfilled:

(i)   the servant agrees that, in consideration of a wage or other remuneration, he will provide his own work and skill in the performance of some service for his master;

(ii) he agrees, expressly or impliedly, that in the performance of that service, he will be subject to the other's control in a sufficient degree to make that other master;

(iii) the other provisions of the contract are consistent with its being a contract of service ...

In this case, MacKenna J said that the 'obligations are more consistent, I think, with a contract of carriage than one of service'.

Note ———————————————————————————————

This case is not authority for the proposition that the presence or absence of the obligation to render personal service decides whether a person is an employee or not. The significance of the case is the emphasis placed by MacKenna J on the three factors outlined in his judgment. In fact, the multiple test is very similar to the economic reality test in seeking to avoid one all-embracing phase, such as a 'control' or 'integration'. *Hall (Inspector of Taxes) v Lorimer* (see 1.2.3, above) is really an example of the multiple test.

Note ———————————————————————————————

The Court of Appeal's decision in *Express & Echo Publications Ltd v Tanton* (1999) that a right to provide a substitute is inherently inconsistent with the existence of a contract of employment.

1.2.5 The mutual obligations test

O'Kelly and Others v Trusthouse Forte plc (1983) CA

The applicants were employed on a 'regular casual' basis at the Grosvenor House Hotel.

Held, by the Court of Appeal, that they were self-employed. There were a number of reasons in favour of their being employees: they were not in business on their own account (see 1.2.4, above); they were subject to the conditions of the hotel (see 1.2.1, above); and their work was organised on a weekly rota and they needed permission to take time off from rostered duties. However, it was held that there was no mutuality of obligation, in the sense that the applicants had no contractual right to claim if they were not offered work and, on their part, they were not bound to accept work which was offered.

Nethermere (St Neots) Ltd v Taverna and Gardiner (1984) CA

The respondents were employed as 'homeworkers'. One of them, Mrs Taverna, used a sewing machine provided by the appellant. She had no fixed hours for doing the work and was paid weekly according to the number of garments which she made. Mrs Gardiner, another homeworker, originally used her own machine, but was then provided with one. Each day, she usually made 200 pockets and put them onto trousers, but there was no contractual obligation to do this; if she did not wish to do so much, she simply told the driver who delivered the materials. The only rule was that she had to make it worthwhile for the driver to call on her.

Held, by the Court of Appeal, that they were employees. *Per* Dillon LJ:

> There was a regular course of dealing between the parties for years, under which garments were supplied daily to the outworkers, worked on, collected and paid for. If it is permissible on the evidence to find that by such conduct, a contract had been established between each applicant and the company, I see no necessity to conclude that that contract must have been a contract for services and not a contract of service.

Kerr LJ, however, dissented and observed:

> A course of dealing can be used as a basis for implying terms into individual contracts which are concluded pursuant thereto, but I can find no authority for the proposition that even a lengthy course of dealing can somehow convert itself into a contractually binding obligation – subject only to reasonable notice – to continue to enter into individual contracts, or to be subject to some 'umbrella' contract.

Q   Is it possible to distinguish between *O'Kelly* and *Nethermere*? Do you prefer Kerr LJ's dissenting judgment in *Nethermere*? If so, why?

Carmichael v National Power plc (1999) HL

The appellants were guides at power stations, where they took visitors on conducted tours. They worked on a 'casual as required' basis, under which they were offered, and accepted, work as it arose. They were not obliged to take work and the company did not guarantee that work would be available. They were paid only for the hours which they worked and tax and National Insurance contributions were deducted. They claimed a statement of terms and conditions of employment in accordance with s 1 of the Employment Protection (Consolidation) Act 1978, a right which is now contained in s 1 of the Employment Rights Act 1996.

Held, by the House of Lords, that they were not employees for the purposes of s 1. Although they might have had the status of employees when actually working as guides (this point was not decided), they did not have a contract which would entitle them to a statement under s 1 and, clearly, it followed that they would not have continuity of employment to enable them to claim other employment rights. Irvine LC, who delivered the leading opinion and with whom the other Law Lords agreed, said that: 'The parties incurred no obligations to accept or provide work, but at best assumed moral obligations of loyalty in a context where both recognised that the best interests of each lay in being accommodating to the other.' He said that the words 'casual as required basis' meant that the appellants 'were doing no more than intimate that they were ready to be invited to attend for casual work as station guides as and when the CEGB required their services'. The 'irreducible minimum of moral obligation necessary to create a contract of service', which was present, for example, in *Clark v Oxfordshire Health Authority* (1998), was not present here. Furthermore, on 17 occasions, one of the appellants had not been available for work and, on eight occasions, the other applicant had not been available, but in no case did any question of disciplining them arise. Accordingly, the appellants did not have 'their relationship regulated by contract' when they were not working as guides.

Lord Hoffman held that the ascertainment of the terms of the agreement was a question of fact, and not law, which could be ascertained from the conduct of the parties and oral exchanges as well as from the actual agreement. Accordingly, such a finding of fact by an employment tribunal should not be interfered with on appeal.

1.2.6 The description given by the worker

Ferguson v John Dawson and Partners (Contractors) Ltd (1976) CA

The plaintiff was a building worker. He was subject to the defendant's orders as to what he did, and the defendant provided tools. However, when the plaintiff went to work for the defendant, the site agent said in evidence that 'I did inform him that there were no cards; we were purely working as a lump labour force'.

Held, by the Court of Appeal, that the plaintiff was an employee. Megaw LJ held that, on the evidence, this was clearly so; any declaration by the parties that he was self-employed would be disregarded:

> I find difficulty in accepting that the parties, by a mere expression of intention as to what the legal relationship should be, can in any way influence the conclusion of law as to what the relationship is. I think that it would be contrary to the public interest if that were so, for it would mean that the parties, by their own whim, by the use of verbal formula, unrelated to the reality of the relationship, could influence the decision on whom the responsibility for the safety of workmen, as imposed by statutory regulations, should rest.

Q   Do you consider that the decision of the Court of Appeal was influenced by the fact that this was a claim for injury at work and, if Ferguson had not been held to be an employee, he may not have received any compensation?

Note ──

Megaw LJ said that he had found the reasoning in both the *Market Investigations* (see 1.2.3, above) and *Ready Mixed Concrete* cases (see 1.2.4, above) useful, which indicates, as said above, that the 'economic reality' test and the 'multiple' test have similarities. See, also, *Davis v New England College of Arundel* (1977). Note, also, the statement by Lord Denning MR in *Massey v Crown Life Assurance Co* (1978): '... if the parties deliberately arrange to be self-employed to obtain tax benefits, that is strong evidence that that is the real relationship.'

Q   Do you agree with Lord Denning MR's remark in *Massey*?

1.2.7 A question of fact or law?

Lee v Chung and Shun Sing Construction and Engineering Co Ltd (1990) PC
Lee was a stonemason who was injured whilst working on a construction site for the employers. He was provided with tools and told where to work, but was then left to proceed with the job. He was not paid a set wage, but was paid according to the amount of work which he did. However, he was expected to be on site when there was work for him to do.

Held, by the Judicial Committee of the Privy Council, that Lee was an employee. Lord Griffiths said:

> ... whether or not a person is employed under a contract of service is often said in the authorities to be a mixed question of fact and law. Exceptionally,

if the relationship is dependent solely upon the true construction of a written document, it is regarded as a question of law: see *Davies v Presbyterian Church of Wales* (1986). But where, as in the present case, the relationship has to be determined by an investigation and evaluation of the factual circumstances in which the work is performed, it must now be taken to be firmly established that the question of whether or not the work was performed in the capacity of an employee or as an independent contractor is to be regarded by an appellate court as the question of fact to be determined by the trial court.

McMeechan v Secretary of State for Employment (1995) CA

McMeechan worked for an employment agency under a series of temporary contracts, which provided that he was self-employed. He was not obliged to accept any assignment, but, if he did so, he was subject to the normal obligations owed by an employee of fidelity, confidentiality, and obedience to lawful instructions. He was paid weekly by a specified hourly rate and the employees could instruct him to end an assignment at any time. However, he did not have to work for a specified number of hours and he did not receive hourly pay.

Held, by the EAT, that he was an employee. Mummery J said that there was no rule that those working for an employment agency were self-employed. He also said:

> ... where the relevant contract is, as here, wholly contained in a document or documents, the question whether the contract is one of employment is a question of law to be determined upon the construction of the document in its factual matrix.

Note ──

The judgment of Mummery J in this case can be seen as, to some extent, a retreat from the principle in *Lee* that the question of employee status is one of the fact and not law, although Mummery J confined his remarks to cases where the contract of employment is in writing.

───

The Court of Appeal agreed with the EAT that McMeechan was an employee but, instead of Mummery J's general reasoning, it distinguished between the status of agency workers in two situations:

(a) an agency worker can have the status of an employee in relation to a particular engagement;

(b) however, such a worker may not have employee status under the general terms of his agreement because, for example, there may be a lack of obligations.

See, also, *Clifford v Union of Democratic Mineworkers* (1991), where the approach in *Lee v Chung* (that is, that the question is one of fact) was followed.

1.3 Rights of employees to be provided with a statement of initial employment particulars

Employment Rights Act 1996

Section 1

(1) Where an employee begins employment with an employer, the employer shall give to the employee a written statement of particulars of employment.

(2) The statement may (subject to s 2(4)) be given in instalments and (whether or not given in instalments) shall be given not later than two months after the beginning of the employment.

(3) The statement shall contain particulars of:

(a) the names of the employer and employee;

(b) the date when the employment began; and

(c) the date on which the employee's period of continuous employment began (taking into account any employment with a previous employer which counts towards that period).

(4) The statement shall also contain particulars, as at a specified date not more than seven days before the statement (or the instalment containing them) is given, of:

(a) the scale or rate of remuneration or the method of calculating remuneration;

(b) the intervals at which remuneration is paid (that is, weekly, monthly or other specified intervals);

(c) any terms and conditions relating to hours of work (including any terms and conditions relating to normal working hours);

(d) any terms and conditions relating to any of the following:

(i) entitlement to holidays, including public holidays, and holiday pay (the particulars given being sufficient to enable the employee's entitlement, including any entitlement to accrued holiday pay on the termination of employment, to be precisely calculated);

(ii) incapacity for work due to sickness or injury, including any provision for sick pay; and

(iii) pensions and pension schemes.

(e) the length of notice which the employee is obliged to give and entitled to receive to terminate his contract of employment;

(f) the title of the job which the employee is employed to do or a brief description of the work for which he is employed;

(g) where the employment is not intended to be permanent, the period for which it is expected to continue or, if it is for a fixed term, the date when it is to end;

(h) either the place of work or, where the employee is required or permitted to work at various places, an indication of that and of the address of the employer;

(i) any collective agreements which directly affect the terms and conditions of the employment including, where the employer is not a party, the persons by whom they were made; and

(j) where the employee is required to work outside the UK for a period of more than one month:

    (i) the period for which he is to work outside the UK;

    (ii) the currency in which remuneration is to be paid while he is working outside the UK;

    (iii) any additional remuneration payable to him, and any benefits to be provided to or in respect of him, by reason of his being required to work outside the UK; and

    (iv) any terms and conditions relating to his return to the UK.

(5) Sub-section (4)(d)(iii) does not apply to an employee of a body or authority if:

(a) the employee's pension rights depend on the terms of a pension scheme established under any provision contained in or having effect under any Act; and

(b) any such provision requires the body or authority to give to a new employee information concerning the employee's pension rights or the determination of questions affecting those rights.

Section 2

(1) If, in the case of a statement under s 1, there are no particulars to be entered under any of the heads of para (d) or (k) of sub-s (4) of that section, or under any of the other paragraphs of sub-s (3) or (4) of that section, that fact shall be stated.

(2) A statement under s 1 may refer the employee for particulars of any of the matters specified in sub-s (4)(d)(ii) and (iii) of that section to the provisions of some other document which is reasonably accessible to the employee.

(3) A statement under s 1 may refer the employee for particulars of either of the matters specified in sub-s (4)(e) of that section to the law or to the provisions of any collective agreement directly affecting the terms and conditions of the employment which is reasonably accessible to the employee.

(4) The particulars required by s 1(3) and (4)(a)–(c), (d)(i), (f) and (h) shall be included in a single document.

(5) Where before the end of the period of two months after the beginning of an employee's employment, the employee is to begin to work outside the UK for a period of more than one month, the statement under s 1 shall be given to him no later then the time when he leaves the UK in order to begin so to work.

(6) A statement shall be given to a person under s 1, even if this employment ends before the end of the period within which the statement is required to be given.

Section 3

(1) A statement under s 1 shall include a note:

(a) specifying any disciplinary rules applicable to the employee or referring the employee to the provisions of a document specifying such rules which is reasonably accessible to the employee;

(b) specifying (by description or otherwise):

(i) a person to whom the employee can apply if dissatisfied with any disciplinary decision relating to him; and

(ii) a person to whom the employee can apply for the purpose of seeking redress of any grievance relating to his employment, and the manner in which any such application should be made; and

(c) where there are further steps consequent on any such application, explaining those steps or referring to the provisions of a document explaining them which is reasonably accessible to the employee.

Note

Section 3(2) provides that the requirements in s 3(1) do not apply to rules, procedures, etc, relating to health and safety at work. Section 3(3) exempts small firms (where, on the date when the employee's employment began, the number of employees was less than 20) from most of the requirements set out in s 3(1). Section 3(5) requires the note which is given under s 3(4) to state whether there is in force a contracting-out certificate (issued in accordance with Pt III of the Pension Schemes Act 1993), stating that the employment is contracted-out employment for the purpose of Pt III.

1.3.1 Statement of changes

Section 4(1)

If, after the material date, there is a change in any of the matters particulars of which are required by ss 1 and 3 to be included or referred to in a statement under s 1, the employer shall give to the employee a written statement containing particulars of the change.

Note ───────────────────────────────────

Section 4 also provides that any statement of changes may refer the employee to some reasonably accessible document, the general law or a collective agreement for the details of those changes in cases where the original written statement would have allowed such a reference. In addition, it provides that, where the name and the identity of the employee changes, the employee does not have to be issued with a statement under s 1, unless continuity of employment is broken by the change of identity or there are changes in any of the matters (other than the names of the parties) which are required to be included in the written statement.

Note ───────────────────────────────────

The following are excluded from the right to receive a written statement of employment particulars (see s 5):
(a) self-employed persons (s 230);
(b) employees working wholly or mainly outside Great Britain (s 196);
(c) employees who are employed for less than one month (s 198);
(d) mariners (s 199).

1.3.2 Reasonably accessible document or collective agreement

Section 6

In ss 2–4, references to a document or collective agreement which is reasonably accessible to an employee are references to a document or collective agreement which:

(a) the employee has reasonable opportunities of reading in the course of his employment; or

(b) is made reasonably accessible to the employee in some other way.

1.3.3 Power to require particulars of further matters

Section 7

The Secretary of State may by order provide that s 1 shall have effect as if particulars of such further matters as may be specified in the order were included in the particulars required by that section; and, for that purpose, the order may include such provisions amending that section as appear to the Secretary of State to be expedient.

Gascol Conversions v Mercer (1974) CA

The employer had sent to the employee a document containing written terms of employment, which the employee signed. One term stated that the employee's normal working week was 40 hours. When he was dismissed for redundancy, he claimed that as he worked 14 hours overtime, his normal working week should be 54 hours, which would have increased his redundancy pay.

Held, by the Court of Appeal, that the written contract was binding. It could not, in accordance with normal contractual principles, be varied by extraneous evidence. Lord Denning MR observed that:

> It is settled that, where there is a written contract of employment, as there was here, and the parties have reduced it to writing, it is the writing which governs their relations. It is not permissible to say they intended something different.

System Floors (UK) Ltd v Daniel (1981) EAT

The applicant had started work for the employers on an agency basis in September 1979 and it was then agreed that he would be employed directly by them from 26 November. However, his statement of (what is now called) employment particulars stated that he began as an employee on 19 November. The difference was significant in deciding whether the applicant could claim for unfair dismissal, the length of continuous employment then required being 52 weeks.

Held, by the EAT, that the employer could adduce evidence that the starting date was different. *Mercer* was distinguished, as that was the case of an individual contract whereas this concerned the statutory statement. Browne Wilkinson J drew a clear distinction between the status of these two types of documents:

> In that case, Mr Mercer had signed a document which he confirmed was a new contract of employment and that it set out the terms and conditions of his employment. The Court of Appeal treated that as being a contract in writing, as indeed it was, having been signed by both parties. But in the case of an ordinary statutory statement served pursuant to the statutory obligation, the document is a unilateral one merely stating the employer's view of what those terms are. In the absence of an acknowledgment by the parties that the statement itself is a contract and that the terms are correct, such as that contained in the *Mercer* case, the statutory statement does not itself constitute a contract in writing.

In the present case, all that the employee did was to sign an acknowledgment that he had received the statement. In no sense did he sign it as a contract or acknowledge the accuracy of the terms in it. We therefore think that the industrial tribunal erred in law in treating the date of commencement mentioned in the statement as decisive, because it was a contractual term. In our view, the statement is no more than persuasive, though not conclusive, evidence of the date of commencement.

Note

See, also, *Robertson v British Gas Corp* (1983) (which confirmed the approach in *Systems Floors v Daniel*) and *Jones v Associated Tunnelling Co Ltd* (1981) (dealing with the situation where an employer changes the terms of a statement and the employee works under the changed terms). It seems that, where the statement favours the employee, it is more likely to be felt to represent strong evidence of the terms of the contract. (See Ackner LJ in *Robertson v British Gas Corp*.)

1.3.4 Enforcement of the duty to supply initial employment particulars

Section 11(1) of the ERA 1996 gives an employee the right to complain to an employment tribunal on the grounds that either he has not been given a statement or that the statement given did not contain the particulars required by s 1(1). He may also complain on the grounds that proper notice has not been given of a change in the particulars.

The employment tribunal may determine what matters should have been included in the particulars, or whether any particulars which were included are to be confirmed, amended or substituted.

Note

The powers of industrial tribunals under s 11 are simply to find out what has been agreed between the parties and, if required, to amend the statement so that it reflects that agreement. In *Cuthbertson v AML Distributors* (1975), the industrial tribunal was held to have acted correctly in refusing to decide what length of notice would have been reasonable as this would have meant interpreting the contract. See, also, on the same point, *Construction Industry Training Board v Leighton* (1978).

2   Terms of the Contract of Employment

2.1   Express terms

An example of an express term inserted by statute is found in s 1(1) of the Equal Pay Act 1970:

> If the terms of a contract under which a woman is employed at an establishment in Great Britain do not include (directly or by reference to a collective agreement or otherwise) an equality clause, they should be deemed to include one.

In addition, contracts of employment will contain express terms which have actually been agreed by the parties. (See 1.3.3, above, for cases on the relationship between the express terms of the contract and the statement of initial employment particulars.)

2.2   Implied terms

2.2.1   When will the courts imply a term into a contract of employment?

Shirlaw v Southern Foundries (1939) CA
McKinnon LJ said:

> *Prima facie*, that which in any contract is left to be implied and need not be expressed is something so obvious that it goes without saying; so that, if while the parties were making their bargain, an officious bystander were to suggest some express provision for it in the agreement, they would testily suppress him with a common 'Oh, of course'.

Courtaulds Northern Spinning Ltd v Sibson (1988) CA
Slade LJ said that, where the court is asked to imply a term into a contract of employment with regard to place of work:

> ... the court does not have to be satisfied that the parties, if asked, would in fact have agreed the term before entering into the contract. The court

merely has to be satisfied that the implied term is one which the parties would probably have agreed if they were being reasonable.

Ali v Christian Salvesen Food Services Ltd (1997) CA

Employees were obliged by their contracts to work a certain number of hours (1,824) per year, after which they were entitled to overtime pay. They were dismissed before they had worked 1,824 hours

Held, by the Court of Appeal, reversing the EAT, that there was no implied term that they would be paid overtime for every week in which they had worked for over 40 hours. The fact that this point was not dealt with in the relevant collective agreement did not mean that the courts should imply a term to this effect.

2.2.2 Terms implied by custom

Sagar v Ridehalgh & Son Ltd (1931) CA

Held, by the Court of Appeal, that a custom which was followed by most mills in Lancashire that deductions would be made from employees' wages if work was not done with reasonable care and skill were incorporated into individual contracts of employment. *Per* Lawrence LJ:

> The practice of making reasonable deductions for bad work has continually prevailed at the defendant's mill for upwards of 30 years and, during the whole of that time, all weavers employed by the defendants have been treated alike in that respect. The practice was therefore firmly established at the defendant's mill when the plaintiff entered upon his employment there. Further, I think it is clear that the plaintiff accepted employment in the defendant's mill on the same terms as others employed at that mill ...

2.2.3 Can a term be implied by work rules and Codes of Practice?

Dryden v Greater Glasgow Health Board (1992) EAT

An employee, who was a heavy smoker, left his employment and claimed constructive dismissal when his employer introduced a no smoking policy in the hospital where he worked.

Held, by the EAT, that his claim failed, because works rules banning smoking were not part of his contract, but were within the discretion of the employer. *Per* Lord Coulsfield: 'There can, in our view, be no doubt that an employer is entitled to make rules for the conduct of employees in their place of work ...'

Note ———————————————————————————
See, also, *Secretary of State for Employment v ASLEF (No 2)* (1972), where Lord Denning MR stated that work rules: '... are in no way part of the

contract of employment. They are only instructions to a man on how he is to do his work.'

Wandsworth London Borough Council v D'Silva and Another (1998) CA

The respondents had a Code of Practice on staff sicknesses, which included procedures for monitoring and reviewing different categories of absence. They changed certain provisions and two employees argued that, as the Code formed part of their contract of employment, it could not be altered unilaterally.

Held, by the Court of Appeal, that the Code was not part of the contract of employment. It was simply giving guidance to supervisors as to what was expected to happen where employees had been absent from work and, accordingly, the employers could change it unilaterally (but see, also, 2.6, below).

Taylor v Secretary of State for Scotland (1999) Court of Session

A management circular to employees, setting out an equal opportunities policy, included an undertaking not to discriminate on the grounds of age. The applicant, a prison officer, had been allowed to continue in employment beyond the normal retirement age, but had then been dismissed in pursuance of a policy to achieve a younger workforce. He claimed that his dismissal was in breach of contract.

Held, by the Court of Session, that, although the equal opportunities policy was part of his contract, he had not been dismissed in breach of it on the grounds of age, because the employers retained a discretion on the nature of any retirement policy and this discretion could not have been intended by the parties to be fettered by age considerations.

2.2.4 Collective agreements as a source of contractual terms

Section 179 of the Trade Union and Labour Relations (Consolidation) Act 1992

(1) A collective agreement shall be conclusively presumed not to have been intended by the parties to be a legally enforceable contract unless the agreement:

(a) is in writing; and

(b) contains a provision which (however expressed) states that the parties intend that the agreement shall be a legally enforceable contract.

(2) A collective agreement which does satisfy these conditions shall be conclusively presumed to have been intended by the parties to be a legally enforceable contract.

(3) If a collective agreement is in writing and contains a provision which (however expressed) states that the parties intend that one or more parts of the agreement specified in that provision, but not the whole of the agreement, shall be a legally enforceable contract, then:

   (a) the specified part or parts shall be conclusively presumed to have been intended by the parties to be a legally enforceable contract; and

   (b) the remainder of the agreement shall be conclusively presumed not to have been intended by the parties to be such a contract.

(4) A part of a collective agreement which by virtue of sub-s (3)(b) is not a legally enforceable contract may be referred to for the purpose of interpreting a part of the agreement which is such a contract.

Section 17 of the Employment Relations Act 1999

(1) The Secretary of State may make regulations about cases where a worker:

   (a) is subjected to detriment by his employer, or

   (b) is dismissed,

   on the grounds that he refuses to enter into a contract which includes terms which differ from the terms of a collective agreement which applies to him.

Note ───

The object of this provision is to protect workers from being dismissed, or subjected to a detriment, because they have refused to enter into a contract which contains terms which differ from those of a collective agreement which applies to them.

Q   What effect does a collective agreement have on individual contracts of employment?

National Coal Board v Galley (1958) CA

The defendant, a pit deputy, had a contract of employment which stated that the contract should be regulated by national agreements then in force. Later, his employer and the union agreed a revised national term of agreement, which required pit deputies to work 'such days and part days in each week as may reasonably be required'.

Held, by the Court of Appeal, that the defendant was in breach of his contract by refusing to work on Saturdays. *Per* Pearce LJ:

... by the defendant's personal contract, his wages were to be regulated by national agreements for the time being in force.

Cadoux v Central Regional Council (1986) Court of Session
The employee's letter of appointment stated that he would be employed subject to national conditions of service, which provided, *inter alia*, a non-contributory pension scheme for employees. The defendant employer later unilaterally withdrew the scheme.

Held, by the Court of Session, that this alteration to the conditions of service was not a breach of contract. *Per* Lord Ross:

> The rules contain no express provision regarding amendment and the clear inference from the fact that they are the defenders' rules is that the defenders have power to alter them, the only obligation being to enter the amendments in the rules or otherwise record them for the pursuer to refer to within a stipulated period.

Marley v Forward Trust Group Ltd (1986) CA
Marley's contract of employment expressly incorporated the terms of a collective agreement which had been negotiated with his trade union, and the terms of his contract were made subject to any amendment which the collective agreement might make to it. The contract contained a mobility clause, under which he could be required to work in any department of the company to which he might be sent. An amendment to the collective agreement provided that if employees who were made redundant were then offered a new job with significant changes, such as a new location, they would have the right to a six month trial period. Marley worked in Bristol but, when his post there was made redundant, his employer sought to transfer him to London, relying on the mobility clause. Marley claimed that the redundancy clause in the collective agreement applied.

Held, by the Court of Appeal, that, although the collective agreement made between union and employer itself might have been unenforceable (see s 179 of the Trade Union and Labour Relations (Consolidation) Act 1992, above), that was not, by itself, a bar to the incorporation of the terms of such a collective agreement into an individual contract of employment and the matter was remitted to an industrial tribunal to decide if, in fact, the term in the collective agreement should be incorporated.

Anderson v Pringle of Scotland Ltd (1998) Court of Session
The petitioner sought an interdict (injunction) against the respondents to prevent any redundancy selection procedure other than on the 'last in, first out' basis, because this basis of selection had been agreed in a collective agreement which, he claimed, was incorporated into his contract of employment.

Held, by the Court of Session, that this was correct, and an interim interdict would be granted preventing redundancy selection other than on this basis.

Q   Why do you consider that the court should have come to this decision?

2.3   Duties of the employer and the employee

2.3.1   Duties of the employer

To pay wages
See, also, 2.7, below.

Miles v Wakefield Metropolitan District Council (1987) HL
The applicant was a superintendent registrar of births, marriages and deaths. His employer withheld three-37ths of his pay, because of his refusal, as part of industrial action, to carry out marriages on Saturday mornings.

Held, by the House of Lords, that the employers were entitled to make the deduction. *Per* Lord Templeton:

> For my part ... I take the provisional view that, on principle, a worker who, in conjunction with his fellow workers, declines to work efficiently with the object of harming his employer, is no more entitled to his wages under the contract than if he declined to work at all. The worker whose industrial action takes the form of 'going slow' inflicts intended damage which may be incalculable and non-apportionable, but the employer, in order to avoid greater damage, is obliged to accept the reduced work the worker is willing to perform. In those circumstances, the worker cannot claim that he is entitled to his wages under the contract, because he is deliberately working in a manner designed to harm the employer. But the worker will be entitled to be paid on a *quantum meruit* basis for the amount and value of the reduced work performed and accepted.

Wiluszynski v London Borough of Tower Hamlets (1989) CA
The employee, along with others, was engaged in limited industrial action which meant that, in his case, he did not deal with enquiries from councillors about the housing problems of their ward members. His employer had told him that, if he did turn up for work without being prepared to carry out all of his duties, any work which he did would be regarded as voluntary and his pay would be withheld.

Held, by the Court of Appeal, that his employers were entitled not to pay him at all for the days he was engaged in industrial action. Nicholls LJ said that it was not the case that his employers had accepted the service which the employee had performed and must therefore pay him for it. Nicholls LJ observed, '... a person is not treated by the law as having chosen to accept that which is forced down his throat, despite his objection', that is, that although the employer had not physically prevented the employee from continuing to come to his place of work, that did not mean that the employer had accepted the work which the employee did perform.

Hanley v Pease and Partners Ltd (1915) HC

The plaintiff failed to turn up for work and, when he did turn up the following day, he was suspended without pay for one day.

Held, by the High Court (KBD), that, although the employers might have dismissed the employee, they did not, and because the contract then continued, they were obliged to pay him. *Per* Lush J:

> But in the present case, after declining to dismiss the workman – after electing to treat the contract as a continuous one – the employers took upon themselves to suspend him for one day; in other words, to deprive the workman of his wages for one day, thereby assessing their own damages for the servant's misconduct at the sum which would be represented by one day's wages. They have no possible right to do that. Having elected to treat the contract as continuing, it was continuing. They might have had a right to claim damages against the servant, but they could not justify their act in suspending the workman for the one day and refusing to let him work and earn wages.

Q   What legal options would be open today to an employee who was suspended without pay?

Note ————————————————————————

See *Devonald v Rosser & Sons* (1906) and *Browning v Crumlin Valley Collieries Ltd* (1926).

To provide work

Collier v Sunday Referee Publishing Co Ltd (1940) HC

The employee was employed as subeditor on a newspaper. When the newspaper was sold, the new employer did not wish to use his services, and so the previous employer continued to pay him, but did not provide him with any work.

Held, by the High Court (KBD), that his employer did not have a duty to provide him with work. *Per* Asquith LJ:

> It is true that a contract of employment does not necessarily, or perhaps normally, oblige the master to provide the servant with work. Provided I

pay my cook her wages regularly, she cannot complain if I choose to take any or all of my meals out. In some exceptional cases, there is an obligation to provide work. For instance, where the servant is remunerated by commission, or where (as in the case of an actor or singer) the servant bargains, among other things, for publicity, and the master, by withholding work, also withholds the stipulated publicity.

However, in this case, the employers were liable to the employee for breach of contract because, by selling the newspaper, they had 'destroyed the office to which they had appointed him', that is, chief subeditor.

Q   How would the case be dealt with today in the light of s 218 of the Employment Rights Act 1996 (ERA) and the Transfer of Undertakings (Protection of Employment) Regulations 1981?

Langston v Amalgamated Union of Engineering Workers (No 2) (1974) NIRC
The employee objected to the 'closed shop' principle and refused to join a union. As a result, industrial action was taken by his fellow employees and, eventually, his employer suspended him without pay.

Held, by the National Industrial Relations Court, that, as the employee was entitled under his contract to be paid premium rates for night shifts and overtime, the denial to him of an opportunity to work meant the denial of an opportunity to earn those payments and, therefore, the employer was in breach of contract. In the Court of Appeal (*Langston v Amalgamated Union of Engineering Workers (No 1)* (1974)), Lord Denning MR proposed overruling Asquith LJ in *Collier* and replacing the principle in that case with a rule that 'an employer, when employing a skilled man, is bound to provide him with work'.

Breach v Epsylon Industries Ltd (1976) EAT
The applicant worked as a chief engineer, but when the contracts on which he worked were transferred overseas, he was left with no work; he claimed that the failure to provide him with work amounted to constructive dismissal.

Held, by the EAT, that the question was whether there should be an implied term in the employee's contract that he should be provided with work. The case was remitted to the industrial tribunal to decide whether, on the facts, a term should be implied and, in doing so, the EAT emphasised that there was no principle of law that, in all circumstances, there was no obligation on an employer to provide an employee with work.

Not to damage the relationship of trust and confidence which should exist between an employer and an employee

Isle of Wight Tourist Board v Coombes (1976) EAT

Mrs Coombes was personal secretary to the director of the Tourist Board. After she had had an argument with him, the director said to another employee in her presence: 'She is an intolerable bitch on a Monday morning.'

Held, by the EAT, that the relationship between the director and his personal secretary must be one of complete confidence and, by his words, the director had shattered that confidence. Accordingly, the implied term of trust and confidence had been broken, resulting in her constructive dismissal.

Post Office v Roberts (1980) EAT

A bad report was written on the employee by a senior official, which concluded that she was unfit for promotion. The report was written without consideration of the employee's record.

Held, by the EAT, that she had been constructively dismissed. Talbot J emphasised that there was no requirement that the action alleged to constitute a repudiatory breach of contract should be deliberate or done in bad faith. He referred with approval to the words of Kilner-Brown J in *Robinson v Crompton Parkinson Ltd* (1978):

> In a contract of employment and in conditions of employment, there has to be mutual trust and confidence between master and servant.

Talbot J then added:

> In stating that principle, in our view, Kilner-Brown J does not set out any requirement that there should be deliberation, intent or bad faith.

Note ———————————————————————————

See, also, to the same effect, *Woods v WM Car Services (Peterborough) Ltd* (1982) and also 4.2.3, below (constructive dismissal).

To take reasonable steps to bring to the attention of employees rights of which the employees could not have been expected to be aware

Scally and Others v Southern Health and Social Services Board (1991) HL

The plaintiffs were doctors employed in the health service in Northern Ireland. Their employer had failed to tell them of their right to purchase added years so as to enhance their pension contributions.

Held, by the House of Lords, that a term would be implied. Lord Bridge laid down the following conditions which must be satisfied before the courts in a case such as this one would imply a term imposing an obligation on the employer:

(a) the terms of the contract of employment have not been negotiated with the individual employee, but result from negotiation with a representative body or are otherwise incorporated by reference;

(b) a particular term of the contract makes available to the employee a valuable right, contingent upon action being taken by him to avail himself of its benefit;

(c) the employee cannot, in all the circumstances, be reasonably expected to be aware of the term, unless it is drawn to his attention.

To take reasonable care to ensure an employee's health and safety

Johnstone v Bloomsbury Area Health Authority (1991) CA

The plaintiff was employed by the defendant as a Senior House Officer in a hospital. Clause 4b of his contract provided that, in addition to his standard working week of 40 hours, he should be available on call for an average of a further 48 hours a week. The plaintiff alleged that, in some weeks, he had been required to work over 100 hours a week; this had resulted in his suffering from stress and depression. The plaintiff sought to strike the claim out on the ground that it disclosed no reasonable cause of action.

Held, by the Court of Appeal, that the claim would not be struck out. Browne-Wilkinson VC said:

> In my judgment, there must be some restriction on the Authority's rights. In any sphere of employment other than that of junior hospital doctors, an obligation to work up to 88 hours in any one week would be rightly regarded as oppressive and intolerable. But even that is not the limit of what the Authority claims. Since the plaintiff's obligation is to be available 'on average' for 48 hours per week, the Authority claims to be entitled to require him to work more than 88 hours in some weeks, regardless of possible injury to his health. Thus, the plaintiff alleges that he was required to work for 100 hours during one week in February 1989 and 105 hours during another week in March 1989. How far can this go? Could the Authority demand of the plaintiff that he worked 130 hours (out of a total of 168 hours available) in any one week if this would manifestly involve injury to his health? In my judgment, the Authority's right to call for overtime under cl 4(b) is not an absolute right, but must be limited in some way. There is no technical legal reason why the Authority's discretion to call for overtime should not be exercised in conformity with the normal implied duty to take reasonable care not to injure their employee's health.

Note

Legatt LJ dissented and held that the express term of the contract dealing with hours of work could not be varied by an implied term.

Waltons and Morse v Dorrington (1997) EAT

The appellant, a non-smoker, left her employment in protest at the employer's failure to deal adequately with her complaints about being exposed to cigarette smoke from other employees.

Held, by the EAT, that the employer was in breach of an implied term to provide and monitor, as far as reasonably practicable, a working environment which is reasonably suitable for the performance by employees of their contractual duties.

See, also, Chapter 3.

To take care when providing references

Spring v Guardian Assurance plc (1994) HL

The plaintiff claimed damages from his former employer for supplying a reference to a prospective employer which, he alleged, contained inaccurate statements about him.

Held, by the House of Lords, that a duty of care could arise in the giving of a reference. Lord Slynn was not impressed with the argument that to impose a duty would mean that employers only gave bland references or none at all. He dealt with the policy arguments as follows:

> I do not accept the *in terrorem* arguments that to allow a claim in negligence will constitute a restriction on freedom of speech, or that in the employment sphere, employers will refuse to give references or give such bland or adulatory ones as is forecast. They should be and are capable of being sufficiently robust as to express frank and honest views, after taking reasonable care both as to the factual content and as to the opinion expressed. They will not shrink from the duty of taking reasonable care when they realise the importance of the reference both to the recipient (to whom it is assumed that a duty of care exists) and to the employee (to whom it is contended on existing authority that there is no such duty). They are not being asked to warrant absolutely the accuracy of the facts or the incontrovertible validity of the opinions expressed, but to take reasonable care in compiling or giving the reference and in verifying the information on which it is based. The courts can be trusted to set a standard which is not higher than the law of negligence demands. Even if it is right that the number of references given will be reduced, the quality and value will be greater, and it is by no means certain that to have more references is more in the public interest than to have more careful references.

27

Those giving references can make it clear what are the parameters within which the reference is given, such as stating their limited acquaintance with the individual either as to time or as to situation. This issue does not arise in the present case, but it may be that employers can make it clear to the subject of the reference that they will only give one if he accepts that there will be a disclaimer of liability to him and to the recipient of the reference.

Note ───

Lord Goff based the existence of a duty of care in the giving of a reference on the principles in *Hedley Byrne v Heller* (1964), whereas Lords Slynn, Lowry and Woolf looked at the matter from the point of view of proximity and breach of an implied term in a contract. In addition, Lord Woolf suggested that, where the employee seeks a reference in a situation where it is normal practice to require a reference from a previous employer, then that employer is under a contractual duty, based on an implied term, to supply one.

Bartholomew v London Borough of Hackney (1999) CA

The respondents had given the appellant, an ex-employee, a reference which stated that he had taken voluntary severance following the deletion of his post and that, when he left, he was suspended on a charge of gross misconduct and disciplinary action had commenced against him. It also stated that this action automatically lapsed when he left the respondent's employment. All of this was true, but the applicant claimed that the reference was unfair, in that it gave no details of the gross misconduct and did not mention that he strongly denied the charge, or that he was given six weeks pay in lieu of salary.

Held, by the Court of Appeal, that, although an employer is under a duty to provide a reference which is in substance true, accurate and fair, the employer in this case was not in breach of this duty. The misconduct was in fact financial, but the court did not feel that knowing this extra information would have had any effect on the prospective employer, which was another local authority for whom he was applying for a job as a resident social worker. The fact that he denied the charge was implicit in the fact that the proceedings were ongoing, and the mention in the reference of voluntary severance indicated that the appellant must have received some payment. Moreover, had the employer omitted to mention the suspension and the disciplinary proceedings, it could have been in breach of its duty to other local authorities, their ratepayers and their clients.

2.3.2 Duties of the employee

Duty to obey orders

Morrish v Henlys (Folkestone) Ltd (1973) NIRC

The employee was a stores driver and it was his duty to draw diesel oil for his vehicle. He drew five gallons of diesel oil, but the manager changed it to seven gallons. The employee protested about this to the manager, stating that he was not prepared to have false entries recorded in respect of the vehicle which he drove, but the manager instructed him to leave the records as they stood, that is, as altered. When the employee refused, he was dismissed.

Held, by the National Industrial Relations Court, that the dismissal was unfair. *Per* Sir Hugh Griffiths:

> The respondents, that is, the employers, contended that, as there was evidence before the tribunal that it was a common practice to alter the records in this way to cover deficiencies, it was unreasonable of the appellant to object, and he should have accepted the manager's instructions. Accordingly, his refusal to do so was an unreasonable refusal to obey an order, which justified dismissal. We cannot accept this submission. It involves the proposition that it is an implied term of an employee's contract of service that he should accept an order to connive at the falsification of one of his employer's records. The proposition only has to be stated to be seen to be untenable. In our view, the appellant was fully entitled to refuse to be in any way party to a falsification of this record, and the tribunal was manifestly right in holding that he had been unfairly dismissed. The cross-appeal therefore fails.

Ottoman Bank v Chakarian (1930) PC

The employee worked for the bank in Turkey. He had previously narrowly escaped execution by the Turkish forces and asked for a transfer outside Turkey. When this was refused, he left Turkey anyway, and was dismissed by the bank.

Held, by the Judicial Committee of the Privy Council, that the dismissal was wrongful. *Per* Lord Thankerton:

> The risk of personal danger which caused the respondent's flight from Constantinople, in disregard of the appellants' repeated refusals to allow him to leave, was real and justified from the point of view of his personal safety ... It was not seriously maintained by the appellants that their order to the respondent to remain in Constantinople was a lawful order which the respondent was bound to obey at the grave risk to his person.

In their Lordships' opinion, the risk to the respondent was such that he was not bound to obey the order, which was therefore not a lawful one.

Note ──

This case was referred to by Lord Browne-Wilkinson in *Johnstone v Bloomsbury Area Health Authority* (see 2.3.1, above) for the proposition that a term can be implied in an employee's contract that the employer will safeguard the employee's health, even though this may conflict with the express terms of the contract. In *Walmsley v Udec Refrigeration Ltd* (1972), it was held that an employee was not justified in refusing to work in Eire because of a generalised fear of IRA activity. Reference to the job title in an employee's statement of initial employment particulars (s 1(4)(f) of the ERA 1996) will help to determine whether an order is lawful or not.

──

Duty to adapt to new methods of doing the job

Cresswell v Board of Inland Revenue (1984) HC

The High Court held that employees who worked in the Inland Revenue had a contractual duty to adapt to a new computerised system which replaced the traditional manual system of tax coding. Walton J distinguished between the method of doing the job and the actual job which, in this case, remained unchanged. He observed:

> ... there can really be no doubt as to the fact that an employee is expected to adapt himself to new methods and techniques introduced in the course of his employment.

Duty to exercise reasonable care in the performance of contractual duties

Lister v Romford Ice and Cold Storage Co Ltd (1957) HL

The appellant was a lorry driver employed by the respondents. He negligently injured a fellow employee, X, who happened to be his father, whilst acting in the course of employment. X sued the respondents and was awarded damages against them, on the basis that they were vicariously liable for the appellant's negligence. The respondents' insurers sued the appellant for a contribution from him towards the damages paid as a result of his negligence, as he was a joint tortfeasor and, more relevantly to employment law, damages for breach of an implied term in his contract of employment that he would exercise reasonable care in driving the lorry.

Held, by the House of Lords, that there was such an implied term. Viscount Simonds was in no doubt:

> It is, in my opinion, clear that it was an implied term of the contract that the appellant would perform his duties with proper care.

Furthermore, the House of Lords held that there is no implied term that an employer will not seek to be indemnified by an employee against liability in cases such as this, although Lord Radcliffe dissented and was prepared to imply such a term.

Note

See *Harvey v RG O'Dell Ltd* (1958), where it was held that the employer's right of indemnity did not apply where the employee, who was employed as a storekeeper, drove his motorcycle combination on his employer's instructions and with a fellow employee as passenger, in order to do some repair work. In the course of the journey, there was an accident, and the question arose whether the employee was liable to indemnify the employer when the employer had to pay compensation for injuries caused by the employee's negligence. McNair J held that, in this case, the employee was not obliged to do this. He was impressed by the fact that the employee had willingly made his motorcycle available for his employer's business when he was not normally employed to drive it.

Does an employee owe a duty to disclose his own misdeeds and those of fellow employees?

Sybron Corp v Rochem (1983) CA

A Mr Roques was a director of G, a company which was owned by the respondent company. After Roques retired, it was found that, during his employment, he had been preparing with others to set up in competition with G, and the respondents sought the return of payments which had been made by his employer into a pension scheme, together with the lump sum payment which he was given when he retired.

Held, by the Court of Appeal, that the respondents were entitled to recover these payments because, had they known what Roques was doing, they could have dismissed him for gross misconduct, in which case, the payments would never have been made. Stephenson LJ then referred to the speech of Lord Atkin in *Bell v Lever Bros Ltd* (1932) on whether an employee has a duty to disclose his own misdeeds:

It is said that there is a contractual duty of the servant to disclose his past faults. I agree that the duty in the servant to protect his master's property may involve the duty to report a fellow servant whom he knows to be wrongfully dealing with that property. The servant owes a duty not to steal but, having stolen, is there superadded a duty to confess that he has stolen? I am satisfied that to imply such a duty would be a departure from the well established usage of mankind and would be to create obligations entirely outside the normal contemplation of the parties concerned.

On the issue of whether an employee has a duty to disclose to his employer the misdeeds of fellow employees, Stephenson LJ said:

> ... there is no general duty to report a fellow servant's misconduct or breach of contract; whether there is such a duty depends on the contract and on the terms of employment of the particular servant.

Stephenson LJ added that whether there was such a duty might depend on whether the employee was so placed in the hierarchy 'as to have a duty to report such misconduct'.

Duty of fidelity

Secretary of State for Employment v ASLEF (No 2) (1972) CA
Railway workers took part in a work to rule and overtime ban in support of a pay claim.

Held, by the Court of Appeal, that the action was in breach of their contracts of employment. *Per* Lord Denning MR:

> Now I quite agree that a man is not bound positively to do more for his employer than his contract requires. He can withdraw his goodwill if he pleases. But what he must not do is wilfully to obstruct his employer as he goes about his business ... If he, with the others, takes steps wilfully to disrupt the undertaking, to produce chaos so that it will not run as it should, then each one who is a party to those steps is guilty of a breach of contract. It is no answer for any of them to say 'I am only obeying the rule book or I am not bound to do more than a 40 hour week'. That would be all very well if done in good faith without any wilful disruption of services, but what makes it wrong is the object with which it is done.

Note ———————————————————————————————————
The case can be considered either as an example of the duty of fidelity or as an example of the duty of employees to co-operate with their employer. See, also, *Ticehurst v British Telecommunications plc* (1992).

Hivac Ltd v Park Royal Scientific Instruments Ltd (1946) CA
The plaintiff company manufactured hearing aids. Two of its employees worked for a rival employer (X) in their spare time and also tried to persuade other employees to do the same. However, they did not pass on confidential information to X.

Held, by the Court of Appeal, that an injunction would be granted restraining the employees from working for X, because to do so was a breach of their common law duty of fidelity to their employers. Lord Green MR observed:

> ... it would be deplorable if it were laid down that a workman could, consistently with his duty to his employer, knowingly, deliberately and

secretly set himself to do in his spare time something which would inflict great harm on his employer's business.

On the other hand, he observed that the law also needed to be aware of placing an undue restriction on the right of the workman, particularly a manual workman, to make use of his leisure for his profit.

Misuse of confidential information

Faccenda Chicken Ltd v Fowler (1986) CA

Fowler was employed as the sales manager of the chicken marketing business of Faccenda Chicken Ltd. He then left, along with eight other employees, in order to set up a business of their own, selling chickens in competition with Faccenda Chicken Ltd. The company claimed that Fowler had used confidential sales information, and that this was a breach of an implied term in his contract not to disclose the information. There was no express term in Fowler's contract which imposed any restriction on his activities after leaving Faccenda's employment.

Held, by the Court of Appeal, that the information was not confidential and, therefore, Faccenda's action failed. Neill LJ, in a significant judgment, laid down the following precepts relating to the use of information by ex-employees:

(1) Where the parties are, or have been, linked by a contract of employment, the obligations of the employee are to be determined by the contract between him and his employer: see *Vokes Ltd v Heather* (1945).

(2) In the absence of any express term, the obligations of the employee in respect of the use and disclosure of information are the subject of implied terms.

(3) While the employee remains in the employment of the employer, the obligations are included in the implied term, which imposes a duty of good faith or fidelity on the employee. For the purpose of the present appeal, it is not necessary to consider the precise limits of this implied term, but it may be noted:

   (a) that the extent of the duty of good faith will vary according to the nature of the contract (see *Vokes Ltd v Heather*);

   (b) that the duty of good faith will be broken if the employee makes or copies a list of the customers of the employer for use after his employment ends or deliberately memorises such a list, even though, except in special circumstances, there is no general restriction on an ex-employee canvassing or doing business with customers of his former employer (see *Robb v Green* (1895) and *Wessex Dairies Ltd v Smith* (1935)).

(4) The implied term which imposes an obligation on the employee as to his conduct after the determination of the employment is more restricted in its scope than that which imposes a general duty of good faith. It is clear that the obligation not to use or disclose information may cover secret processes of manufacture, such as chemical formulae (*Amber Size and Chemical Co v Menzel* (1913)) or designs or special methods of construction (*Reid and Sigrist Ltd v Moss and Mechanism Ltd* (1932)) and other information which is of a sufficiently high degree of confidentiality as to amount to a trade secret.

The obligation does not extend, however, to cover all information which is given to or acquired by the employee while in his employment and, in particular, may not cover information which is only 'confidential' in the sense that an unauthorised disclosure of such information to a third party while the employment subsisted would be a clear breach of the duty of good faith.

(5) In order to determine whether any particular item of information falls within the implied term so as to prevent its use or disclosure by an employee after his employment has ceased, it is necessary to consider all the circumstances of the case. We are satisfied that the following matters are among those to which attention must be paid:

(a) The nature of the employment. Thus, employment in a capacity where 'confidential' material is habitually handled may impose a high obligation of confidentiality, because the employee can be expected to realise its sensitive nature to a greater extent than if he were employed in a capacity where such material reaches him only occasionally or incidentally.

(b) The nature of the information itself. In our judgment, the information will only be protected if it can properly be classed as a trade secret or as material which, while not properly to be described as a trade secret, is in all the circumstances of such a highly confidential nature as to require the same protection as a trade secret *eo nomine*.

(c) Whether the employer impressed on the employee the confidentiality of the information. Thus, though an employer cannot prevent the use or disclosure merely by telling the employee that certain information is confidential, the attitude of the employer towards the information provides evidence which may assist in determining whether or not the information can properly be regarded as a trade secret.

(d) Whether the relevant information can easily be isolated from other information which the employee is free to use or disclose.

Duty to account

Reading v Attorney General (1951) HL

Reading was a sergeant in the army, stationed in Egypt. He agreed, on a number of occasions, to accompany civilian lorries carrying illicit spirits, his uniform guaranteeing that the lorries would not be inspected. He was paid about £20,000 for his services. He was arrested and imprisoned, and the Crown impounded the £20,000. When he was released from prison, he claimed the £20,000 back. The House of Lords rejected his claim. *Per* Lord Porter:

> ... it is a principle of law that, if a servant, in violation of his duty of honesty and good faith, takes advantage of his service to make a profit for himself, in this sense, that the assets of which he has control, or the facilities which he enjoys, or the position which he occupies, are the real cause of his obtaining money ... that is, if they play a predominant part in his obtaining the money, then he is accountable for it to the master. It matters not that the master has not lost any profit, nor suffered any damage.

2.3.3 Employees' inventions

Patents Act 1977

Section 39   Right to employees' inventions

(1) Notwithstanding anything in any rule of law, an invention made by an employee shall, as between him and his employer, be taken to belong to his employer for the purposes of this Act and all other purposes if:

  (a) it was made in the course of the normal duties, or in the course of duties falling outside his normal duties, but specifically assigned to him, and the circumstances in either case were such that an invention might reasonably be expected to result from the carrying out of his duties; or

  (b) the invention was made in the course of the duties of the employee and, at the time of making the invention, because of the nature of his duties and the particular responsibilities arising from the nature of his duties, he had a special obligation to further the interests of the employer's undertaking.

(2) Any other invention made by an employee shall, as between him and his employer, be taken for those purposes to belong to the employee.

Section 40   Compensation of employees for certain inventions

(1) Where it appears to the court or the comptroller on an application made by an employee within the prescribed period that the employee has made an invention belonging to the employer for which a patent

has been granted, that the patent is (having regard among other things to the size and nature of the employer's undertaking) of outstanding benefit to the employer and that, by reason of those facts, it is just that the employee should be awarded compensation to be paid by the employer, the court or the comptroller may award him such compensation of an amount determined under s 41, below.

(2) Where it appears to the court or the comptroller on an application made by an employee within the prescribed period that:

(a) a patent has been granted for an invention made by and belonging to the employee;

(b) his rights in the invention, or in any patent or application for a patent for the invention have, since the appointed day, been assigned to the employer or an exclusive licence under the patent or application has since the appointed day been granted to the employer;

(c) the benefit derived by the employee from the contract of assignment, assignation or grant or any ancillary contract ('the relevant contract') is inadequate in relation to the benefit derived by the employer from the patent; and

(d) by reason of those facts, it is just that the employee should be awarded compensation to be paid by the employer, in addition to the benefit derived from the relevant contract,

the court or comptroller may award him such compensation of an amount determined under s 41, below.

(3) Sub-sections (1) and (2) above shall not apply to the invention of an employee where a relevant collective agreement provides for the payment of compensation in respect of inventions of the same description as that invention to employees of the same description as that employee.

(4) Sub-section (2) above shall have effect notwithstanding anything in the relevant contract or any agreement applicable to the invention (other than any such collective agreement).

(5) If it appears to the comptroller on an application under this section that the application involves matters which would be more properly be determined by the court, he may decline to deal with it.

(6) In this section:

'the prescribed period', in relation to proceedings before the court, means the period prescribed by rules of court; and

'relevant collective agreement' means a collective agreement within the meaning of the Trade Union and Labour Relations Act 1974, made by, or on behalf of, a trade union to which the employee belongs, and by the employer or an employers' association to which the employer belongs, which is in force at the time of the making of the invention.

Note
This definition of a collective agreement is now contained in s 178 of the Trade Union and Labour Relations (Consolidation) Act 1992.

(7) References in this section to an invention belonging to an employer or employee are references to it so belonging as between the employer and the employee.

Section 41   Amount of compensation

(1) An award of compensation to an employee under s 40(1) or (2) above, in relation to a patent for an invention, shall be such as will secure for the employee a fair share (having regard to all the circumstances) of the benefit which the employer has derived, or may reasonably be expected to derive, from the patent or from the assignment, assignation or grant to a person connected with the employer of the property or any right in the invention or the property in, or any right in or under, an application for that patent.

(2) For the purposes of sub-s (1) above, the amount of any benefit derived or expected to be derived by an employer from the assignment, assignation or grant of:

(a) the property in, or any right in or under, a patent for the invention or an application for such a payment; or

(b) the property or any right in the invention,

to a person connected with him shall be taken to be the amount which could be reasonably be expected to be so derived by the employer if that person had not been connected with him.

(3) Where the Crown or a Research Council in its capacity as employer assigns or grants the property in, or any right in or under, an invention, patent or application for a patent to a body having among its functions that of developing or exploiting inventions resulting from public research, and does so for no consideration or only a nominal consideration, any benefit derived from the invention, patent or application by that body shall be treated for the purposes of the foregoing provisions of this section as so derived by the Crown or, as the case may be, Research Council.

In this sub-section, 'Research Council' means a body which is a Research Council for the purposes of the Science and Technology Act 1965.

(4) In determining the fair share of the benefit to be secured for an employee in respect of a patent for an invention which has always belonged to an employer, the court or the comptroller shall, among other things, take the following matters into account, that is to say:

    (a) the nature of the employee's duties, his remuneration and the other advantages he derives or has derived in relation to the invention under this Act;

    (b) the effort and skill which the employee has devoted to making the invention;

    (c) the effort and skill which any other person has devoted to making the invention jointly with the employee concerned, and the advice and other assistance contributed by any other employee who is not a joint inventor of the invention; and

    (d) the contribution made by the employer to the making, developing and working of the invention by the provision of advice, facilities and other assistance, by the provision of opportunities and by his managerial and commercial skill and activities.

(5) In determining the fair share of the benefit to be secured for an employee in respect of a patent for an invention which originally belonged to him, the court or the comptroller shall, among other things, take the following matters into account, that is to say:

    (a) any conditions in a licence or licences granted under this Act or otherwise in respect of the invention or the patent;

    (b) the extent to which the invention was made jointly by the employee with any other person; and

    (c) the contribution made by the employer to the making, developing and working of the invention as mentioned in in sub-s (4)(d), above.

(6) Any order for the payment of compensation under s 40 above may be an order for the payment of a lump sum or for periodical payment, or both.

Section 42 Enforceability of contracts relating to employees' inventions

(1) This section applies to any contract (whenever made) relating to inventions made by an employee, being a contract entered into by him:

    (a) with the employer (alone or with another); or

    (b) with some other person at the request of the employer or in pursuance of the employee's contract of employment.

(2) Any term in a contract to which this section applies which diminishes the employee's rights in inventions of any description made by him after the appointed day and date of the contract, or in or under patents

for those inventions or applications for such patents, shall be unenforceable against him to the extent that it diminishes his rights in an invention of that description so made, or in or under a patent for such an invention or an application for any such patent.

(3) Sub-section (2) above shall not be construed as derogating from any duty of confidentiality owed to his employer by an employee by virtue of any rule of law or otherwise.

Note ──

References in the Act to 'the court' means the Patents Court and references to 'the comptroller' means the Comptroller of Patents. See *Reiss Engineering Co Ltd v Harris* (1985), one of the main cases so far decided on this area.

2.4 Duty of mutual trust and confidence

Malik v Bank of Credit and Commerce International SA (In Liquidation) (1997) HL

The two appellants were long serving employees of a bank which collapsed as a result of a massive fraud perpetrated by those controlling it. The appellants were unaware of the fraud. After the bank went into liquidation, they were made redundant and claimed that they had suffered by their association with the bank and, accordingly, claimed 'stigma compensation'. This, they claimed, arose from the fact that they had been put at a disadvantage in the labour market due to their employer's breach of implied terms in their contracts of employment that the employer would not conduct the business in a manner calculated or likely to destroy or seriously damage the relationship of trust and confidence between them.

Held, by the House of Lords, that, in principle, their employers were in breach of this implied term and that the appellant's action succeeded. The decision is of great significance because:

(a) Although the implied term of mutual trust and confidence has often been considered in determining constructive dismissal for the purpose of an unfair dismissal action, this was the first time that it had been considered by the courts in an action founded solely on the breach of the contract of employment. As Lord Steyn pointed out, the evolution of the implied term was part of a 'change in legal culture', of which other examples are *Scally and Others v Southern Health and Social Services Board* (1991) and *Spring v Guardian Assurance plc* (1994). As Lord Steyn observed:

It is true that the implied term adds little to the employee's implied obligations to serve his employer loyally and not to act contrary to his employer's interests. The major importance of the implied duty of trust and confidence lies in its impact on the obligations of the employer ... And the implied obligation so formulated is apt to cover the great diversity of situations in which a balance has to be struck between an employer's interest in managing his business as he sees fit, and the employee's interest in not being unfairly and improperly exploited.

(b) In *Addis v Gramophone Co* (1909), the House of Lords had decided that any losses suffered by an employee from the very fact of dismissal itself were not recoverable. This would include damages for injured feelings and what were called in the present case 'stigma compensation'. Lord Nicholls held that any observations in *Addis* 'cannot be read as precluding the recovery of damages where the manner of dismissal involved a breach of the trust and confidence term and this caused financial loss'. He pointed out that this implied term had not been formulated at the date of the decision in *Addis* and thus neatly sidestepped the issue of whether *Addis* was no longer good law. Nevertheless, in so far as *Addis* was thought to prevent the recovery of losses of the kind alleged in *Malik*, and possibly also damages for injured feelings, it is clear that *Malik* is now the authority to be relied on.

Bank of Credit and Commerce International v Ali (No 3) (1999) HC

This case followed the decision of the House of Lords in *Malik* (see above). Once it had been held that claims for stigma damages were possible, five employees were selected to bring claims to determine whether the dishonest conduct of BCCI (the bank) was of sufficient gravity to constitute a breach of the implied term of mutual trust and confidence and, if so, what loss the employees suffered as a result of the breach and whether that loss was compensatable in damages.

Held, by the High Court, that:

(a) there was a breach of the implied term of mutual trust and confidence. To amount to such a breach, the misconduct on the part of the employer must be so serious as to amount to constructive dismissal (see 4.2.3, below). Carrying on a business in a corrupt or dishonest manner could be a breach but, in deciding whether there has been a breach, one needs to look at the degree of dishonesty, the size and number of dishonest transactions, the level of employees involved and the importance and prevalence of the wrongdoing, in the context of the employer's business as a whole. One can then form a view as to whether it would be unfair or improper exploitation of the employees to continue to require them to be employed in such a business.

(b) However, the employees failed to establish that the publicity given to the bank's wrongdoing blighted their chances of obtaining fresh employment. As Lightman J put it: 'Damages can only be recoverable if the "stigma in the marketplace" results in financial loss.' Damages for stigma as such are not recoverable.

Note ──────────────────────────────────

The duty of mutual trust and confidence has also been considered in a number of other recent cases. See:

(a) *French v Barclays Bank plc* (1999). A decision by an employee bank to change the terms of a relocation loan made to an employee was held to be a breach;

(b) *University of Nottingham v (1) Eyett (2) The Pensions Ombudsman* (1999). A failure by an employer to warn an employee that, by not delaying his retirement for a few days, he was making a financial mistake in view of how his pension entitlements were calculated was not a breach of the duty;

(c) *Johnson v Unisys Ltd* (1999). The Court of Appeal held that, where there has been an express dismissal, then *Addis* remained the authority for the proposition that damages for wrongful dismissal cannot include damages for the manner of the dismissal, the employee's injured feelings, or stigma compensation. Accordingly, the remarks in the House of Lords in *Malik* on the status of the decision in *Addis* were held to be limited to cases where the complaint related to a breach of trust and confidence by the employee. This was a surprising decision and was clearly an attempt by the Court of Appeal to limit the scope of *Malik*;

(d) *Brown v Merchant Ferries Ltd* (1998). The Northern Ireland Court of Appeal held that, in deciding whether there has been a breach of the duty of mutual trust and confidence so as to amount to constructive dismissal, the test is whether the employer's conduct so impacted on the employee that, viewed objectively, the employee could properly conclude that the employer was repudiating the contract;

(e) *Macari v Celtic Football and Athletic Co Ltd* (1999). The Court of Session held that, where an employee carries on working when the employer has broken the implied term of mutual trust and confidence, the employee cannot, on the ground of the employer's breach of that term, disregard the employer's lawful and legitimate instructions regarding his work.

2.5 Doctrine of restraint of trade

Herbert Morris v Saxelby (1916) HL

Lord Parker explained:

> I cannot find any case in which a covenant against competition by a servant
> has, as such, ever been upheld by the court. Wherever such covenants have
> been upheld, it has been on the grounds, not that the servant or apprentice
> would, by reason of his employment and training, obtain the skill or
> knowledge necessary to equip him as a possible competitor in the trade,
> but that he might obtain such personal knowledge of, and influence over,
> the customers of his employer that, on such an acquaintance with his
> employer's trade secrets as would enable him, if competition were
> allowed, to take advantage of his employer's trade connections or utilise
> information confidentially obtained.

Nordenfelt v Maxim Nordenfelt Guns and Ammunition Co Ltd (1894) HL

Lord Macnaghten's formulation is the beginning of the modern doctrine of
restraint of trade:

> The true view at the present time, I think, is this: the public have an interest
> in every person's carrying on his trade freely; so has the individual. All
> interference with individual liberty of action in trading, and all restraints
> of trade of themselves, if there is nothing more, are contrary to public
> policy and therefore void. That is the general rule. But there are exceptions:
> restraints of trade and interference with individual liberty of action may be
> justified by the special circumstances of a particular case. It is sufficient
> justification and, indeed, it is the only justification, if the restriction is
> reasonable – reasonable, that is, in reference to the interest of the parties
> concerned and reasonable in reference to the interests of the public, so
> framed and so guarded as to afford adequate protection to the party in
> whose favour it is imposed, while at the same time, it is in no way injurious
> to the public.

Note ───

See *Forster v Suggett* (1918) for an example of a valid clause which
protected trade secrets and *Home Counties Dairies v Skilton* (1970) for an
example of a valid clause which protected customer connections.

Mason v Provident Clothing and Supply Co Ltd (1913) HL

The defendant was employed by the plaintiffs to canvass business and
collect payments in a part of Islington. A clause in his contract prevented
him from doing similar work within 25 miles of London for three years
after leaving his employment with the plaintiffs.

Held, by the House of Lords, that the restraint was too wide and therefore void as being unreasonable. Lord Moulton said:

> The nature of the employment of the appellant in this business was solely to obtain members and collect their instalments. A small district in London was assigned to him, which he canvassed and in which he collected the payments due, and outside that small district, he had no duties. His employment was therefore that of a local canvasser and debt collector, and nothing more.

> Such being the nature of the employment, it would be reasonable for the employer to protect himself against the danger of his former servant canvassing or collecting for a rival firm in the district in which he had been employed. If he were permitted to do so before the expiry of a reasonably long interval, he would be in a position to give to his new employer all the advantages of that personal knowledge of the inhabitants of the locality and, more especially, of his former customers, which he had acquired in the service of the respondents and at their expense. Against such a contingency, the master might reasonably protect himself, but I can see no further or other protection which he could reasonably demand.

Littlewoods v Harris (1977) CA

The defendant was the creative director of the plaintiff's mail order business. The plaintiff's principal rival was Great Universal Stores Ltd (GUS Ltd). The defendant's contract provided that, for 12 months after leaving the plaintiff's employment, the defendant would not 'Enter into a contract of service or other agreement of a like nature with GUS Ltd, or any company subsidiary thereto or be directly or indirectly engaged concerned or interested in the trading or business of the said GUS Ltd or any such company aforesaid'.

The defendant left the employment of the plaintiff company, but refused to give an undertaking that he would not work for GUS Ltd within the following 12 months.

Held, by the Court of Appeal, that the clause was binding. The difficulty was with reference to 'any company subsidiary thereto' which, it was argued by the defendant, was too wide, because many of GUS Ltd's subsidiaries had no connection with the mail order business. However, the court was prepared to construe the clause in the following way:

> 'Any company subsidiary thereto' means any subsidiary which, at any relevant moment of time during the period covered by the covenant, is concerned wholly or partly in the mail order business carried on in the UK. That would include, for example, a subsidiary which was concerned with the buying of goods which were going to be used by some other company

in the group in the mail order business in the UK. It would include any subsidiary in which it was sought to employ the defendant, whatever the function of that subsidiary, and whether or not there might be any reference thereto in his contract of service to deal in any way with, or advise in any way, or give anyone information relating to the mail order business in the UK. It will, I hope, be clear from what I have said that I am not suggesting that the covenant requires to be re-written. I am interpreting the covenant as I understand it ought to be interpreted in the circumstances which exist in this case, as I conceive to have been done in the cases which I have cited [*per* Megaw LJ].

Note ──

This approach had also been taken in *Home Counties Dairies v Skilton* (1970), where the Court of Appeal dealt with a clause in a milkman's contract of employment which provided that he was not to 'serve or sell milk or dairy products' to any customer of the dairy within one year of leaving their employment. This could have prevented him from serving a customer of the dairy with cheese whilst working in a grocer's shop, but the Court of Appeal limited the restraint to activities as a milkman.

Scully UK Ltd v Lee (1998) CA

The defendant was employed by the plaintiffs and his contract of employment contained a clause prohibiting him from being involved in any business dealing with the type of equipment provided by the plaintiffs.

Held, by the Court of Appeal, that the clause was unreasonable and invalid, because it applied to businesses which were not in competition with the plaintiffs. Nor was it possible, on the facts, to follow the approach in *Home Counties Dairies v Skilton* (1970) and limit the clause to activities which were reasonable.

Greer v Sketchleys Ltd (1979) CA

The plaintiff was a director of the defendant company, who ran a dry cleaning business in the Midlands and London. His contract of employment prevented him, for 12 months after leaving the defendant's employment, from being engaged in a similar business in any part of the UK.

Held, by the Court of Appeal, that the restraint was too wide and was therefore void as being unreasonable, because it applied to the whole of the UK. Lord Denning MR said that the clause provided that:

... he shall not engage in any part of the UK in any similar business. If Sketchleys operated all over England, Scotland and Wales, it might be reasonable to have such a covenant, but Sketchleys did not operate as widely. In 1974, their operations were confined to the Midlands and the south of England, excluding Wales, Cornwall and Devon and Lancashire right up to the north. Sketchleys did not cover any of that area. Was it reasonable for them to have a covenant restraining Mr Greer from going to any of these other parts of England, Scotland and Wales? Suppose, for instance, there had been a group of dry cleaning shops in the Tyne and Wear conurbation or in the Lancashire conurbation or Glasgow and Edinburgh or down in Devon; Sketchleys did not have any kind of operation in those areas then. Was it reasonable to restrain him from engaging in any of those businesses or with any of those groups which were in those areas in which Sketchleys did not operate at all? It is said by Mr Buckley that they might expand into those areas in the future. Now, over three years later, they have not expanded into Devon or Cornwall or into Yorkshire or Lancashire or into the north of England or into Scotland. It seems to me that that problematical and possible expansion into all these other areas is much too vague and much too wide to justify restraint over every part of the UK.

Q   Can the approach taken in *Littlewoods v Harris* be reconciled with that in *Greer v Sketchleys*? If not, which do you feel is preferable?

2.5.1 Non-solicitation by agreement

TSC Europe (UK) Ltd v Massey (1999) HC
The defendant had set up a company in the field of call centre and customer management applications. This company was then bought by the plaintiff, who continued to employ the defendant. The defendant's contract of employment included a non-solicitation clause, under which he agreed, for either three years from the date of the agreement or one year from the date of termination of his contract, not to solicit any employees of either the plaintiff's or of his own company to leave their employment.

Held, by the High Court, that an employer has a legitimate interest in maintaining a stable, trained workforce and, therefore, non-solicitation clauses can be valid. However, the present clause went beyond the limits of reasonableness in that it prohibited solicitation of any employee, without reference to his or her importance in the business, and it applied to any employee who joined the company during the prohibited period, including those whose employment began after the defendant had ceased to be an employee. Therefore, the restraint was unreasonable and invalid.

2.5.2 Exclusive service contracts

A Schroeder Music Publishing Co Ltd v Macaulay (1974) HL

The respondent, then a young unknown songwriter, made a contract with the appellant, under which he gave his services exclusively to the appellant for five years. The agreement, which was the standard agreement used by the appellant, provided that the appellant should have full copyright in all the respondent's songs which he composed up to the end of the five year period. They agreed to pay him one sum of £50 as an advance against future royalties. The appellant could terminate the agreement at any time by one month's notice, but the respondent had no reciprocal right. Similarly, whereas the appellant could assign the agreement, the respondent could not and, most importantly, the appellant was under no obligation to publish the respondent's work.

Held, by the House of Lords, that, given the inequality of bargaining power between the parties, the fact that as it was on a standard form, there was no opportunity for negotiation, and the fact that the terms of the agreement were totally one-sided, it was contrary to public policy and void. Lord Diplock pointed out that, when music publishers negotiated with songwriters whose success had already been established, they did not use such a form of contract. The implication was that, in using them in the case of inexperienced songwriters, they were taking advantage of that inexperience.

2.5.3 Doctrine of severance

Scorer v Seymour-Johns (1966) CA

The defendant was employed by the plaintiff in sole charge of the Kingsbridge office of their estate agents' business. There was another office in Dartmouth. The defendant's contract provided that he would not, for three years after the termination of his contract of employment, 'undertake or carry on either alone or in partnership or be employed or interested directly or indirectly in any capacity whatsoever in the business of an auctioneer surveyor or estate agent or in any ancillary business carried on by [the plaintiff] at [the Kingsbridge and Dartmouth offices] within a five mile radius thereof ...'.

Held, by the Court of Appeal, that, whereas the prohibition in respect of the Kingsbridge office was valid and enforceable, that in respect of the Dartmouth office was not, but, as the restraints were quite separate, the prohibition in respect of the Dartmouth office could be severed.

2.5.4 Attempts to prevent a claim that a clause in a contract is an unlawful restraint of trade

Rock Refrigeration Ltd v Jones and Another (1997) CA

The Court of Appeal considered the effect of a provision in the defendant's contract which stated that restraint of trade clauses would still apply to him in the event of termination of his contract of employment 'howsoever occasioned'.

Held, by the Court of Appeal, that the rule in *General Billposting v Atkinson* (1909) still applied – a restraint of trade clause would not apply if the employee was wrongfully dismissed. However, Simon Brown and Morritt LJJ held that, although the attempt by the employer to make the clause apply even in the event of a breach of contract by the employer did not succeed, that did not mean that the clause was by itself unlawful and unreasonable.

2.5.5 Enforcement of a valid restraint

Jack Allen (Sales and Service) Ltd v Smith (1999) Court of Session

The Court of Session held that an interim interdict (injunction), restraining a restraint of trade clause in a contract, should not be granted on the basis of a *prima facie* case, but the employer must point to 'a perceived actual or potential harm which is real and not fanciful, which would justify interim restraint to avoid such harm being inflicted'.

2.6 Changing the contract of employment

Wandsworth London Borough Council v D'Silva and Another (1998) CA

The actual decision in this case (see 2.2.3, above) was that a Code of Practice was not part of a contract of employment. However, Lord Woolf MR made the following observations on when the parties to an employment contract can vary it unilaterally and, although these are *obiter*, they are of great interest:

> The general position is that contracts of employment can only be varied by agreement. However, in the employment field, an employer or, for that matter, an employee, can reserve the ability to change a particular aspect of the contract unilaterally by notifying the other party as part of the contract that this is the situation. However, clear language is required to reserve to one party an unusual power of this sort. In addition, the court is unlikely to favour an interpretation which does more than enable a party to vary contractual provisions with which that party is required to comply.

2.7   Payment of wages

2.7.1 Right to an itemised pay statement

Section 8 of the Employment Rights Act 1996
(1) An employee has the right to be given by his employer, at or before the time at which any payment of wages or salary is made to him, a written itemised statement.

(2) The statement shall contain particulars of:

(a) the gross amount of wages or salary;

(b) the amounts of any variable, and (subject to s 9) any fixed, deductions from that gross amount and the purposes for which they are made;

(c) the net amount of wages or salary payable; and

(d) where different parts of the net amount are paid in different ways, the amount and method of payment of each part-payment.

2.7.2 Deductions from wages

Right not to suffer unauthorised deductions

Section 13 of the Employment Rights Act 1996
(1) An employer shall not make a deduction from wages of a worker employed by him, unless:

(a) the deduction is required or authorised to be made by virtue of a statutory provision or a relevant provision of the worker's contract; or

(b) the worker has previously signified in writing his agreement or consent to the making of the deduction.

(2) In this section, 'relevant provision', in relation to a worker's contract, means a provision of the contract comprised:

(a) in one or more written terms of the contract of which the employer has given the worker a copy on an occasion prior to the employer making the deduction in question; or

(b) in one or more terms of the contract (whether express or implied and, if express, whether oral or in writing), the existence and effect, or combined effect, of which in relation to the worker the employer has notified to the worker in writing on such an occasion.

(3) Where the total amount of wages paid on any occasion by an employer to a worker employed by him is less than the total amount of the wages properly payable by him to the worker on that occasion (after deductions), the amount of the deficiency shall be treated for the

purposes of this Part as a deduction made by the employer from the worker's wages on that occasion.

(4) Sub-section (3) does not apply in so far as the deficiency is attributable to an error of any description on the part of the employer affecting the computation by him of the gross amount of the wages properly payable by him to the worker on that occasion.

(5) For the purposes of this section, a relevant provision of a worker's contract having effect by virtue of a variation of the contract does not operate to authorise the making of a deduction on account of any conduct of the worker, or any other event occurring, before the variation took effect.

(6) For the purposes of this section, an agreement or consent signified by a worker does not operate to authorise the making of a deduction on account of any conduct of the worker, or any other even occurring, before the agreement or consent was signified.

(7) The section does not affect any other statutory provision by virtue of which a sum payable to a worker by his employer, but not constituting 'wages' within the meaning of this Part, is not to be subject to a deduction at the instance of the employer.

2.7.3 Meaning of 'wages'

Section 27 gives a lengthy definition, but the most important provision is s 27(1)(a):

(1) In this Part 'wages', in relation to a worker, means any sums payable to the worker in connection with his employment, including:

(a) any fee, bonus, commission, holiday pay or other emolument referable to his employment, whether payable under his contract or otherwise.

Delaney v Staples (1992) HL
The applicant was summarily dismissed and her employer gave her a cheque for £82 as payment in lieu of notice. The employer then stopped the cheque, alleging that he had been entitled to dismiss the applicant without notice, on the ground that she had broken her contract by taking away with her confidential information.

Held, by the House of Lords, that the term 'wages', in what is now s 27 of the ERA 1996, does not cover payments in lieu of notice, because the Act defines the term 'wages' as including 'any sums payable to the worker by his employer in connection with his employment'. Payments in lieu of notice, however, are damages for breach of contract and therefore can be claimed as such, but not as an unlawful deduction from wages.

Note ───

The applicant also claimed outstanding commission of £18 and accrued holiday pay of £37.50. The Court of Appeal held that these were cases of straightforward non-payment, and so could be recovered in an action for unlawful deductions from wages. The Court of Appeal was not impressed with an argument based on a distinction between non-payment and deduction; what is now s 13 of the ERA 1996 applies, in principle, to both. Nicholls LJ observed that 'any shortfall in the amount of wages properly payable was to be treated as a deduction'. (This point was not appealed to the House of Lords.) Other recent cases on deductions from wages are *Kent Management Services Ltd v Butterfield* (1992), which held that a discretionary or *ex gratia* payment could be challenged as an unlawful deduction, because what is now s 27(1)(a) of the ERA 1996 refers to sums 'whether payable under his contract or otherwise', and *Fairfield Ltd v Skinner* (1992). In the latter case, an employer claimed the right to make a deduction for alleged damage to a van and for phone calls and mileage in excess of an agreed figure. The EAT held that, even though, in principle, an employer may be entitled to make a deduction, he can still be required to substantiate the amount where the deduction was found to be excessive.

2.7.4 Deductions to which the Employment Rights Act 1996 does not apply

Section 14

(1) Section 13 does not apply to a deduction from a worker's wages made by his employer where the purpose of the deduction is the reimbursement of the employer in respect of:

(a) an overpayment of wages; or

(b) an overpayment in respect of expenses incurred by the worker in carrying out his employment,

made (for any reason) by the employer to the worker.

(2) Section 13 does not apply to a deduction from a worker's wages made by his employer in consequence of any disciplinary proceedings, if those proceedings were held by virtue of a statutory provision.

(3) Section 13 does not apply to a deduction from a worker's wages made by his employer in pursuance of a requirement imposed on the employer by a statutory provision to deduct and pay over to a public authority amounts determined by that authority as being due to it from the worker, if the deduction is made in accordance with the relevant determination of that authority.

(4) Section 13 does not apply to a deduction from a worker's wages made by his employer in pursuance of any arrangements which have been established:

    (a) in accordance with a relevant provision of his contract to the inclusion of which in the contract, the worker has signified his consent or agreement in writing; or

    (b) otherwise with the prior agreement or consent of the worker signified in writing,

and under which the employer is to deduct and pay over to a third person amounts notified by the employer to that person as being due to him from the worker, if the deduction is made in accordance with the relevant notification by that person.

(5) Section 13 does not apply to a deduction from a worker's wages made by his employer where the worker has taken part in a strike or other industrial action and the deduction is made by the employer on account of the worker's having taken part in that strike or other action.

(6) Section 13 does not apply to a deduction from a worker's wages made by his employer with his prior agreement or consent signified in writing, where the purpose of the deduction is the satisfaction (whether wholly or in part) of an order of a court or tribunal requiring the payment of an amount by the worker to the employer.

Hussman Manufacturing v Weir (1998) EAT

The appellant was employed on the night shift, which meant that he was entitled to a shift allowance. His employers then introduced a new shift system, as a result of which he was switched to another shift, which meant that his allowance was reduced by £17 a week. He claimed that he had suffered an unauthorised deduction from wages in breach of s 13 of the ERA 1996.

Held, by the EAT, that he had not suffered an unauthorised deduction, because his employers were entitled, under the terms of his contract, to change his shifts; the alteration in his wages was simply a consequence of that. *Per* Lord Johnston:

    ... the fact that the consequence of a permitted and lawful act may have an economic impact upon the earnings of the employee does not in itself render that impact ... an unauthorised deduction in terms of the legislation.

2.7.5 Remedies for unlawful deductions from wages

Sections 23–26 of the ERA 1996 provide that a complaint must be made to an industrial tribunal within three months of the last deduction or payment, although the tribunal has a discretion to extend this time limit if satisfied that it was not reasonably practicable to present a claim within this time. The tribunal can order repayment of amounts improperly deducted.

2.7.6 National Mininum Wage Act 1998

Section 1

(1) A person who qualifies for the national minimum wage shall be remunerated by his employer in respect of his work in any pay reference period at a rate which is not less than the national minimum wage.

(2) A person qualifies for the national minimum wage if he is an individual who:

(a) is a worker;

(b) is working, or ordinarily works, in the UK under his contract;

(c) has ceased to be of compulsory school age.

(3) The national minimum wage shall be such single hourly rate as the Secretary of State may from time to time prescribe.

(4) For the purposes of this Act, a 'pay reference period' is such period as the Secretary of State may prescribe for the purpose.

(5) ...

3 Health and Safety at Work

3.1 Liability of the employer under the tort of negligence

3.1.1 Duty of care

Williams and Clyde Coal Co Ltd v English (1938) HL
The respondent was employed by the appellants at a colliery. At the end of a day shift, the respondent was proceeding underground to the pit-bottom, but he was then crushed when a haulage plant was set in motion. He claimed that it was recognised mining practice that the haulage plant should be stopped when day shift men were being raised to the surface. The appellants claimed that they had discharged their duty to provide a safe system of work by appointing a qualified manager.

Held, by the House of Lords, that the duty to provide a safe system of work was a personal one and rested on an employer, even where the actual performance of the duty had been delegated to an agent. *Per* Lord Wright:

> I think the whole course of authority consistently recognises a duty which rests on the employer, and which is personal to the employer, to take reasonable care for the safety of his workmen, whether the employer be an individual, a firm or a company, and whether or not the employer takes any 'share in the conduct of the operations'.

Square D Ltd v Cook (1992) CA
The respondent was employed by the appellants as an electronics engineer and was sent to Saudi Arabia, where his task was to complete work on four computer control systems. The premises where he worked were occupied by another company, and yet another company was the main contractor. Some tiles had been removed from the floor of a corridor in order to complete wiring work, which had left holes in the floor and, whilst seeking to avoid these holes, the respondent's foot became jammed in them and he suffered injuries to his knee.

Held, by the Court of Appeal, that the appellants were not liable. Although an employer can be liable for injuries occurring at the premises of third parties, whether or not an employer is actually held liable will depend on all the circumstances, and here, as Farquharson LJ put it:

> The suggestion that the home-based employer may have a responsibility for the daily events of a site in Saudi Arabia has an air of unreality.

On the general principle, he observed:

> It is clear that, in determining an employer's responsibility, one has to look at all the circumstances of the case, including the place where the work is to be done, the nature of the building on the site concerned (if there is a building), the experience of the employee who is so despatched to work at such a site, the nature of the work he is required to carry out, the degree of control that the employer can reasonably exercise in the circumstances and the employer's own knowledge of the defective state of the premises ...

Hudson v Ridge Manufacturing Co Ltd (1957) HC

One of the defendants had engaged in practical jokes for many years and, in particular, he often tripped up fellow employees. He had often been reprimanded by the foreman, but no other action had been taken against him. He then tripped up the plaintiff, a cripple, and injured him.

Held, by the High Court (QBD), that his employers were liable to the plaintiff, because they had been aware of the employee's misconduct for some time and had not taken proper steps to put an end to it.

White and Others v Chief Constable of South Yorkshire Police and Others (1999) HL

The respondents were police officers who had been on duty at Hillsborough football stadium when 96 persons were crushed to death and many more injured. They claimed damages in negligence against the Chief Constable of South Yorkshire on the ground that he owed them a duty of care as employees/rescuers to avoid exposing them to unnecessary risk of physical or psychiatric injury.

Held, by the House of Lords, that their claim failed. A claimant who is not within the range of foreseeable physical injury is a 'secondary' victim and, in order to recover compensation for psychiatric injury, must satisfy the control mechanism set out by the House of Lords in *Allcock v Chief Constable of South Yorkshire Police* (1992). This requires, *inter alia*, that there must be close ties of love and affection between the claimant and the victim which, obviously, could not be the case here. Accordingly, the police officers could not recover, and the fact that they were employees was no reason in itself for treating them as primary victims and allowing them to recover.

Walker v Northumberland County Council (1995) HC

The plaintiff was employed by the defendants as an area social services officer. The volume of his work rose but, despite the plaintiff making representations calling for increased staffing levels, nothing was done, and the plaintiff suffered a nervous breakdown. When he returned to work, it was agreed to provide him with extra assistance but, after a month, it was withdrawn. He suffered a second breakdown five months later and was subsequently dismissed on the ground of permanent ill health.

Held, by the High Court (QBD), that his employer owed the plaintiff a duty of care. *Per* Goulding J, '... although there was little judicial authority on the extent to which an employer owes to his employees a duty not to cause them psychiatric damage by the volume or character of the work which the employees are required to perform', there was no reason why the risk of psychiatric damage should be excluded from the employer's duty of care. However, he emphasised that claims based on psychiatric damage 'will often give rise to extremely difficult evidential problems of foreseeability and causation'. What was crucial in this case was that the plaintiff's first breakdown meant that he 'was exposed in his job to a reasonably foreseeable risk to his mental health' and, therefore, the standard of care required the local authority to provide additional assistance to the plaintiff. In fact, the extra help provided was withdrawn after one month.

Note ——————————————————————————————————————
See, also, *Johnstone v Bloomsbury Area Health Authority* (see 2.3.1, above).

Q   In *Walker v Northumberland County Council*, Goulding J held that the local authority's duty was owed irrespective of its staffing problem caused by lack of resources. What do you consider to be the implications of this view?

3.1.2   The standard of care

Latimer v AEC Ltd (1953) HL
The respondents owned a large factory which was flooded by an unusually heavy rainstorm. The water then mixed with an oily liquid and collected in channels on the floor; as a result, the floor surface became very slippery. The respondents had kept a stock of what they believed would be sufficient sawdust to cover all eventualities but, in fact, there was not enough sawdust to cover the whole area. The appellant, an employee, slipped on an untreated part of the floor and injured his ankle.

Held, by the House of Lords, that the employers were not liable. *Per* Lord Tucker:

> The only question was: 'Has it been proved that the floor was so slippery that, remedial steps not being possible, a reasonably prudent employer would have closed down the factory rather than allow his employees to run the risks involved in continuing work?' ... The absence of any evidence

that anyone in the factory during the afternoon or night shift, other than the appellant, slipped, or experienced any difficulty, or that any complaint was made by or on behalf of the workers, all points to the conclusion that the danger was, in fact, not such as to impose on a reasonable employer the obligation placed on the respondents by the trial judge.

Note ───
The judge in the High Court had held the employers liable.

Paris v Stepney Borough Council (1951) HL

The appellant, who was blind in one eye, worked for the respondents as a garage hand. Whilst attempting to remove a bolt which held the springs of an axle, he hit the bolt with a hammer, causing a piece of metal to fly into his other eye, with the result that he became totally blind.

Held, by the House of Lords, that the respondents were liable for negligence in failing to supply him with suitable goggles, even though they might not have owed such a duty to a fully sighted employee. *Per* Lord Morton of Henryton:

> ... if A and B, who are engaged on the same work, run precisely the same risk of an accident happening, but if the results of an accident will be more serious to A than to B, precautions which are adequate in the case of B may not be adequate in the case of A, and it is a duty of the employer to take such additional precautions for the safety of A as may be reasonable. The duty to take reasonable precautions against injury is one which is owed by the employer to every individual workman.

Withers v Perry Chain Co Ltd (1961) CA

The plaintiff had an attack of dermatitis due to a reaction to grease used in her job. When she returned to work, she suffered further attacks of dermatitis and sued her employer for negligence in employing her on work which it either knew, or ought to have known, could cause dermatitis.

Held, by the Court of Appeal, that the employers were not liable. Although on the principle in *Paris v Stepney Borough Council*, an employer in such a case may have a duty to take special precautions to protect the employee, there was no suggestion here that there were any special precautions which could have been taken to protect the employee.

Pape v Cumbria County Council (1991) CA

The appellant was employed as a cleaner by the respondents. Her work involved the use of chemical cleaning agents; cleaners, although provided with rubber gloves, hardly ever used them. They were not warned of the dangers of dermatitis resulting from the skin coming into contact with chemical cleaning agents. The appellant contracted eczema as a result and sued her employers for negligence.

Held, by the High Court, that they were liable. *Per* Waite J:

> The dangers of dermatitis or acute eczema from the sustained exposure of unprotected skin to chemical cleansing agents is well known, well enough known to make it the duty of a reasonable employer to appreciate the risks it presents to members of his cleaning staff, but at the same time, not so well known as to make it obvious to his staff without any necessity for warning or instruction.

> There was a duty on the defendants to warn their cleaners of the dangers of handling chemical cleaning materials with gloves at all times ... no such warning or instruction was given, and that is sufficient to place the defendants in breach of their duty of care ...

Q   How can *Withers v Perry Chain Co Ltd* and *Pape v Cumbria County Council* be distinguished? Consider also the approach taken by s 25 of the Health and Safety at Work Act 1974 (see 3.2, below) to the question of dangerous articles and substances.

Pickford v ICI plc (1998) HL

The respondent was employed as a secretary by the appellants and claimed that she suffered repetitive strain injury (RSI) in her hands because she had been typing for prolonged periods without proper rest breaks.

Held, by the House of Lords, that the High Court judge was entitled to find, on the medical evidence available, that it could not be said whether her condition was organic or psychogenic. It was, therefore, for the respondent to prove that her condition was organic and she had failed to do this. In particular, it was found that she had exaggerated the amount and nature of her typing work, especially as it was found that 25% of her work was not typing. She could, therefore, plan her work so as to avoid undue strain and her employers were not negligent in failing to warn her of the need for rest breaks. As Lord Hope put it: 'She did not need to be told what to do.'

Note ────────────────────────────

In *Sheriff v Klyne Tugs* (1999), the Court of Appeal held that an employment tribunal had jurisdiction to award compensation by way of damages for personal injury, including both physical and psychiatric injury, caused by the 'statutory tort' of unlawful discrimination. It was, therefore, an abuse of process to claim such damages in a county court action when an action brought in an employment tribunal claiming such damages had been settled. See, also, Chapter 9.

See, also, *James v Hepworth & Grandage Ltd* (1968) and *Reid v Rush and Tomkins Group plc* (1989).

3.1.3 Employer's Liability (Defective Equipment) Act 1969

Section 1   Extension of employer's liability for defective equipment

(1) Where, after the commencement of this Act:

    (a) an employee suffers personal injury in the course of his employment in consequence of a defect in equipment provided by his employer for the purposes of the employer's business; and

    (b) the defect is attributable wholly or partly to the fault of a third party (whether identified or not),

the injury shall be deemed to be also attributable to negligence on the part of the employer (whether or not he is liable in respect of the injury apart from this sub-section), but without prejudice to the law relating to contributory negligence and to any remedy by way of contribution or in contract or otherwise which is available to the employer in respect of the injury.

(2) In so far as any agreement purports to exclude or limit any liability of an employer arising under sub-s (1) of this section, the agreement shall be void.

Coltman v Bibby Tankers Ltd (1987) HL

A ship, *The Derbyshire*, sank with all hands, and it was alleged that the ship had been defectively built due to the negligence of the manufacturer.

Held, by the House of Lords, that the word 'equipment' in s 1(1) (above) could include the actual workplace provided by the employer, such as a ship, as here, as well as equipment in the more usual sense, such as tools.

3.1.4 Contributory negligence

The Law Reform (Contributory Negligence) Act 1945

Section 1   Apportionment of liability in case of contributory negligence

(1) Where any person suffers damage as the result partly of his own fault and partly of the fault of any other person or persons, a claim in respect of that damage shall not be defeated by reason of the fault of the person suffering the damage, but the damages recoverable in respect thereof shall be reduced to such extent as the court thinks just and equitable, having regard to the claimant's share in the responsibility for the damage.

Stapley v Gypsum Mines Ltd (1953) HL

The appellant claimed damages against the respondents in respect of the death of her husband, who was killed by the fall of a roof in the mine where he was working. The husband and a fellow employee, who worked together, had been told to bring the roof down to make the area safe to work in but, finding it difficult to bring the roof down, they decided to disregard these instructions and continued working in the area, despite the roof being unsafe.

Held, by the House of Lords, that the respondents were vicariously liable for the negligence of the other employee, who was the senior of the two. However, it was probable that, if the other employee had insisted on first bringing the roof down, the deceased would have agreed with him. That being so, the deceased's own conduct amounted to contributory negligence; damages payable to his widow were reduced by 80%.

3.1.5 *Volenti non fit injuria*

Bowater v Rowley Regis Borough Council (1944) CA

The plaintiff was employed by the defendants as a carter. He was told to take out a horse which had tried to run away on several previous occasions and, therefore, the plaintiff said that he did not wish to take out that particular horse. However, he was ordered to do so by the borough surveyor. Whilst the plaintiff was driving the horse, it bolted and he was thrown to the ground and injured.

Held, by the Court of Appeal, that the employers were liable and that *volenti* did not apply. Goddard LJ:

> The maxim *volenti non fit injuria* is one which, in the case of master and servant, is to be applied with extreme caution. Indeed, I would say that it can hardly ever be applicable where the act to which the plaintiff is said to be *volens* arises out of his ordinary duty, unless the work for which the plaintiff is engaged is one in which danger is necessarily involved. Thus, a man in an explosives factory must take the risk of an explosion occurring, in spite of the observance and provision of all statutory regulations and safeguards.

Note ———————————————————————————————————
See, also, *Imperial Chemical Industries v Shatwell* (1964).

3.2 Health and Safety at Work Act 1974

Section 2   General duties of employers to their employees

(1) It shall be the duty of every employer to ensure, so far as is reasonably practicable, the health, safety and welfare at work of all his employees.

(2) Without prejudice to the generality of an employer's duty under the preceding sub-section, the matters to which that duty extends include, in particular:

(a) the provision and maintenance of plant and systems of work that are, so far as is reasonably practicable, safe and without risks to health;

(b) arrangements for ensuring, so far as is reasonably practicable, safety and absence of risks to health in connection with the use, handling, storage and transport of articles and substances;

(c) the provision of such information, instruction, training and supervision as is necessary to ensure, so far as is reasonably practicable, the health and safety at work of his employees;

(d) so far as is reasonably practicable as regards any place of work under the employer's control, the maintenance of it in a condition that is safe and without risks to health and the provision and maintenance of means of access to and egress from it that are safe and without such risks;

(e) the provision and maintenance of a working environment for his employees that is, so far as is reasonably practicable, safe, without risks to health, and adequate as regards facilities and arrangements for their welfare at work.

Edwards v National Coal Board (1949) CA

A colliery worker, whilst walking along a travelling road in a coal mine, was killed when part of the side of the road fell away. His widow claimed damages from the National Coal Board (NCB) for breach of their statutory duty to make the road secure, but the NCB relied on the defence provided by s 102(8) of the Coal Mines Act 1911, which provided that there would be no liability if it was not 'reasonably practicable' to avoid a breach of statutory duty. In this case, the NCB argued that the number of travelling roads and the difficulties of knowing when a fall in the road was likely to occur meant that it was not reasonably practicable for them to make all travelling roads secure.

Held, by the Court of Appeal, that the defendants had failed to establish that this was not reasonably practicable. Asquith LJ said that:

'Reasonably practicable' is a narrower term than 'physically possible' and seems to me to imply that a computation must be made by the owner, in which the quantum of risk is placed in one scale and the sacrifice involved in the measures necessary for averting the risk (whether in money, time or trouble) is placed in the other.

Although the case dealt with the interpretation of the phrase 'reasonably practicable' in other legislation, it can still be a useful guide to the interpretation of this phrase in the Health and Safety at Work Act 1974.

Q   Compare this decision with that in *Latimer v AEC Ltd* (1953).

Section 3   General duties of employers and self-employed to persons other than their employees

(1) It shall be the duty of every employer to conduct his undertaking in such a way as to ensure, so far as is reasonably practicable, that persons not in his employment who may be affected thereby are not thereby exposed to risks to their health or safety.

(2) It shall be the duty of every self-employed person to conduct his undertaking in such a way as to ensure, so far as is reasonably practicable, that he and other persons (not being his employees) who may be affected thereby are not thereby exposed to risks to their health or safety.

R v Associated Octel Co Ltd (1996) HL

The defendants ran a chemical plant, designated by the Health and Safety Executive as a 'major hazard site' and, for a number of years, they had used a small firm of specialist contractors for repairs. The contractor's eight employees were employed virtually full time on the defendant's site. One employee was engaged in cleaning a tank, using the light from an electric light bulb, when the light bulb broke, causing a bucket of highly inflammable acetone, which was being used for the cleaning, to ignite. The employee was, in consequence, badly burned in the resulting flash fire.

Held, by the House of Lords, that the defendants were guilty of a criminal offence under s 3 of the Health and Safety at Work Act 1974. The duty imposed by s 3 was not the same as the common law principle under which an employer is not normally liable for the acts of independent contractors. The question under s 3 was, *per* Lord Hoffman: '... whether the activity in question can be described as part of the employer's undertaking.' Here, the repairing of a tank clearly was such an activity. Accordingly, the issue was then whether the defendants had taken all reasonably practicable steps to avoid risk to the contractor's employees, and it was unanimously held that a jury, properly instructed on the law, would undoubtedly have held that the defendants had not, and, therefore, would have convicted them. In addition, the House of Lords doubted the reasoning in *RMC Roadstone Products Ltd v Jester* (1994), where the

Divisional Court held that an employer was not guilty of an offence under s 3 of the Health and Safety at Work Act when he did not exercise control over what the independent contractors were doing.

Note

See, also, *R v Board of Trustees of the Science Museum* (1993), where an inspection showed that legionella bacteria in the cooling system of the museum could be a danger to persons outside the building. The Court of Appeal held that an offence could be committed under s 3 where there was a risk of possible harm, and the prosecution did not need to prove that any members of the public had actually been at risk.

In *R v British Steel plc* (1995), it was held that a corporate employer could not avoid liability for an offence under s 3 on the basis that the company at senior management level had taken all reasonable care to delegate supervision of the work.

Section 6   General duties of manufacturers, etc, as regards articles and substances for use at work

(1) It shall be the duty of any person who designs, manufacturers, imports or supplies any article for use at work or any article of fairground equipment:

(a) to ensure, so far as is reasonably practicable, that the article is so designed and constructed that it will be safe and without risks to health at all times when it is being set, used, cleaned or maintained by a person at work;

(b) to carry out or arrange for the carrying out of such testing and examination as may be necessary for the performance of the duty imposed on him by the preceding paragraph;

(c) to take such steps as are necessary to secure that persons supplied by that person with the article are provided with adequate information about the use for which the article is designed or has been tested, and about any conditions necessary to ensure that it will be safe and without risks to health at all such times as are mentioned in para (a) above and when it is being dismantled or disposed of; and

(d) to take such steps as are necessary to secure, so far as is reasonably practicable, that persons so supplied are provided with all such revisions of information provided to them by virtue of the preceding paragraph as are necessary by reason of its becoming known that anything gives rise to a serious risk to health or safety.

Section 7   General duties of employees at work

It shall be the duty of every employee while at work:

(a) to take reasonable care for the health and safety of himself and of other persons who may be affected by his acts or omissions at work; and

(b) as regards any duty or requirement imposed on his employer or any other person by or under any of the relevant statutory provisions, to co-operate with him so far as is necessary to enable that duty or requirement to be performed or complied with.

Section 8   Duty not to interfere with or misuse things provided pursuant to certain provisions

No person shall intentionally or recklessly interfere with or misuse anything provided in the interests of health, safety or welfare in pursuance of any of the relevant statutory provisions.

Section 9   Duty not to charge employees for things done or provided pursuant to certain specific requirements

No employer shall levy or permit to be levied on any employee of his any charge in respect of anything done or provided in pursuance of any specific requirement of the relevant statutory provisions.

Section 21   Improvement notices

If an inspector is of the opinion that a person:

(a) is contravening one or more of the relevant statutory provisions; or

(b) has contravened one or more of those provisions in circumstances that make it likely that the contravention will continue or be repeated,

he may serve on him a notice (in this Part referred to as 'an improvement notice'), stating that he is of that opinion, specifying the provision or provisions as to which he is of that opinion, giving particulars of the reasons why he is of that opinion, and requiring that person to remedy the contravention or, as the case may be, the matters occasioning it within such period (ending not earlier than the period within which an appeal against the notice can be brought under s 24) as may be specified in the notice.

Section 22   Prohibition notices

(1) This section applies to any activities which are being or are [likely] to be carried on by or under the control of any person, being activities to or in relation to which any of the relevant statutory provisions apply or will, if the activities are so carried on, apply.

(2) If as regards any activities to which this section applies an inspector is of the opinion that, as carried on or [likely] to be carried on by or under

the control of the person in question, the activities involve or, as the case may be, will involve a risk of serious personal injury, the inspector may serve on that person a notice (in this Part referred to as 'a prohibition notice').

Section 25   Power to deal with cause of imminent danger

(1) Where, in the case of any article or substance found by him in any premises which he has power to enter, an inspector has reasonable cause to believe that, in the circumstances in which he finds it, the article or substance is a cause of imminent danger of serious personal injury, he may seize it and cause it to be rendered harmless (whether by destruction or otherwise).

Section 47   Civil liability

(1) Nothing in this Part shall be construed:

(a) as conferring a right of action in any civil proceedings in respect of any failure to comply with any duty imposed by ss 2 to 7 or any contravention of s 8; or

(b) as affecting the extent (if any) to which breach of a duty imposed by any of the existing statutory provisions is actionable; or

(c) as affecting the operation of s 12 of the Nuclear Installations Act 1965 (right to compensation by virtue of certain provisions of that Act).

R v F Howe & Son (Engineers) Ltd (1999) CA

The company was convicted of a number of offences under the Health and Safety at Work Act 1974, resulting from the death of an employee who had been electrocuted through a cable being in a dangerous state of repair. A circuit breaker had been deliberately interfered with, resulting in it becoming inoperable. The company was fined £48,000 at the Crown Court, having pleaded guilty.

Held, by the Court of Appeal, that the fine was excessive, because the Crown Court judge should have given more weight to the means of the company (which was small); therefore, the fine was reduced to £5,000.

Nevertheless, the court held that, in general, the level of fines for health and safety offences was too low and, subject to the court's remarks about the need to take the means of a company into account, any fine must be large enough to bring the message home that the object of prosecutions was to achieve a safe environment for workers and those members of the public who may be affected.

3.3 Working Time Regulations 1998

Regulations 4(1) and (2) provide that:

1   Subject to reg 5, a worker's working time, including overtime, in any reference period which is applicable in his case, shall not exceed an average of 48 hours for each seven days.

2   An employer shall take all reasonable steps, in keeping with the need to protect the health and safety of workers, to ensure that the limit specified in para (1) is complied with in the case of each worker employed by him in relation to whom it applies.

Note ───

Regulation 5, referred to in reg 4(1) above, deals with opt-out agreements.

───

Barber v RJB Mining (UK) Ltd (1998) HC

Held, by the High Court, that the requirement in reg 4(1) (above) is mandatory and is incorporated into the contracts of employment of all workers. Accordingly, an employee required to work in breach of reg 4(1) can bring a civil action for a declaration and/or an injunction. Employees were not limited to the remedies provided for in the Regulations of protection against detriment and unfair dismissal. Nor was it the case that reg 4(1) had to be read subject to reg 4(2), which would have the effect of limiting the employer's obligations, because it used the phrase 'all reasonable steps'. Regulation 4(2) was separate, and breach of it is a criminal offence.

Note, also:

(a) *R v Attorney General for Northern Ireland ex p Burns* (1999) – definition of a night worker.

(b) *Gibson v East Riding of Yorkshire Council* (1999), where the EAT held that Art 7 of the Working Time Directive (dealing with annual leave) was capable of direct enforcement against an emanation of the State. This opened the door to a challenge to other parts of the Working Time Regulations, provided that they were held capable of direct enforcement, on the basis that they did not implement the Working Time Directive.

4 Terminating the Contract

4.1 Termination not involving dismissal

4.1.1 By resignation

East Sussex County Council v Walker (1972) NIRC
After a disagreement with her employers, the applicant was strongly encouraged to resign. When she claimed a redundancy payment, the employer alleged she had not been dismissed but had voluntarily resigned.

Held, by the National Industrial Relations Court, that, where an employee is prevailed upon to resign by pressure, that is not a valid resignation but, rather, in practice, a dismissal. *Per* Brightman J:

> ... if an employee is told she is no longer required in her employment and is expressly invited to resign, a court of law is entitled to come to the conclusion that, as a matter of common sense, the employee was dismissed.

Note ————————————————————————
See, also, *Scott v Formica Ltd* (1975).

Sheffield v Oxford Controls Co Ltd (1979) EAT
The applicant and his wife were employed as directors of the Oxford Controls Co Ltd. Further to a disagreement between the applicant's wife and the controlling shareholders of the company, the shareholders insisted on her dismissal. As a consequence, a dispute then arose between the applicant and the shareholders, resulting in the applicant receiving a letter threatening dismissal if he did not resign. Later, an agreement was signed, setting out the financial terms for his resignation. The applicant claimed he had been unfairly dismissed.

Held, by the EAT, that the applicant had not been dismissed, as he had clearly agreed to terminate his employment on mutually acceptable terms. The threat of dismissal was not a sufficiently causative factor in the applicant's decision to resign; rather, he had willingly resigned because of the satisfactory terms that were offered to him to do so.

Note

See, also, *Staffordshire County Council v Donovan* (1981); *Jones v Mid Glamorgan County Council* (1997) and 4.1.2, below.

Martin v MBS Fastening Ltd (1983) CA

During a meeting between the applicant and his employer, the applicant explained that he was being prosecuted for drunk driving. He was advised that there would have to be an inquiry and it would probably end in dismissal. His employer suggested that it would be in the applicant's best interests if he resigned. The applicant followed the advice, but later made an application for unfair dismissal. An industrial tribunal concluded that this was not a dismissal. The applicant's appeal was allowed by the EAT.

Held, by the Court of Appeal, that there were no grounds to intervene in the industrial tribunal's conclusion that there had not been a dismissal in law. It is for the industrial tribunal to determine whether, on the evidence, the employer or employee terminated the employment; the court will only intervene if the tribunal's decision was so perverse that no reasonable tribunal could have come to that conclusion. Here, the tribunal's decision (on the facts) that the degree of pressure applied was not sufficient to induce the employee's resignation was commensurate with the evidence submitted.

Caledonian Mining Co Ltd v Bassett (1987) EAT

The defendant company wrote to all employees at a particular colliery, informing them that a number of jobs would be lost there. The applicants were interviewed for other work with the company, but, eventually, were not offered alternative jobs. Instead, it was arranged for them to find work with other employers. The applicants then terminated their employment with the defendants and claimed a redundancy payment. The defendants argued that, as the applicants had resigned to take other jobs, they had not been dismissed and so were not able to make a redundancy claim.

Held, by the EAT, that, in these circumstances – where the employers had caused the employees to leave employment and the employers' purpose in finding the applicants other employment was to avoid having to make redundancy payments – resignation was not the reason for the termination of the contract of employment; the applicants had been dismissed.

Hellyer Brothers v Atkinson and Dickinson (1994) CA

The plaintiff employees had been employed for a number of years on the employer's fishing boats under a series of 'crew agreements'. These agreements lasted for a specified period of time, unless (as listed in the contract) they were terminated by mutual agreement, by notice or by loss of the vessel. Due to the company decommissioning their boats, the plaintiffs 'signed off' from the latest crew agreement.

The employees claimed a redundancy agreement on the basis that their employment had been terminated once they had been informed of the decommissioning. The employer argued that, as termination was neither by loss of the vessel nor by notice, it must have been terminated by mutual consent when they 'signed off' from the crew agreement.

Held, by the Court of Appeal, that unilateral termination had taken place when the employees had been told that the boats on which they were employed would not be sailing again. It could not be accepted that termination must have been by mutual agreement under the contract. When the employees 'signed off', they were only signifying acceptance of what was, in practice, a *fait accompli*, and were merely waiving their right to receive notice of dismissal.

Kwik Fit (GB) Ltd v Lineham (1992) EAT

Lineham was a manager of one of the company's depots. After a security officer reported an incident, Lineham was disciplined by the divisional sales manager. During a heated interview between them, Lineham threw his keys down on the counter and left. The divisional sales manager informed personnel that Lineham should not be re-employed. When Lineham claimed unfair dismissal, the employers argued he had not been dismissed, as he had unambiguously resigned at the end of the interview with the divisional sales director.

Held, by the EAT, that, where an employee unambiguously resigns, by actions or words, with immediate effect, an employer is entitled to assume them as genuine and treat them as such by accepting the repudiation of the contract immediately (following *Sothern v Franks Charlesly & Co* (1981)). However, in cases where the words are spoken or the actions are taken under pressure and in the heat of the moment, an employer should allow a reasonable period of time to elapse (a day or two) before accepting a resignation at face value. During this period, facts may emerge which cast doubt upon whether the resignation was truly intended to be taken seriously. Furthermore, although an employer is not under a duty to investigate the circumstances of such a 'resignation', it may be prudent to do so to ascertain whether the employee really did intend to resign. On these facts, the employer was not entitled to assume that what had actually occurred was a genuine resignation.

Note ──

In the earlier decision of the EAT in *Barclay v City of Glasgow District Council* (1983), the court held that the employer was not entitled to treat as a notice of termination an unequivocal oral resignation by an employee who had serious learning difficulties. Employers are expected to take account of the special circumstances of each employee when determining whether the 'resignation' was a conscious and rational decision. See, also, the Court of Appeal's decision in *Sovereign House Security Services Ltd v Savage* (1989).

Ely v YKK Fasteners Ltd (1994) CA

The employee informed his employers that he wished to give up his job to move to Australia. When he was asked some months later for a firm date for his last day at work, he said he had changed his mind and wished to stay. The employers had made arrangements for a replacement and said that, as far as they were concerned, he had resigned when he informed them of his intention to leave.

Held, by the Court of Appeal, that the employee's intimation of an intention to resign did not amount to a formal notice of termination of his contract. The employee had expressed an intention to resign in the near future; it was not an unequivocal actual resignation. Consequently, by insisting that he had resigned and should leave their employment, the employer had dismissed the employee.

Note

Although the employee succeeded in establishing that he had been dismissed, on the facts of the case, it was held that he had not been unfairly dismissed.

London Transport Executive v Clarke (1981) CA

The applicant, who was employed as a bus mechanic, requested unpaid leave to visit family in Jamaica. His application was refused. The applicant was told that, should he go without permission, his name would be removed from the books. When the applicant went on holiday, the employers wrote to his home address, requesting an explanation as to his absence. Later, they wrote to say that if no explanation was forthcoming, it would be assumed that he did not wish to continue in employment and had resigned from his job. Some time later, when the applicant presented himself at work, he was refused entry. The employers argued that the applicant had not been dismissed, but that he had left of his own accord.

Held, by a majority of the Court of Appeal, that the employee's contract of employment had not been terminated by his own conduct in absenting himself from work for seven weeks without permission. Where an employee has engaged in a repudiatory breach (serious misconduct), an employer will normally terminate the employee's contract (thereby accepting the breach) by formal written means. Here, acceptance of the repudiatory breach and subsequent termination of contract occurred when the employer refused to allow the employee to return to work.

This decision was of some importance, as the Court of Appeal clearly rejected the notion of 'constructive resignation'. As the contract of employment is not automatically terminated by breach, it is the employer who must accept the repudiation and expressly or impliedly terminate.

Q   What would have been the practical consequences if the courts had found that an employee's fundamental breach of contract could, by itself, terminate the contract?

4.1.2 By subsequent agreement

McAlwane v Boughton Estates (1973) NIRC

The employee, a painter and decorator, was given notice of termination of employment by his employer. A week before the expiry of notice, the employee orally asked to leave immediately in order to start a new job. The employer granted the request. The employee subsequently applied for a redundancy payment and unfair dismissal compensation. The employer argued that, as the employee had himself requested permission to leave before the expiry of notice, this was now a case of an agreed termination of the contract, rather than a dismissal.

Held, by the National Industrial Relations Court, that this was not a consensual termination, but merely an agreed variation of notice; consequently, the dismissal remained effective. *Per* Donaldson J:

> ... tribunals should not find an agreement to terminate employment unless it is proved that the employee really did agree, with full knowledge of the implications it had for him.

Igbo v Johnson Matthey Ltd (1986) CA

Mrs Igbo had requested, and had been given, extended unpaid leave to visit relatives in Nigeria. Before she left, she signed a holiday agreement which stated, *inter alia*: '... you have agreed to return to work on 28 September 1983. If you fail to do this, your contract of employment will automatically terminate on that date.' Although Mrs Igbo returned to the UK before that date, she did not report for work, as she was sick. The employers argued that, as she had failed to comply with the agreement, her employment was terminated in accordance with the terms of the contract.

Held, by the Court of Appeal (overruling *British Leyland (UK) Ltd v Ashraf* (1978)), that such termination agreements went against s 140 of the Employment Protection (Consolidation) Act 1978 (now s 203 of the Employment Rights Act 1996), which holds that any term in a contract which purports to limit or exclude rights (for example, to claim unfair dismissal) provided by the statute is void and unenforceable.

Note
The Court of Appeal commented that, if such an agreement could bring a contract to an end, it would be possible for an employer to insert a clause in an employment contract stating that lateness for work would be treated as a reason for automatic termination, thereby excluding any unfair dismissal claim in such circumstances.

Q   Would it have made any difference if Mrs Igbo had received a financial or other inducement to sign the document?

Humber and Birch v University of Liverpool (1985) CA
The university employers sent round a circular requesting volunteers for premature retirement. Humber and Birch volunteered, and received enhanced retirement payments. On the termination of their employment contracts, the applicants argued that they had been dismissed, as it was the employer who had formally terminated their contracts, and so they were entitled to statutory redundancy payments.

Held, by the Court of Appeal, that this was a genuine agreement (not imposed as in *Igbo*, above) facilitated by the financial benefit provided to the employees. Employment had been terminated by the employee's offer to retire, accepted by the university. Consequently, this was a case of termination by mutual agreement, not dismissal.

Note
See, also, *Burton, Allton & Johnson Ltd v Peck* (1975); *Morley v CT Morley Ltd* (1985); and *Scott v Coalite Fuels Ltd* (1988).

Logan Saltan v Durham County Council (1989) EAT
The applicant was employed as a social worker. As a result of a disciplinary hearing, he was redeployed to a new team on the same grade. Due to further disputes with the employer, the applicant was given notice of another disciplinary hearing and a recommendation that he be dismissed. In order to forestall possible dismissal, the applicant's union representative negotiated a financial package for the applicant's agreement to the termination of his contract. The applicant argued that he had been unfairly dismissed, as the contract he had entered into was void for duress or, alternatively, that it was void by virtue of s 203 of the Employment Rights Act 1996.

Held, by the EAT, that this was not a dismissal, but an example of a valid and enforceable, mutually agreed termination agreement. The employee entered into the agreement for financial reasons, without duress and after taking appropriate union advice. *Per* Wood J:

... in the resolution of ... disputes, it is in the best interests of all concerned that a contract made without duress, for good consideration, preferably after proper and sufficient advice and which has the effect of terminating a contract of employment by mutual agreement (whether at once or on some future date) should be effective between the contracting parties, in which case, there probably will not have been a dismissal.

Note ────────────────────────────

The EAT also distinguished this case from *Igbo*, as there had not been (as there had been in *Igbo*) a variation of an existing contract. Neither did termination depend on the happening of a future event. Rather, a separate contract had been negotiated about an immediate termination.

4.1.3 Frustration by illness

Poussard v Spiers (1876) HC

The plaintiff was an opera singer who agreed to sing at the defendant's theatre for a period of three months. Just before the opening night, the plaintiff was taken ill. Because the defendant was unsure how long the illness might continue, an understudy was appointed. The understudy performed the part for the first two weeks. On recovery, the plaintiff expected to resume the role. However, the defendant, satisfied with the performance of the understudy, refused to allow the plaintiff to return.

Held, by the High Court, that, in these circumstances, the illness which had prevented the plaintiff from performing went to the root of the contract and performance of the contract was radically different from envisaged at the time the contract was agreed. As such, the defendants were automatically discharged from further obligations to the plaintiff.

Condor v Barron Knights Ltd (1966) HC

The plaintiff entered into a contract whereby he agreed to act as the drummer for the defendant rock band for a period of five years. Due to the stress of the work and subsequent illness, the plaintiff was unable to perform on the number of nights specified in the contract. On the termination of the contract, the plaintiff claimed he had been wrongfully dismissed.

Held, by the High Court, that there was a likelihood that the plaintiff would suffer continual damage to his mental and physical health if he continued to perform at the level specified in the contract. Therefore, as it was impossible for him to continue, his illness was a sufficiently grave event to frustrate the contract.

Marshall v Harland Woolf (1972) NIRC

The applicant was a shipyard fitter who was absent from work (without pay) for 18 months because of illness. Due to a decision by the employers to shut down their business, the applicant was dismissed (with the rest of the workforce). The applicant was refused a redundancy payment, as his employers argued, *inter alia*, that his contract of employment had been terminated by frustration.

Held, by Sir John Donaldson in the National Industrial Relations Court, that, in the context of incapacity due to sickness, whether or not a contract had been determined by frustration depended upon whether, in accordance with the general test elaborated in *Davis Contractors Ltd v Fareham Urban District Council* (1956), the employee's incapacity, looked at before the purported dismissal, was of such a nature, or appeared likely to continue for such a period, that further performance of obligations in the future would be either impossible or would be a thing radically different from that undertaken by the employee and accepted by the employer under the agreed terms of employment.

Note ————————————————————————————————

In this particular case, Sir John Donaldson believed that, as the employee might well recover and resume work, further performance of the employee's obligations were neither impossible nor radically different from that undertaken under his contract. Accordingly, the relationship had not been terminated by frustration.

Egg Stores Ltd v Leibovici (1976) EAT

Mr Leibovici was injured in an accident and was absent from work for four months. The employers had taken on a replacement worker and refused to allow him back.

Held, by the EAT, *per* Phillips J:

... if an event such as an accident or illness occurs, the course and outcome of which is uncertain ... there will have been frustration of the contract if the time arrives when, looking back, one can say that, at some point, matters had gone on so long, and the prospects for future employment were so poor, that it was no longer practical to regard the contract as still subsisting. Among the matters to be taken into account in such a case in reaching a decision are these:

(1) the length of the previous employment;

(2) how long it had been expected that the employment would continue;

(3) the nature of the job;

(4) the nature, length and effect of the illness or disabling event;

(5) the need of the employer for the work to be done, and the need for a replacement to do it;

(6) the risk to the employer of acquiring obligations in respect of redundancy payments or compensation for unfair dismissal to the replacement employee;

(7) whether wages have continued to be paid;

(8) the acts and the statements of the employer in relation to the employment, including the dismissal of, or failure to dismiss, the employee; and

(9) whether, in all these circumstances, a reasonable employer could have expected to wait any longer.

Harman v Flexible Lamps Ltd (1980) EAT

The plaintiff had been employed as a quality control inspector for two years. In the first year of employment, she had been off sick for 13 weeks. At the beginning of the second year, she was sick for two months. This absence resulted in her employers informing her that they regarded her employment as at an end.

Held, by Bristow J in the EAT, that the discharge of contracts of employment by frustration cannot normally occur where the contract is determinable by notice, as, otherwise, the provisions of the Employment Protection (Consolidation) Act 1978 (now the Employment Rights Act 1996), protecting against unfair dismissal, would be too easily avoided. In a case like this, where notice could be, and was, provided, a dismissal had taken place, not a termination of the contract by operation of law.

Notcutt v Universal Equipment Co (1986) CA

Notcutt had worked for Universal Equipment Co as a milling machine operator for over 28 years. In 1983, he suffered a disabling heart attack. After several months of absence, the employers requested a medical report from his doctor. The prognosis was that he was unlikely to return to work. Consequently, some eight months after his heart attack, he was given notice by his employers. Due to a dispute over sick pay, the employers argued his contract had been terminated by frustration before notice was given.

Held, by the Court of Appeal, that there was no reason in principle why a contract of employment determinable by notice should not be subject to the long established doctrine of frustration. Bristow J's view in *Harman v Flexible Lamps Ltd,* that the doctrine did not formally apply in such cases, could not be sustained. In this case, *per* Lord Justice Dillon:

> ... the coronary which left the complainant unable to work again was an unexpected occurrence which made his performance of the contractual obligations to work impossible and brought about such a change in the significance of the mutual obligations that the contract, if performed, would be a different thing than that contracted for.

Williams v Watsons Coaches (1990) EAT

The applicant was employed as a part time typist. Due to an accident at work, she was absent from work for 18 months. On the sale of her employer's business, there was no work available for her when she returned.

Held, by the EAT, that, in the present case, the industrial tribunal's decision that her contract had been frustrated was flawed, as the tribunal had failed to fully consider the legal issues in reaching that decision. The tribunal should ensure that the factors outlined by Phillips J in *Leibovici* are properly considered in determining whether, in reality, the contract has been terminated by frustration. In addition, the tribunal should also consider whether there is a prospect of recovery and return to employment, and whether sick pay is provided during the period of incapacity.

Note

The EAT also counselled that the courts should be wary of allowing the doctrine to apply too readily when redundancy occurs or where there is evidence that, in reality, a dismissal by reason of disability has occurred. Furthermore, if the employer has caused the injury which results in the employee being off work, the employer cannot rely on the doctrine of frustration, as they are at fault in creating the frustrating event.

Villella v MFI Furniture Centres Ltd (1999) HC

The claimant's contract of employment included a permanent health insurance scheme, whereby incapacity benefit was payable indefinitely where the claimant was absent due to sickness. After being absent for a number of years due to sickness, the employer terminated payments to the claimant. On initiating legal proceedings under the contract, the claimant's employer argued that his contract of employment had been terminated by frustration, due to his long term absence.

Held, by the High Court, that the claimant's long term incapacity had not frustrated the contract. Although a contract of employment is capable of frustration by long term incapacity of sufficient duration to strike at the root of the contract, an occurrence, as here, which is both foreseen and provided for by the contract is incapable of being a frustrating act.

4.1.4 Frustration of the contract by imprisonment

Hare v Murphy Brothers (1974) CA

The applicant was a foreman who had been employed for 25 years. He was sentenced to 12 months' imprisonment for unlawful wounding outside of work. On his release from prison, he went back to his employers, who told him his post had been filled. He subsequently claimed unfair dismissal.

Held, by the Court of Appeal, that, in the light of the length of time the applicant was away from his work and was unable to perform his obligations under the contract, the sentence of imprisonment imposed by the court was a frustrating event. *Per* Lord Denning MR:

> ... where the man committed an unlawful act and was sentenced to 12 months' imprisonment, the event was so unforeseen and the delay so long that the contract of employment was brought automatically to an end when the sentence was imposed.

Norris v Southampton City Council (1982) EAT

The applicant had been convicted of several driving offences over an 18 month period, which culminated in a conviction for reckless driving whilst disqualified. He was remanded in custody prior to sentencing. It was anticipated that he would receive a substantial custodial sentence. On hearing of these circumstances, his employers sent him a letter terminating his employment.

Held, by Kilner Brown J in the EAT, that, where a person by his own conduct makes the performance of his contract of employment impossible, that is normally a repudiatory breach which entitles the employer to dismiss him or her. Frustration can only apply where there is no fault of either party (such as in a case of illness). Where there is fault, such as where the contract cannot be performed due to the employee's own conduct in committing a criminal offence, then the doctrine of frustration cannot arise. Thus, in this case, his contract had not automatically come to an end through frustration, but rather the employee had committed a repudiatory breach which the employer accepted by sending the letter of termination, which was a dismissal in law.

Note

In the course of his judgment, Kilner Brown J criticised the decisions in *Harrington v Kent County Council* (1980) and *Chakki v United Yeast Co* (1982) by different divisions of the EAT. In both these cases, the EAT held that a sentence of imprisonment could result in termination by frustration. Kilner Brown J regarded them as being of 'doubtful authority', as they had misinterpreted the Court of Appeal's judgment in *Hare v Murphy Brothers* by according too much credence to the opinion of Lord Denning MR. However, see below for a more recent decision of the Court of Appeal on the issue of fault and frustration.

FC Shepherd & Co Ltd v Jerrom (1986) CA

The employee was a apprentice plumber who was sentenced to 6 months' detention after being convicted of offences arising out of his involvement in a gang fight. His employer terminated his contract and refused to allow him to resume his training. The employee submitted a claim of unfair dismissal.

Held, by the Court of Appeal, that the imposition of a custodial sentence on an employee was capable in law of frustrating a contract of employment, even though performance of the contract had been rendered impossible by an act that was the fault of one of the parties. The principle that the frustrating act must have occurred without the fault of either of the parties is to ensure that the party against whom frustration is asserted cannot rely on his own misconduct to avoid the legal consequences of his actions. Otherwise, to permit an employee to improve his position by asserting that an event which would otherwise bring about a discharge by frustration did not do so because it was caused by his own fault would, *per* Mustill LJ: '... be an affront to common sense and an infringement of what Diplock LJ, in *Hong Kong Fir Shipping Co v Kawasaki Kischen Kaisha* (1962), described as "the fundamental legal and moral rule that a man should not be allowed to take advantage of his own wrong".'

Note ───

Balcombe LJ came to the same conclusion as Mustill LJ, but argued from the position (agreeing with Lord Denning MR in *Hare v Murphy Brothers*) that it was not the actual crime which caused the frustrating event, but the imposition of the sentence by the court, which was independent of the 'fault' of the plaintiff.

───

Q   Considering the effect of the doctrine of frustration on the remedy of unfair dismissal and redundancy, should it be excluded by statute as an operative reason for the termination of an employment contract?

4.2   Termination by dismissal

4.2.1   Express dismissal with or without notice

Section 95(1) of the Employment Rights Act 1996

... an employee shall be treated as dismissed by his employer if ...

(a) the contract under which he is employed is terminated by the employer, whether it is so terminated with or without notice ...

(b) ...

(c) ...

Futty v D & D Brekkes Ltd (1974)

The applicant was a fish filleter at Hull Docks who often engaged in abusive 'banter' with fellow workers and his supervisors. During one bantering session, the exchanges became more acrimonious and the applicant was told by his supervisor, 'If you don't like the job, fuck off'. The applicant took the supervisor at his word and left the premises, later claiming he was unfairly dismissed.

Held, by the industrial tribunal, that the meaning of these words had to be considered against the background of the custom and practice of the fish trade and the circumstances of the job. Here, where the use of 'industrial' language and light hearted conflict was common, the words did not necessarily mean the applicant was dismissed. Instead, the words amounted to general criticism and an exhortation to the applicant to take a 'cooling down' break from work. Thus, the applicant had terminated his own contract by leaving and subsequently finding another job.

Tanner v DT Kean Ltd (1978) EAT

Tanner had received orders from his employer not to use the company van outside working hours and had received finance from his employer to buy a car for personal use. On hearing that Tanner had still been using the company van for his own use, the employer exclaimed: 'What's my fucking van doing outside; you're a tight bastard. I've just lent you £275 to buy a car and you are too tight to put juice in it. That's it, you're finished with me.' Tanner claimed he had been dismissed unfairly.

Held, by the EAT, that the industrial tribunal, considering all the factual circumstances of the case, was entitled to hold that the employer had merely spoken in the heat of the moment and had not intended to bring the contract to an end, and so dismiss the employee. In determining whether the words or actions of an employer constituted a dismissal in law, an additional question to consider is how a reasonable employee would in all the circumstances have understood what the employer intended by what he said or did. In these circumstances, a reasonable employee would have understood that the words were spoken as a reprimand and not as an intended dismissal.

Q   Could the behaviour of the employer have amounted to a breach of the implied term of trust and confidence and, therefore, have resulted in a constructive dismissal of the employee?

J and J Stern v Simpson (1983) EAT

The applicant was employed as a general manager of a business owned by Mrs Stern and her son. During a heated discussion between the applicant and the owners, Mrs Stern shouted 'Go, get out, get out'. The applicant left the premises and later on, on his return, found himself locked out of his office. The industrial tribunal held that he had been dismissed in law.

Held, by the EAT, that, in order to determine whether there has been a dismissal in law, the correct test is to construe the words in the context of the facts to ascertain whether the words used clearly establish that a dismissal has taken place. Only if there is some ambiguity should the further test – of whether a reasonable employer or employee in the surrounding circumstances of the case might have understood the words to amount to a termination of the contract – be applied. In this case, the tribunal had failed to consider the relevance of the heated argument when deciding the phrase 'Go, get out, get out' amounted to a dismissal, and so the appeal was allowed.

Haseltine Lake & Co v Dowler (1981) EAT

The applicant was informed by the employer that he had no future with the firm and was advised to look for alternative work; otherwise, he would have to be dismissed. He was told that he ought to leave before 'the end of the summer'. After being periodically reminded that he was expected to find another job, the applicant resigned and claimed unfair dismissal.

Held, by the EAT, that the applicant had not been dismissed. A contract can only be terminated where there is a known date for termination or where the circumstances are such that the date of termination can be ascertained. The present case was not one where the employers had threatened immediate dismissal if the applicant did not resign or said that he would be dismissed at a particular future date. The employers had merely issued a warning that, at some point in the future, he may be dismissed.

Note

On the necessity for a dismissal to have an ascertainable date, see, also, *Doble v Firestone Tyre Co Ltd* (1981) and *Tunnel Holdings Ltd v Woolf* (1976).

Halfpenny v Ige Medical Systems Ltd (1999) CA

After the end of her maternity leave, the applicant was too ill to return to work on the agreed date. Her employer took the view that, as she did not exercise her right to return to work, her contract of employment had lapsed and, therefore, there was no dismissal in law. The EAT held that the contract of employment does continue to subsist after an employee goes on maternity leave, but only for the purposes of permitting the employee to revive it when she exercises her statutory right of return. If she fails to exercise that right, the contract comes to an end by implied agreement.

Held, by the Court of Appeal, that the EAT decision could not be supported. The process of exercising the right to return is complete once the appropriate notices have been given for the notified date of return. The contract of employment is then revived, and a failure by an employer to permit a return to work is an express termination by the employer; that is, a dismissal.

Note ————————————————————————————
See, also, *Hilton Hotels Ltd v Kaissi* (1994) and *Cress v Royal London Insurance* (1998).

Alcan Extrusions v Yates (1996) EAT
On the imposition of a new shift system, which worsened the terms and conditions of employment, Yates and others informed the employer that they would only work the new shift system under protest and would reserve their right to claim unfair dismissal. Subsequently, they put in an application for unfair dismissal while continuing to work under protest.

Held, by the EAT, that, where an employer introduces a fundamental change in employment terms without obtaining an employee's consent, that could constitute an express dismissal. *Per* Judge Smith QC:

... where an employer unilaterally imposes radically different terms of employment, applying the principle in *Hogg v Dover College* (1990), there is a dismissal under [s 95(1)(a)] if, on an objective construction of the relevant letters or other conduct on the part of the employer, there is a removal or withdrawal of the old contract.

Note
There is great significance in identifying a unilateral change of contract as an express dismissal, rather than a repudiatory breach for the purposes of constructive dismissal (see 4.2.3, below). In a situation where a contract has been imposed on an employee, he or she may claim unfair dismissal, although still technically employed so long as the 'acceptance' of the changes was under protest and so without prejudice to his or her statutory rights. However, it should also be noted that this decision has attracted a substantial degree of academic criticism, as it seems to contradict previous case law that a contract of employment is not terminated 'automatically' on repudiatory breach by an employee or employer, but that the other party must positively 'elect' to terminate: see *London Transport Executive v Clarke* (1981), 4.1.1, above.

4.2.2 Expiration of a fixed term contract

Section 95(1) of the Employment Rights Act 1996
... an employee shall be treated as dismissed by his employer if:

(a) ...

(b) where under the contract he is employed for a fixed term, that term expires without being renewed ...

(c) ...

Dixon v BBC (1979) CA

The employee was employed as a porter under a series of fixed term contracts that were determinable by one week's notice. When the final contract expired, the BBC failed to renew it and Dixon claimed he had been unfairly dismissed. The BBC argued that, where a contract includes a term providing for termination before the end of the fixed term, it could not be a 'fixed term contract' for the purposes of the Act.

Held, by the Court of Appeal, that Dixon had been dismissed within the meaning of s 95(1)(b) when his fixed term contract had not been renewed, even though the contract included a term that it could be determined by one week's notice within that period. To decide otherwise would, *per* Lord Denning:

> ... mean that an employer could always evade the Act by inserting a simple clause 'determinable by one week's notice'. That can never have been the intention of the legislature at all.

Note

The Court of Appeal, in coming to this conclusion, had to directly contradict the decision of the Court of Appeal in *BBC v Ioannou* (1975) that, if a notice clause is included in a contract, it is not a 'fixed term' contract for the purposes of the statute. The decision in *Dixon* was justified by a finding that the *Ioannou* judgment was given *per incuriam* (that the court had failed to consider other relevant matters – that is, the true intention behind the legislation). Also, see on fixed term contracts and the exclusion of employment rights: *Housing Services v Cragg* (1997); *Bhatt v Chelsea and Westminster Health Care Trust* (1997); and *BBC v Kelly-Phillips* (1998).

Wiltshire County Council v NATFHE and Guy (1980) CA

The applicant had been employed as a part time teacher for several years at a college in Wiltshire. At the beginning of each academic year, she entered into a fresh contract to teach certain courses on specified days and for a specified number of hours. The contracts would terminate at the end of the academic year, when the courses she taught had finished. At the beginning of the academic year for 1977, her appointment was not renewed and she claimed this amounted to a non-renewal of a fixed term contract and that she had been dismissed in law. Her employer argued that the circumstances of her engagement amounted to a contract for specified work which, when the courses ended, was discharged by performance.

Held, by the Court of Appeal, that this was a fixed term contract within the meaning of the statute. A fixed term contract has a defined beginning and a defined end. This contract satisfied this requirement. As the applicant was employed for the academic session ending on the last day of the summer term, it was known when the contract would cease, so it did have a defined or determinable end.

Note ───

The Court of Appeal accepted the argument that, if it had been shown that it was a contract to perform a specified task – to teach certain courses the length of which were not known when the contract was made – she would not have been employed for a fixed term.

Brown v Knowsley Borough Council (1986) EAT

The employee had been employed as a temporary teacher under a series of fixed term contracts. At the start of the academic year 1983, she was offered a contract which stipulated, *inter alia,* that: 'The appointment will last only as long as sufficient funds are provided either by the Manpower Services Commission or by other sponsors to fund it.' Later in the year, she was informed that, due to the failure of the college to attract sufficient funding for these courses, the contract would terminate in accordance with the above clause.

Held, by the EAT, that the contract came to an end automatically when the event specified in the letter took place, that is, when funds for the course were not provided by the Manpower Services Commission. The employee had not been employed on a fixed term contract, but for a specific purpose. When that specific purpose was completed or came to an end, the contract was discharged by performance. Thus, in such circumstances, there was no dismissal within the meaning of the statutory definition.

Q   Do you think an argument based on s 203 of the Employment Rights Act 1996 should have succeeded in this case?

Note ───

Further cases on the discharge of a 'task contract' by performance – *Ryan v Shipboard Maintenance Ltd* (1980) and *Ironmonger v Movefield Ltd* (1988). See, also, *Cress v Royal London Insurance* (1998).

4.2.3 Constructive dismissal

Section 95(1)

... an employee shall be treated as dismissed by his employer if:

(a) ...

(b) ...

(c) the employer terminates that contract with or without notice, in circumstances such that he is entitled to terminate it without notice by reason of the employer's conduct.

Western Excavating (ECC) Ltd v Sharp (1978) CA

The applicant had been suspended without pay by the employer as a disciplinary measure for taking a day off work without permission. This put the applicant in severe financial difficulties. In order to obtain accrued holiday pay and to pursue an unfair dismissal claim, he resigned, arguing he had been constructively dismissed on the grounds that the employer had acted unreasonably by refusing him a loan or an advance on his holiday pay.

Held, by the Court of Appeal, that the employer's conduct did not amount to constructive dismissal. *Per* Lord Denning:

> If the employer is guilty of conduct which is a significant breach going to the root of the contract of employment, or which shows that the employer no longer intends to be bound by one or more of the essential terms of the contract, then the employee is entitled to treat himself as discharged from any further performance. If he does so, then he terminates the contract by reason of the employer's conduct. He is constructively dismissed. The employee is entitled in these circumstances to leave at the instant without giving any notice at all or, alternatively, he may give notice and say that he is leaving at the end of the notice. But the conduct must in either case be sufficiently serious to entitle him to leave at once.

Note

This case finally established that an employee is not entitled to claim constructive dismissal merely on an allegation the employer has engaged in 'unreasonable behaviour'. The conduct of the employer must be such that a repudiatory breach of contract has occurred. See the earlier cases – *Pepper v Webb* (1969); *Marriot v Oxford Co-op Society* (1970); *Wetherall Ltd v Lynn* (1978); *Turner v London Transport Executive* (1977); and *Burroughs Machines Ltd v Timmoney* (1977).

Courtaulds Ltd v Andrew (1979) EAT

Andrew was an experienced supervisor with an unblemished service record. During a heated argument with a member of management, the manager exclaimed, in earshot of others, 'You can't do the bloody job anyway'. Andrew reacted by leaving and claiming he had been constructively dismissed, due to the conduct of the manager.

Held, by the EAT, that there is an important implied term in a contract of employment that an employer will not conduct themselves in a manner likely to destroy or seriously damage the relationship of trust and confidence that must exist between the employee and employer in order for the contract to function effectively. Where the employer has criticised the applicant without good reason in earshot of others, this is conduct which destroys the relationship of trust between the parties and is a fundamental breach that goes to the root of the contract, justifying the employee to claim he had been constructively dismissed.

Lewis v Motorworld Garages Ltd (1985) CA

Lewis had been demoted from his position as sales manager. As a consequence, he lost his office, was given a smaller company car and a salary increase was withheld from him. After numerous incidents of senior management criticising his work, the applicant left his job and claimed that he had been constructively dismissed. He argued that their overall conduct was such that a repudiatory breach of contract had occurred, namely, the implied term of trust and confidence which exists between employer and employee.

Held, by the Court of Appeal, that, even though the applicant had not treated the original breach of the express contractual terms (the demotion) as a wrongful repudiation, he was, *per* Glidewell LJ:

> ... entitled to add such a breach to the other actions, which, taken together, may cumulatively amount to a breach of the implied obligation of trust and confidence ... the tribunal (should) consider the breaches of the express contractual terms as part of the background material in evaluating the respondent's subsequent conduct and, if those breaches were also breaches of the implied term of trust and confidence, to add them to any other breaches ... to support an allegation that there had been a course of conduct which cumulatively constituted a breach of the implied obligation of sufficient gravity to justify the appellant in claiming that he had been constructively dismissed.

Also, the employer's argument that their actions were not repudiatory on the grounds that they never intended to repudiate the contract or believed their actions were repudiatory could not be accepted. Conduct was repudiatory if, viewed objectively, it evinced an intention no longer to be bound by the contract.

Bracebridge Engineering Ltd v Darby (1990) EAT

The applicant had been sexually harassed and assaulted by two fellow employees at work. The applicant complained to the general manager, who, after speaking to the two employees, decided that no further action was required. Believing that her complaint had not been taken seriously by her employers, she resigned and claimed unfair dismissal and sex discrimination.

Held, by the EAT, that the implied term relating to mutual trust and confidence is extremely important in circumstances of harassment such as this. Given that the applicant had suffered shock and trauma as a consequence of the incident and that the incident had not been treated with the gravity it deserved, the industrial tribunal was correct to conclude that the employee was entitled to resign and treat herself as being constructively dismissed.

Note

For further analysis of this subject, see Chapter 9.

Hilton Hotels (UK) Ltd v Protopapa (1990) EAT

After being severely reprimanded by her immediate supervisor in front of other employees, the applicant left her employment and claimed she had been constructively dismissed. The industrial tribunal held that the supervisor had behaved in an 'officious and insensitive manner' and that the applicant had been 'humiliated, intimidated and degraded to such an extent that there was a breach of trust and confidence which went to the root of the contract'. The employers appealed, arguing that the applicant had not been constructively dismissed, as the supervisor had no authority to dismiss the applicant.

Held, by the EAT, that the action of the supervisor was conduct on the part of the employer. There was no requirement for the purposes of the section that the supervisor had to have express authority to dismiss. Whether the repudiatory conduct by the supervisor which brings about the wrongful termination of contract binds the employer depends on the application of the general law of vicarious liability; that is, whether the act of the supervisor was done in the course of employment. Since it was conceded that the supervisor was acting within the scope of her employment in reprimanding the applicant, the employer was liable for her actions.

Brown v Merchant Ferries Ltd (1998) CA (NI)

The applicant resigned and claimed he had been constructively dismissed on the grounds that, due to a re-organisation of work, he was unsure of his future role within the organisation and, consequently, felt 'undermined' by the changes taking place.

Held, by the Northern Ireland Court of Appeal, that the employer's conduct was not serious enough to justify the applicant's decision to resign and claim constructive dismissal. In determining whether there had been a breach of the implied term of trust and confidence such as to amount to a constructive dismissal, the test to be applied is whether the employer's conduct so impacted on the employee that, viewed objectively, the employee could properly conclude that the employer was repudiating the contract. Seriously unreasonable conduct may provide sufficient evidence that there has been such a breach; in the present case, it did not.

Note ───

For further examples of repudiatory breaches of the implied term of trust and confidence, see: *Isle of Wight Tourist Board v Coombes* (1976); *Robinson v Crompton Parkinson Ltd* (1978); *Pulmanor Ltd v Cedron* (1978); *Post Office v Roberts* (1980); *Woods v WM Car Services* (1981); *Warnes v Cheriton Oddfellows Social Club* (1993); and *BCCI v Ali* (1999).

Greenaway Harrison Ltd v Wiles (1994) EAT

Mrs Wiles was employed as a daytime telephonist. Due to a decision to re-organise the service so as to provide additional evening cover, Mrs Wiles was informed that she would have to work a new shift system, including evening work. Mrs Wiles found this impossible due to family commitments. During negotiations over these changes, Mrs Wiles believed she would be unable to change the management's mind and so left her employment, claiming she had been constructively dismissed. Her employer argued that she had not been constructively dismissed, as there had been no threat to break the contract (by varying the contract unilaterally) or any actual breach of contract. Rather, the upshot of the negotiations was a threat to terminate the old contract lawfully by giving due notice under the contract.

Held, by the EAT, that, in these circumstances – where there is a threat to give due notice if an employee does not agree to new terms – the employer's conduct is an anticipatory breach of a fundamental term of the contract of employment. Proposing to vary the contractual terms and to give the applicant due notice if she did not agree to this amounted to a repudiatory breach which entitled the employee to regard herself as having been constructively dismissed according the principle established in *Western Excavating v Sharp* (see above). Otherwise, if this was not the case, *per* Judge Hague QC:

> ... an employer who wished to make a fundamental alteration to the contract of employment could avoid the effect of (s 95(1)(c)) simply by making a threat of notice of termination.

Note ───

For other examples of repudiatory breaches of contract, see *Hill Ltd v Mooney* (1981) and *Reid v Camphill Engravers* (1990) – failure to pay agreed wages; *McNeil v Charles Grimm Ltd* (1984) – unjustified demotion or suspension; *Millbrook Ltd v McIntosh* (1981) and *Aparau v Iceland Frozen Foods plc* (1996) – unilateral change in job content and contractual terms; *United Bank v Akhatar* (1989) and *White v Reflecting Roadstuds Ltd* (1991) – unreasonable enforcement of mobility clause; *Waltons and Morse v Dorrington* (1997) – requiring an employee to work in an unhealthy environment; and *BCCI v Ali* (1999) – operating a business in a dishonest and corrupt manner.

Weathersfield Ltd v Sargent (1999) CA

Mrs Sargent, a receptionist for the defendant employers, was given instructions to refuse services to individuals from the ethnic minority community. Upset by this policy, she resigned, but did not inform her employers why she did so.

Held, by the Court of Appeal, that, where no reason for the employee's resignation is communicated to the employer, the tribunal may conclude that the repudiatory conduct was not the reason for the employee's actions. However, in order to substantiate a claim of constructive dismissal, there is no requirement in law that an employee must always state the reason for leaving. All that is required is for the tribunal to determine, on the facts and evidence in each case, that the employee's conduct was due to a repudiatory breach by the employers. The tribunal had correctly determined that, in this case, the evidence pointed to the repudiatory conduct being the sole reason for Mrs Sargent's decision to resign. Thus, Mrs Sargent had been constructively dismissed, notwithstanding that she did not tell her employers she had left because of their unlawful instruction to discriminate.

Note ───

It is inevitably more difficult to substantiate a claim of constructive dismissal where the employee has not communicated (whether by words or conduct) the fact that he or she regards the contract of employment as terminated. See *Day v T Pickles Farms Ltd* (1999) and *Edwards v Surrey Police* (1999).

4.2.4 Summary dismissal

Laws v London Chronicle (1959) CA

Some weeks after joining the defendant's company, the plaintiff was dismissed on the spot for refusing to follow an order given by the managing director to remain at a meeting. The plaintiff argued that her minor act of disobedience had not justified the defendant's actions and that, as she had not received due notice of dismissal, this amounted to a wrongful dismissal in breach of contract.

Held, by the Court of Appeal, that only a wilful disregard of the terms of the contract of employment, amounting to a repudiation of the contract, justified summary dismissal. *Per* Lord Evershed:

... it is generally true that wilful disobedience of a lawful and reasonable order shows a disregard – a complete disregard – of a condition essential to the contract of service, namely, the condition that a servant must obey the proper orders of the master, and that, unless he does so, the relationship, is, so to speak, struck at fundamentally.

However, as this single act of disobedience was neither wilful nor particularly grave or serious, it did not amount to a repudiatory act that justified a summary dismissal. Consequently, the plaintiff was entitled to damages for wrongful dismissal, that is, for dismissal in breach of contract.

Pepper v Webb (1969) CA

The applicant was the head gardener for the defendant, employed only in the mornings until noon. After some cross words between the parties earlier in the morning, the applicant was asked to do some planting of shrubs just before noon. When the applicant indicated he would not do so, the defendant asked why he was making such a fuss. The applicant replied, 'I couldn't care less about your bloody greenhouse and your sodding garden', and then walked away. The defendant then dismissed the applicant instantly.

Held, by the Court of Appeal, that the summary dismissal was lawful, because the employee had repudiated his contract of employment by his wilful refusal to obey a lawful and reasonable order which, in combination with the other incidents of disobedience and insolence, amounted to a repudiation of a fundamental term of the contract.

Note

Compare this case with *Wilson v Racher* (1974), where there had also been an argument between employer and employee over gardening duties. However, here, the resulting summary dismissal was held to be unlawful. There had been no history of unco-operative behaviour by the employee, and so the one-off use of abusive language by the employee did not amount to a fundamental breach of contract.

Blyth v The Scottish Liberal Club (1983) Court of Session

The plaintiff was the secretary of the Scottish Liberal Club. For a number of months, relations had deteriorated between the plaintiff and the Management Committee of the club. Despite an express instruction, the plaintiff refused to attend a meeting to discuss the financial future of the club, and later refused to take minutes when the issue was raised at a Management Committee meeting, as he felt these requests did not fall within the ambit of his job description. Consequently, the defendants terminated the plaintiff's contract summarily.

Held, by the Court of Session, that the refusal of the plaintiff to execute these duties under his contract of employment was wilful and deliberate disobedience, which was sufficient to entitle the employers to terminate the plaintiff's contract instantly. The breaches of contract were material, repudiatory breaches, even though he genuinely, although mistakenly, believed that the work which he had been instructed to do did not fall within his contract.

Q   In what circumstances would it be lawful for an employee to refuse to comply with an order by an employer?

Sinclair v Neighbour (1967) CA

The plaintiff was employed as a manager of a betting shop. In order to place a bet at another betting shop, the plaintiff borrowed £15 from the till of the shop he managed, replacing it with an IOU for the same sum, which he later repaid. The defendant employer, on hearing of what had happened, dismissed the plaintiff immediately. The plaintiff took an action for damages for wrongful dismissal.

Held, by the Court of Appeal, that, although the plaintiff may not have been openly dishonest, he was guilty of a gross breach of good faith when he took money from the till, knowing that such misconduct was specifically forbidden by the employer. In such circumstances, the breach of the obligation to serve the employer faithfully undermined the essential relationship of trust which must exist between the parties, and was behaviour incompatible with his employment. As the working relationship was now seriously damaged, the employee's action did amount to a repudiatory breach of contract justifying the decision of the employer to dismiss the plaintiff summarily.

Denco v Joinson (1991) EAT

The applicant was employed as a temporary supervisor on the night shift and was an AEU shop steward. The applicant was dismissed summarily when the defendant's became aware that he had gained unauthorised access to the computer system containing information as to customers, size of orders, wages, etc.

Held, by the EAT, that, *per* Wood J:

> ... in this modern industrial world, if an employee deliberately uses an unauthorised password in order to enter or attempt to enter a computer known to contain information to which he is not entitled, then that of itself is gross misconduct which *prima facie* will attract summary dismissal ...

Note ──

The EAT went on to hold that the employee's motive is immaterial, as this situation can be compared to dishonesty, such as where an employee enters a manager's office, opens a filing cabinet and takes out and reads a file to which he is not entitled.

Neary v Dean of Westminster (1999)

The claimant was organist and master of choristers at Westminster Abbey, and was dismissed on the grounds of gross misconduct for taking fixed fees from music promoters without the knowledge of the Abbey authorities.

Held, by the Special Commissioner, Lord Jauncey (appointed by Her Majesty the Queen), that, whether particular misconduct is sufficiently gross so as to justify summary dismissal is a question of fact. The character of the institutional employer, the role played by the employee in that institution and the degree of trust required of the employee vis à vis the employer must all be considered in determining the extent of the duty of trust and the seriousness of any breach thereof. In this case, the financial wrongdoing was conduct that fatally undermined the relationship of trust and confidence between employer and employee; therefore, it did amount to gross misconduct.

5   Unfair Dismissal

5.1   Establishing the reasons for dismissal

Section 98 of the Employment Rights Act 1996

(1) In determining for the purposes of this Part whether the dismissal of an employee is fair or unfair, it is for the employer to show:

   (a) the reason (or, if more than one, the principal reason) for the dismissal; and

   (b) that it is either a reason falling within sub-s (2) or some other substantial reason of a kind such as to justify the dismissal of an employee holding the position which the employee held.

(2) A reason falls within this sub-section if it:

   (a) relates to the capability or qualifications of the employee for performing work of a kind which he was employed by the employer to do;

   (b) relates to the conduct of the employee;

   (c) is that the employee was redundant; or

   (d) is that the employee could not continue to work in the position which he held without contravention (either on his part or on that of his employer) of a duty or restriction imposed by or under an enactment.

(3) In sub-s (2)(a):

   (a) 'capability', in relation to an employee, means his capability assessed by reference to skill, aptitude, health or any other physical or mental quality; and

   (b) 'qualifications', in relation to an employee, means any degree, diploma or other academic, technical or professional qualification relevant to the position which he held.

W Devis & Sons Ltd v Atkins (1977) CA

An abattoir manager was dismissed because he refused to comply with his manager's wish that the majority of animals should be bought direct from farmers, rather than through dealers. Later, the employers became aware of an act of misconduct by the plaintiff. At the hearing, the tribunal did not allow the employers to adduce this further evidence about the employee, which had come to light since the dismissal, in order to justify their decision to dismiss the plaintiff.

Held, by the House of Lords, dismissing the employer's appeal, that the determination of whether the dismissal was fair or not depended on 'the reason shown by the employer' (in accordance with s 98(1) of the Employment Rights Act 1996 (ERA)) at the time of dismissal. The tribunal must not have regard to matters of which the employer was unaware, since the fundamental issue to consider at this initial stage of establishing the reason for dismissal was the conduct of the employer at the time of dismissal, and not whether the employee had suffered any injustice or because of information which came to light at a later date.

Note
The court did, however, say that the amount of compensation awarded could be reduced to take into account the evidence of misconduct which came to light after the dismissal.

Monie v Coral Racing Ltd (1981) CA
Cash was stolen from the employer's safe in circumstances such that only the employee or an assistant manager could have been responsible. The employer did not know who was responsible and so dismissed them both for dishonesty. The employee appealed internally and was then told that he was not to be dismissed for dishonesty, but for not following proper cash handling procedures.

Held, by the Court of Appeal, that the employers would have been entitled to dismiss for the suspected dishonesty, as there were solid and sensible grounds on which the employers could reasonably suspect dishonesty. However, the determination of whether a dismissal was fair or not depended on the sufficiency of the reason given by the employer at the actual time of the dismissal (the application of *W Devis v Atkins* (above)). Thus, where an employer relies on subsequent and different reasons given at the internal appeal, the dismissal is unfair.

West Midlands Co-operative Society Ltd v Tipton (1986) HL
The employee was summarily dismissed for poor attendance and had been warned about this previously. Despite the fact that he had a contractual right to appeal against the decision, he was not permitted to do so. The industrial tribunal held the dismissal to be unfair, because the employee had not been permitted to exercise his right of appeal. The employers argued, on appeal, that *W Devis v Atkins* decided that whether an employer acted reasonably or unreasonably fell to be determined at the time of dismissal, and so nothing after this date (here, the failure to allow

an appeal) should be taken into account when examining the question of the reasonableness of the employer's action to dismiss the employee.

Held, by the House of Lords, that the appeal process is a necessary element in the overall process of termination of contract; to separate the original decision to dismiss and the decision on appeal introduces an artificiality into the proceedings which is not justified by the language of the statute. A dismissal is thus unfair where the employer has refused to entertain an appeal to which the employee was contractually entitled and thereby denied him the opportunity of showing that, in all the circumstances, the employer's reason for dismissing him was not sufficient. Furthermore, the principle in *W Devis v Atkins* was not relevant to this case, as it decided no more than that conduct of an employee unrelated to the real reason for dismissal is irrelevant to the question of the reasonableness of dismissal for that particular reason.

Note

See, also, *Greenhall Whitley plc v Carr* (1985) and *Whitbread & Co plc v Mills* (1988), where the EAT reiterated in both cases that matters which came to light during the appeal process should be taken into account by the tribunal in considering the reasonableness of the employer's decision to dismiss.

Alboni v Ind Coope Retail Ltd (1998) CA
The applicant received notice of dismissal on 16 May, with dismissal taking effect on 6 July. Between these dates, the employer was willing to consider the applicant's application for a similar post and any other representations regarding dismissal. In allowing the appeal from the tribunal decision that the dismissal was fair, the EAT held that a tribunal was not entitled to take account of what happened after notice of termination had been given.

Held, by the Court of Appeal, that a tribunal, in determining the issue of reasonableness, should have regard to the employer's actions between the date of the dismissal notice and the date the dismissal took effect. In the present case, the tribunal was entitled to hold that the employer had acted reasonably in keeping open the employee's options to make further representations and to apply for a similar post.

Timex Corp v Thomson (1981) CA
The employee had worked for the company for 14 years. Shortly before he was dismissed, he had been appointed to one of three managerial posts. The company re-organised the three management jobs into two positions. The new positions required engineering qualifications that the employee did not possess, and so he was selected for redundancy. At the tribunal, the company also maintained that, as well as lack of qualifications, the

decision to dismiss had also been influenced by the employee's general unsatisfactory performance. The tribunal held that the dismissal was unfair, because the company had failed to establish whether the reason for dismissal was redundancy or lack of capability.

Held, by the EAT, that the tribunal had not erred in holding that the company had failed to satisfy them (as required under s 98(1)) of the true reason for dismissal. *Per* Browne-Wilkinson J: 'Even where there is a redundancy situation, it is possible for an employer to use such a situation as a pretext for getting rid of an employee he wishes to dismiss. In such circumstances, the reason for dismissal will not necessarily be redundancy.' The evidence of unsatisfactory performance here raised the possibility that redundancy was indeed created as a pretext to dismiss the employee, and was not the operative reason for the dismissal.

Adams v Derby City Council (1986) EAT

A refuse collector knocked down and killed a pedestrian whilst driving a dustbin wagon. After an investigation, the employers concluded that he had 'failed to carry out the council's instructions regarding the method to be adopted whilst reversing council vehicles'. The employee was dismissed. At the hearing, the employer claimed the reason for dismissal was gross misconduct under the terms of their disciplinary code. The tribunal found that the offence that he had been charged with was not, in fact, covered by the code; therefore, there was no evidence as to the existence of the reasons cited for dismissal. Nevertheless, the tribunal took the view that the facts before them proved that the employee had committed a dismissable offence and that it was not necessary for an employer in such circumstances to explain the reasons for the decision to dismiss.

Held, by the EAT, that the tribunal had erred in law by holding that it was not necessary for the employer to establish the reason for dismissal. Statute lays the burden on the employer to show the reason for dismissal and, if the employer fails to discharge this burden, the dismissal is automatically unfair. It is, therefore, an error of law for a tribunal simply to consider whether there was a dismissable offence without first having been satisfied as to the employer's reason for the dismissal.

Hotson v Wisbech Conservative Club (1984) EAT

The employee was dismissed after it was found that there was a shortfall in the takings of the bar for which he was responsible; the employee could provide no satisfactory explanation for this. At the tribunal, the employer's notice of appearance suggested the reason for the dismissal was the employee's inefficiency. However, when asked directly whether the reason was really the employee's dishonesty, the employer agreed that it was.

Held, by the EAT, that it was unfair for an employer to dismiss for a reason which was not the real reason, and which only came to light at the prompting of the tribunal chairman, as the employer has clearly not discharged the burden of proof in establishing the true reason for dismissal. Whilst the authorities state that the employer is not tied to the label (see, for example, *Abernethy v Matt, Hay and Anderson* (1974) and *McCory v Magee* (1983)) he happens to put on the particular facts relied on (unless the employee is put at a procedural or evidential disadvantage by a change at a late stage in the proceedings), where the original reason for dismissal is lack of capability, the substitution or addition of suspected dishonesty as a reason, even where it is founded on the same facts, goes a great deal further than a mere change of label and is, in effect, a new and significant allegation.

Note ——

Also, on an employers' failure to establish the true reason for the dismissal, see: *Grootcon (UK) Ltd v Keld* (1984); *Glasgow City Council v Smith* (1987); *Trico-Folberth Ltd v Devonshire* (1989); *Clarke v Trimco Group Ltd* (1993); and *Philip Hodges Ltd v Kell* (1994).

Thomson v Alloa Motor Co Ltd (1983) EAT

The employee was a petrol pump attendant who was learning to drive. After work, she was picked up by her husband. As she drove off, she crashed into a petrol pump. She was dismissed. The employer gave conduct (s 98(2)(b)) as the reason for dismissal.

Held, by the EAT, that the reason for dismissal had not been established. Conduct for the purposes of s 98(2)(b) must relate to acts done in the course of employment that reflect on the employer-employee relationship. Even though the incident took place on the employer's property, this did not affect the way she carried out her duties at work. As no valid statutory reason had been established, the dismissal was unfair.

5.2 Fairness of the dismissal

Section 98 of the Employment Rights Act 1996

(4) Where the employer has fulfilled the requirements of sub-s (1), the determination of the question whether the dismissal is fair or unfair (having regard to the reason shown by the employer):

(a) depends on whether, in the circumstances (including the size and administrative resources of the employer's undertaking), the employer acted reasonably or unreasonably in treating it as a sufficient reason for dismissing the employee; and

   (b) shall be determined in accordance with equity and the substantial
        merits of the case.

5.2.1 Conduct

British Home Stores Ltd v Burchell (1978) EAT
The employee was dismissed for allegedly being involved with a number
of other employees in dishonest staff purchases. The employee had been
implicated by another member of staff during the company's
investigation. The industrial tribunal found that the dismissal was fair. It
was argued that the employer had not shown that the employee was
actually involved in the misconduct relied upon by the employer as the
reason for dismissal.

   Held, by the EAT, that a tribunal should not impose too strict a standard
of proof on the employer. The employer need only show the tribunal that
they 'entertained a reasonable suspicion amounting to a belief in the guilt
of that employee'. The tribunal is not expected to assess whether the
employer's belief in the guilt of the employee was objectively proved. In
order for a dismissal, in these circumstances, to be fair:

(a) the employer must establish the fact that they believed the allegation;

(b) it must be shown that there were reasonable grounds for sustaining
     this belief; and

(c) the employer must have carried out such investigations as were
     reasonable in the circumstances.

The tribunal should not attempt, as the tribunal did here, an objective
evaluation of the material available to the employer to see whether it could
support such a belief on the balance of probabilities or beyond reasonable
doubt. The tribunal should only be concerned about whether evidence
exists which can justify a reasonable conclusion by management.

Royal Society for the Protection of Birds v Croucher (1984) IRLR
The employee was dismissed for fiddling his expenses. He admitted that
this had been going on for many months and, in his defence, claimed he
was merely recovering money which was owed to him in respect of
unclaimed expenses. He appealed to the EAT, after the tribunal had found
that he had been fairly dismissed, arguing that the employer had not
carried out as much investigation of the facts as was reasonable in all the
circumstances.

   Held, by the EAT, that, in a case like this, where dishonest conduct was
admitted, there is little need for the kind of investigation referred to in the
Burchell case; that is, an investigation designed to confirm suspicions or
clear up doubt as to whether or not a particular act of misconduct had
occurred.

British Gas plc v McCarrick (1991) IRLR

The employee was suspected of stealing petrol, but an internal disciplinary hearing found that the allegation had not been proved. However, at a subsequent criminal trial, on counsel's advice, the employee pleaded guilty. The employer initiated fresh disciplinary hearings. Despite the employee's contention that he was innocent and had only pleaded guilty through fear of going to prison, the company dismissed him. The industrial tribunal found that the dismissal was unfair, as a reasonable employer would have believed the employee's story and would have made further enquiries of the employee's legal advisors as to the truth of his story.

Held, by the Court of Appeal, that the tribunal had substituted its own view of what was reasonable, rather than considering what the actions of a reasonable employer would have been when faced with this information. The tribunal merely had to establish that, on the facts known, the employers believed the employee was guilty. Furthermore, where the facts of the conviction were clearly established, it could not be accepted that a reasonable employer would be expected to carry out further investigation of the matter.

P v Nottinghamshire County Council (1992) CA

The employee pleaded guilty to indecent assault on children. As a result, his employer removed him from his job as a schools groundsman and, as no suitable alternative employment could be found, he was dismissed.

Held, by the Court of Appeal (reiterating the principle established in *Burchell*), that, where an employee has pleaded guilty to an offence or has been found guilty, it is reasonable for an employer to believe that the offence has been committed by the employee, without the need for further investigation. A finding by the industrial tribunal that there was a duty on the employer to investigate the circumstances leading up to the conviction and assess the risk to other children, and that due to these failings, it was unreasonable to dismiss, was perverse and could not be upheld.

Note ───

On dishonesty, other criminal activity and the *Burchell* test, see, also, *Scottish Midland Co-op Society Ltd v Cullion* (1991); *Campbell v Secretary of State for Scotland* (1992); and *Lovie Ltd v Anderson* (1999).

Haddon v Van Den Bergh (1999) EAT

Mr Haddon, after 15 years of blameless service, was awarded a good service commendation from his employer at a company ceremony. At the ceremony, Mr Haddon consumed some alcohol and failed to return to work. He was dismissed for disobeying an instruction, given earlier, to return to his shift after the ceremony was over. The tribunal, in applying the range of reasonable responses test (as derived from *Iceland Frozen Foods v Jones* (1982)), concluded that, although many employers would not have dismissed the employee, in these circumstances, it could not be said that no reasonable employer would have done so. The decision to dismiss was, therefore, within the range of reasonable responses of a reasonable employer.

Held, by the EAT, in allowing Mr Haddon's appeal, that the test of fairness in s 98(4) of the ERA 1996 should be applied without embellishment, and that the question for the tribunal is simply, 'is the employer's decision to dismiss reasonable in the circumstances of the particular case having regard to equity and the substantial merits?'. Thus, *per* Morrison J:

> The mantra of the band or range of reasonable responses is not helpful, because it has led tribunals into applying what amounts to a perversity test, which, as is clear from *Iceland* itself, was not its purpose. The moment that one talks of a range or band of reasonable responses, one is conjuring up the possibility of extreme views at either end of the band or range. In reality, it is most unlikely in an unfair dismissal case involving misconduct that the tribunal will need to concern itself with the question whether the deployment of each of the weapons in the employer's disciplinary armoury would have been reasonable. Dismissal is the ultimate sanction. There is, in reality, no range or band to be considered, only whether the employer acted reasonably in invoking that sanction ... Furthermore, the reference to 'equity' in s 98(4) requires at the least a consideration of the case from the employee's perspective.

Wilson v Ethicon Ltd (2000) EAT

The applicant was dismissed for failing to carry out a certain testing procedure. The employment tribunal dismissed her complaint, holding that the decision to dismiss fell within the band of reasonable responses of a reasonable employer.

Held, by the EAT, that the appeal would be allowed, as the employment tribunal had failed to apply the correct test. In cases of unfair dismissal on the grounds of misconduct, the observations of Mr Justice Morrison in *Haddon v Van Den Bergh* would be endorsed. The essential issue to be determined by an employment tribunal is the test of fairness set out in s 98(4) of the ERA 1996. What a tribunal has to do is to stand back from the decision of the employer and assess, in the knowledge of what was known to the employer at the time, whether or not the dismissal was reasonable in the circumstances.

Note

In *Iceland Frozen Foods v Jones*, the EAT had elaborated the 'reasonable responses' test for determining whether a dismissal was unfair. *Per* Browne-Wilkinson J:

> ... the correct approach for the industrial tribunal to adopt in answering the question posed by [s 98(4) of the ERA 1996] is as follows:
>
> (1) the starting point should always be the words of [s 98(4)] themselves;
>
> (2) in applying the section, an industrial tribunal must consider the reasonableness of the employer's conduct, not simply whether they (the members of the industrial tribunal) consider the dismissal to be fair;
>
> (3) in judging the reasonableness of the employer's conduct, an industrial tribunal must not substitute its decision as to what was the right course to adopt for that of the employer;
>
> (4) in many, though not all, cases, there is a band of reasonable responses to the employee's conduct within which one employer might reasonably take one view, [while] another might quite reasonably take another;
>
> (5) the function of the industrial tribunal, as an industrial jury, is to determine whether, in the particular circumstances of each case, the decision to dismiss the employee fell within the band of reasonable responses which a reasonable employer might have adopted. If the dismissal falls within the band, the dismissal is fair; if the dismissal falls outside the band, it is unfair.

Commentators had criticised this test as unduly emphasising the power of managerial prerogative. Now, with the decisions in *Haddon v Van Den Bergh* and *Wilson v Ethicon Ltd*, it would seem that the balance in unfair dismissal law has swung back towards considering the interests of the employee (particularly in cases of misconduct). However, what effect these decisions will have in practice depends on how future tribunals reconcile them with decisions of superior courts, where the *Iceland Frozen Foods* principle has been applied. Furthermore, it is not the situation that all cases decided on the *Iceland Frozen Foods* principle have been wrongly decided. It may be that, in a similar set of factual circumstances, an application of the *Haddon v Van Den Bergh* test would also result in the same decision.

United Distillers v Conlin (1992) EAT

The employee was dismissed for falsely claiming payment for work he had not done. He had previously received a final written warning for this behaviour. The tribunal found that he had been dishonest but, as the fraud involved did not exceed £3, this did not warrant dismissal, especially as this was inconsistent with how the employer had treated other employees involved in similar offences.

Held, by the EAT, that, although consistency of treatment between employees is important in considering the fairness of a dismissal, it is also important that due flexibility should be preserved, so that employers may consider each case on its merits. For these reasons, the dismissal was not unfair.

Proctor v British Gypsum Ltd (1992) EAT

The rules of the company stated fighting 'may result in dismissal'. Notwithstanding the fact that, on a previous occasion, such behaviour resulted only in a suspension for a different employee, Proctor was dismissed for assaulting another employee.

Held, by the EAT, that the requirement that employers must act consistently between all employees means that, before reaching a decision to dismiss, an employer should consider truly comparable cases. The overriding principle must be, however, that each case should be considered on its own facts and mitigating circumstances. Consequently, the industrial tribunal was entitled to find that the employer had investigated the earlier incidents carefully and had decided not to dismiss in those cases, because of different mitigating factors from the present case.

Note

On the issue of different treatment for a similar act of misconduct, see the earlier cases of *Post Office v Fennell* (1981); *Hadjioannou v Coral Casinos Ltd* (1981); and *Cain v Leeds Health Authority* (1990). Further, note that the Court of Appeal in *Paul v East Surrey District Health Authority* (1995) agreed with the reasoning of the EAT in *Proctor*, and further emphasised that, where employers had a known and clear policy on dismissal for a particular act, then it would usually be unfair to dismiss where dismissal had not occurred before.

Frames Snooker Centre v Boyce (1992) EAT

The employee was employed along with two other people as managers. The company was burgled and the police informed the employer that it was 'an inside job'. After other burglaries, the employer decided he had no alternative but to dismiss two of the managers, as he could not genuinely decide who was responsible. He did not dismiss the third manager, because she was his daughter and he trusted her implicitly.

Held, by the EAT, that, where any one of a group of employees could have committed a particular offence, the fact that one or more of them is not dismissed does not render dismissal of the remainder unfair, provided that the employer is able to show (after appropriate investigation) 'solid and sensible grounds' for differentiating between members of the group. There is no 'all or none' principle in the dismissal of a group in this situation.

Note

See, also, on this issue, *Whitbread plc v Thomas* (1988) and *Parr v Whitbread plc* (1990).

East Berkshire Health Authority v Matadeen (1992) EAT

The employee, who was in a position of responsibility, was dismissed for gross misconduct after admitting making nuisance telephone calls to fellow employees. The tribunal, in determining that the dismissal was unfair, found that this was not an act of gross misconduct and, therefore, dismissal was not in the range of reasonable responses of a reasonable employer.

Held, by the EAT, *per* Wood J:

The law as it stands seems to me to indicate that the EAT can only interfere with a decision of the industrial tribunal if, first, there is *ex facie* an error of law, a misdirection or a misapplication of the law. Secondly, that there is a material finding of fact relied upon by the tribunal in the decision, which was unsupported by any evidence or contrary to the evidence before them; thirdly, if there is a finding of perversity – if it is satisfied in the light of its own experience and sound business practice in the industrial field that the decision is one 'to which no reasonable tribunal could come' or 'a conclusion that offends reason'.

On these facts, the tribunal had erred in law in finding that the employee's actions did not amount to gross misconduct. Furthermore, the appeal could also be allowed on the grounds of perversity. The decision to dismiss an employee holding management responsibility for calculated and gross misconduct clearly fell within the band of reasonable responses. A decision to the contrary made absolutely no sense in an industrial relations context and was one that no reasonable tribunal could have reached.

Note

Also, on perversity, see: *Piggott Brothers & Co v Jackson* (1991); *British Railways Board v Jackson* (1994); and *Lock v Cardiff Railway Co Ltd* (1998).

Tower Hamlets Health Authority v Anthony (1988) IRLR

The employee had received a final written warning. Under the employer's disciplinary code, this was a prerequisite to any dismissal. Following further complaints about her work, she was dismissed, notwithstanding the fact that she was appealing against the final written warning.

Held, by the EAT, that, whilst there was no rule of law stating that, where an employee is appealing a previous warning, there should not be a dismissal (after further complaints of misconduct) until the appeal has been heard, an employer acting reasonably should take account of this fact when considering whether dismissal is appropriate. Failure to take this fact into account could reasonably lead a tribunal to consider that dismissal was outside the band of reasonable responses. Therefore, in the present case, the tribunal was entitled to conclude that the employer's failure to take the fact of the pending appeal into account rendered the dismissal unfair.

Whitbread & Co plc v Mills (1988) EAT

The employee suffered a back injury at work and was off work for a number of months. On her return, she was asked to see a company doctor. The employee believed the examination was to do with a compensation claim she had made. In fact, it was in relation to her claim for sick pay. She was not informed that the consultant would carry out a full medical examination. At a hearing relating to sick pay, she made certain allegations of improper conduct against the doctor, which he denied. The employee was invited to a meeting to discuss her allegations further. She was not told that this was a disciplinary hearing and that she risked dismissal. At the meeting, the employee was told that she was being dismissed for making 'scandalous and malicious allegations'. Her internal appeal against the decision (which was in the nature of a general review, rather than a rehearing) failed. At the tribunal, the company argued that, even if they had not behaved as a reasonable employer by not following a fair procedure, any defects in the procedure had been put right at an internal appeal.

Held, by the EAT, that, in certain circumstances, defects in disciplinary and dismissal procedures could be remedied on appeal. If an act or omission had brought about an unfair disciplinary hearing, then whether or not an appeal had rectified the situation depended on the degree of unfairness at the original hearing. Where fundamental breaches of natural justice occur, then that appeal must be of a comprehensive nature, not merely a review of the decision, as here.

Note ——————————————————————————————————

See, also, *Sartar v P & O European Ferries* (1992).

Clark v Civil Aviation Authority (1991) EAT

In breach of her contract with the Civil Aviation Authority, the employee was involved in a travel agency business. After a secret investigation, the employer decided to dismiss the employee, without informing her of the charges or giving her the opportunity to refute the allegations. After dismissal, she was told of the allegations against her and that she had a right of appeal, which she exercised. The appeal was a full review of the evidence and she was given every opportunity to present her case. The dismissal was affirmed by the internal appeal tribunal.

Held, by the EAT, that, even though the original dismissal had been a breach of natural justice, the procedural defects had been rectified by the comprehensive appeal. In normal circumstances, failure to follow a fair procedure will alone be sufficient to render a dismissal unfair. However, the law is now clear (following *Whitbread & Co v Mills* (1988)) that a faulty procedure during the initial stage can be rectified by a full and proper hearing on appeal, if it is, in effect, a re-hearing, so that the applicant has suffered no injustice.

Note

In *obiter* comments, the EAT recommended that, where further investigation of misconduct is required, the proper course for an employer may be to suspend the employee on full pay, followed by a disciplinary hearing and, if necessary, an appeal hearing. Both hearings should fully take account of the rules of natural justice.

Byrne v BOC Ltd (1992) EAT

Whilst the employee was absent from work, an investigation was carried out into her timesheets. A manager, Mr Pegg, became involved in this investigation. On her return, the employee was asked to attend a hastily convened disciplinary hearing, at which she was told she had overclaimed nine and a half hours. This figure had been arrived at by Mr Pegg, who was not at this hearing. She offered no explanation and was dismissed. Her appeal against this decision was heard two days later by Mr Pegg. Mr Pegg went over the case in some detail with the employee but, in the end, supported the decision to dismiss.

Held, by a majority of the EAT, that a person may be disqualified from hearing an appeal not only when he is personally involved in the events that led to the dismissal or in the decision to dismiss, but also through involvement in the investigation. Such a person may become so involved in the matter that he is a judge in his own cause, which, therefore, disentitles him on grounds of natural justice from conducting a fair appeal. Thus, in the present case, the obvious defects in the earlier disciplinary proceedings were not cured by the appeal process, which was itself defective.

Note ───

In *obiter* commentary, the EAT further emphasised that, to determine whether an appeal process was adequate to cure the defects of earlier disciplinary proceedings, it is essential that the appellate process is more than a mere review of the circumstances of dismissal. To make good the deprivation which the employee has suffered by being denied a proper disciplinary hearing at first instance, a comprehensive appeal is required which gives the applicant a full opportunity of stating his or her case.

Note ───

See, also, on 'procedural' unfairness – *Budgen & Co v Thomson* (1976) (failure to permit employee to respond to a misconduct allegation); *RSPCA v Cruden* (1986) (failure to expedite disciplinary proceedings); *Spink v Express Food Group Ltd* (1990) (failure to inform employee of case against him); *Clarke v Trimco Group Ltd* (1993) (failure to allow employee opportunity of defending himself against serious charge of dishonesty); *Stoker v Lancashire County Council* (1992) (failure to follow a full appeal process in a contractually incorporated disciplinary code – but, see contrary decision in *Westminster County Council v Cabaj* (1996); and *Lock v Cardiff Railway Co Ltd* (1998) (failure to have regard to the provisions of the ACAS Code of Practice on disciplinary practice and procedure).

By contrast, see *Royal Naval School v Hughes* (1979) and *Slater v Leicestershire Health Authority* (1989) (natural justice means that the employee must know what is said against him and have the opportunity to be heard. The tribunal must act honestly, but the charge need not be heard before a strictly neutral tribunal); *Retarded Children's Society Ltd v Day* (1978) (circumstances of gross misconduct may justify dismissal without the need for prior warnings – see, also, for example, *Denco v Jonison* (1991)); *Ulsterbus Ltd v Henderson* (1989) (no requirement to carry out an investigation of a quasi-judicial nature); *Fuller v Lloyds Bank* (1991) and *Hussain v Elonex plc* (1999) (a minor procedural error – failure to disclose witness statements prior to disciplinary hearing does not normally render the procedure intrinsically unfair where the employee is already broadly aware of the circumstances of the dismissal).

5.2.2 Capability

Spencer v Paragon Wallpapers Ltd (1976) EAT

The employee had been off work with back trouble for two months. The company asked his doctor (with the employee's permission) how long it would be before he could return to work. On being told it could be four to six weeks, the company dismissed the employee.

Held, by the EAT, that, in cases where an employee is dismissed on grounds of ill health, the basic question which has to be determined is whether, in all the circumstances, the company can be expected to wait any longer and, if so, how much longer? Factors to be taken into account include: the nature of the illness; the likely length of the continuing absence; the need for the employer to have the work done; the work which the employee was engaged to do; and the circumstances of the case. Whilst there should be prior discussion between employer and employee before deciding to dismiss, a written 'warning' of the possibility of dismissal is not appropriate. Rather, a 'more personal touch' is required in the form of consultation as to how the problem may be addressed. In this case, the absence was a sufficient reason for dismissal.

East Lindsey District Council v Daubney (1977) EAT

The employee was dismissed on the ground of ill health. This decision had been reached acting upon the report of the District Community Physician, who had been asked to advise on whether the employee's health was such that he should be retired prematurely.

Held, by the EAT, that the decision to dismiss was unfair, because the employer acted upon a prognosis from their own medical advisor, without giving the employee the opportunity to review the findings, state his case and provide an independent medical opinion. Discussion and consultation with an employee is an important step, as it may bring to light facts and circumstances concerning the employee's medical position of which the employer was unaware. Only in wholly exceptional circumstances will failure to consult be justified since, if the employee is not consulted and given an opportunity to state their case, an injustice may be done.

Eclipse Blinds Ltd v Wright (1992) Court of Session

The employee had been sick for some time. She informed her employers that she thought her health was improving and that she would be back at work within 13 weeks. However, her doctor (whom she had allowed the company to contact) informed the employer that, in fact, her prognosis was not good and that she was highly unlikely to return to work. The company reluctantly decided to dismiss the employee. The director who took the decision knew it was desirable to speak to the employee in person. However, as the employee did not realise the seriousness of her illness, he decided it would be kinder to write to her rather than risk informing her during the interview of her serious condition.

Held, by the Court of Session, that, whilst consultation was necessary in 'normal' cases, it was not necessary in 'wholly exceptional circumstances'. The employer's genuine concern to avoid giving the employee information about her health of which she did not seem to be aware made this an exceptional case justifying the employer's decision not to consult.

Q If an employee refuses to undergo a medical examination, would the employer be acting reasonably by deciding to dismiss anyway without the benefit of a medical prognosis?

London Fire and Civil Defence Authority v Betty (1994) EAT

The employee was falsely accused by his employers of racial discrimination and harassment. As a result, he suffered a nervous breakdown and was unable to return to work. Although the employer had obtained medical reports and had consulted with the employee prior to dismissal, the tribunal found the dismissal unfair, because the illness was the fault of the employer. On appeal, it was argued that the tribunal should not concern itself with the cause of the employee's problems.

Held, by the EAT, that the only question for the tribunal to consider was whether the dismissal was fair, having regard to the employee's medical condition and the procedures that had been followed prior to dismissal. The duty to act fairly was unaffected by considerations as to who was responsible for the employee's unfitness to work. To introduce questions of responsibility for illness or injury would take the tribunal down a path that could lead to endless dispute on matters about which it had no special expertise. In any event, if the injury was caused by the employer, the employee would be entitled and able to recover the appropriate damages in the law of tort or under the contract of employment.

Q Where an employee is off sick intermittently over a substantial period of time and the illness is not verified by appropriate sicknotes, should a resulting dismissal be for reason of misconduct or incapability? See *International Sports Ltd v Thomson* (1980) and *Lynock v Cereal Packaging Ltd* (1988).

Note ———————————————————————————

Also on dismissals on health grounds, see *A Links & Co v Rose* (1991) and *Mitchell v Arkwood Plastics (Engineering) Ltd* (1993). Where incompetence dismissals are concerned, in determining whether the decision to dismiss was within the band of reasonable responses of a reasonable employer, tribunals should consider, *inter alia*, the seriousness of the incompetence, the effectiveness of any employee appraisal system, whether warnings of the problem were given and whether the employee was given any time to improve performance. See on this *Post Office v Mughal* (1977); *Cook v Thomas Linnell & Sons* (1977); *Sutton and Gates v Boxall* (1978); *Taylor v Alidair Ltd* (1978); and *Gair v Bevan Harris Ltd* (1983).

5.2.3 Redundancy

Williams v Compair Maxam Ltd (1982) EAT

Due to severe financial pressures, the company informed the recognised trade union that redundancies would be necessary. There was no consultation with the union or individual employees, nor were employees given prior warning of their dismissal.

Held, by the EAT, that (*per* Browne-Wilkinson J):

The question we have to decide is whether a reasonable tribunal could have reached the conclusion that the dismissal of the applicants in this case lay within the range of conduct which a reasonable employer could have adopted ... there is a generally accepted view in industrial relations that, in cases where the employees are represented by an independent union recognised by the employer, reasonable employers will seek to act in accordance with the following principles:

(1) The employer will seek to give as much warning as possible of impending redundancies so as to enable the union and employees who may be affected to take early steps to inform themselves of the relevant facts, consider possible alternative solutions and, if necessary, find alternative employment in the undertaking or elsewhere.

(2) The employer will consult the union as to the best means by which the desired management result can be achieved fairly and with as little hardship to the employees as possible. In particular, the employer will seek to agree with the union the criteria to be applied in selecting the employees to be made redundant ... and whether selection has been made in accordance with those criteria.

(3) Whether or not an agreement as to criteria to be adopted has been agreed with the union, the employer will seek to establish criteria for selection ... that can be objectively checked against such things as attendance record, efficiency at the job, experience or length of service.

(4) The employer will seek to ensure that the selection is made fairly, in accordance with these criteria, and will consider any representations the union may make as to such selection.

(5) The employer will seek to see whether, instead of dismissing an employee, he could offer him alternative employment.

See, also, 6.4, below, on redundancy procedures.

Polkey v AE Dayton Services Ltd (1987) HL

Due to a re-organisation of duties, the employee was made redundant. The first the employee knew of this was when he was called into the manager's office. He was then immediately dismissed and sent home. A tribunal accepted that the provisions of the ACAS Industrial Relations Code of Practice (now repealed) relating to consultation on redundancy had not been followed. However, applying the principles set out in *British Labour Pump Co Ltd v Byrne* (1979), the tribunal went on to find that the result would have been the same even if there had been a consultation and, consequently, the decision to dismiss was fair.

Held, by the House of Lords, that *British Labour Pump* would be overruled. It is what the employer actually did that was to be judged, not what he might or might not have done. In judging whether the employer acted reasonably (by not consulting), it is necessary to consider whether the employer reasonably believed that, at the time of dismissal, due to exceptional factors, the consultation or warning would have been 'utterly useless' or 'futile' and would not have altered the decision to dismiss. If this was not the case, then failure to observe the requirements of the Code relating to consultation will render a dismissal unfair.

Note

The *Polkey* approach to the relevance of procedure was followed by the Court of Appeal in *Duffy v Yeomans & Partners* (1994).

Ferguson and Others v Prestwick Circuits Ltd (1992) EAT

The employees were made redundant after a business re-organisation. Selection was on the basis of performance, flexibility and future potential. There was no discussion or consultation prior to the redundancies. This was a deliberate decision made by the employer, as three years earlier, the company had gone through the recommended process, prior to redundancies, over a period of three days, only to be told by the workforce that they would have preferred to have been told on the day that they were being made redundant.

Held, by the EAT, that good industrial practice and the law required that, wherever possible, consultation should take place before employees are dismissed on grounds of redundancy. What had happened in the past was not sufficient reason for departing from this, especially as there was no evidence that the present employees had waived their right to consultation.

Heron v Citylink-Nottingham (1993) EAT

Due to a sudden change in business circumstances, the company had to immediately reduce overheads. The employee was immediately dismissed. There was no consultation. The industrial tribunal held that this was sufficient 'exceptional circumstances' to justify the lack of consultation.

Held, by the EAT, that a finding that the requirement to consult was obviated by these exceptional circumstances could only be supported if the circumstances made it necessary to dismiss the employee when they did, and at no later date. In this case, there was no reason why the employer could not have given the employee at least a week or so to consider his future and come up with alternative suggestions to avoid the redundancy. Nor was the failure to consult justified by the employer's belief that the employee was the only person who could be made redundant. The fact that the employer reasonably believed this to be the case does not *per se* reduce the need for consultation. There may be circumstances known to the employee, but not to the employer, which may make the employer change his mind. Consultation may also be useful, even if redundancy is inevitable, to discuss what help the employer can provide to find the employee alternative employment.

Note

Also, on redundancy, see *Vokes Ltd v Bear* (1974) (failure to try to find alternative employment for the redundant employee); *Octavius Atkinson & Sons v Morris* (1989) (no duty to offer an employee a job which came up after dismissal); *Robinson v Ulster Carpets* (1991) (dismissal in breach of an agreed procedure); *FDR v Holloway* (1995) (in order to establish whether the criteria was applied fairly and reasonably discovery of documents is permissible); *King v Eaton Ltd* (1996) (fair consultation implies consultation when the proposals are at the formative stage and that adequate information and time is provided to enable the employee to respond effectively); *John Brown Engineering Ltd v Brown* (1997) (employers must give employees the opportunity to contest the basis of the system used to decide redundancy selection); and *Lloyd v Taylor Woodrow Construction* (1999) (a defect in the consultation process can be corrected at later appeal hearings where the appeal is a re-hearing).

Q Do you think employers would discharge the duty of consultation if they only consulted with employee representatives, that is, a recognised union, rather than each and every individual who is to be made redundant? See *Rolls Royce Motor Cars Ltd v Price* (1993).

Mugford v Midland Bank plc (1997) EAT

The employee was dismissed on the ground of redundancy as part of a restructuring process, which eventually saw 3,000 redundancies. There was no consultation before the employee was identified as being redundant or before he was told of his redundancy, and no steps were taken to contact him before his contract terminated.

Held, by the EAT, *per* Peter Clark J:

Having considered the authorities, we would summarise the position as follows:

(1) where no consultation about redundancy has taken place with either the trade union or the employee, the dismissal will normally be unfair, unless the industrial tribunal finds that a reasonable employer would have concluded that consultation would be an utterly futile exercise in the particular circumstances of the case;

(2) consultation with the trade union over selection criteria does not of itself release the employer from considering with the employee individually his being identified for redundancy;

(3) it will be a question of fact and degree for the industrial tribunal to consider whether consultation with the individual and/or his union was so inadequate as to render the dismissal unfair. A lack of consultation in any particular respect will not automatically lead to that result. The overall picture must be viewed by the tribunal up to the date of termination to ascertain whether the employer has or has not acted reasonably in dismissing the employee on grounds of redundancy.

5.2.4 Some other substantial reason

RS Components Ltd v RE Irwin (1973) NIRC

The employee was dismissed for refusing to agree to a unilateral change in his contract of employment. The tribunal held that this was not a dismissal for 'some other substantial reason', and therefore found that there had been an unfair dismissal.

Held, by the National Industrial Relations Court, that a reason for dismissal 'for some other substantial reason' does not have to be a reason of the same kind or nature as the other heads. The four heads set out in the Act may well be intended to be the common reasons for dismissal, but are not an exhaustive catalogue of all the circumstances in which a company may be justified in dismissing an employee. Although, as a matter of good industrial relations, the words 'some other substantial reason' should not be construed too widely, the words, if construed consistently with the manifest intention of the Act, apply to this situation – a refusal to enter into new terms and conditions of employment.

Chubb Fire Security Ltd v Harper (1983) EAT

The employee was faced with a new contract after a company re-organisation, which he calculated would entail a considerable drop in income. He refused to accept the variation and was dismissed.

Held, by the EAT, that the correct approach in determining whether dismissal is fair in these circumstances is for tribunals to make a finding as to the advantages to the employers of the proposed re-organisation and whether it is reasonable for them to implement it by terminating existing contracts and offering employees new ones. In determining this, the tribunal should have considered whether the employers were acting reasonably in deciding that the advantages to them in implementing the proposed changes, having regard to their business obligations, outweighed any disadvantage which they should have contemplated the employee might suffer.

Note

In coming to this conclusion, the EAT rejected the conclusions of a differently constituted EAT in the earlier case of *Evans v Elementa Holdings Ltd* (1982), where it was held that the tribunal should merely examine the issue from the employee's perspective by assessing whether the terms offered were objectionable and oppressive.

Richmond Precision Engineering Ltd v Pearce (1985) EAT

When the employee's company was taken over, he was informed that there would be no redundancies, but modifications would be made to his contract to bring it into line with the other company's workers. This involved a reduction in income and loss of benefit to the employee, which he refused to accept. He was dismissed.

Held, by the EAT, that, when considering whether an employer has acted reasonably in dismissing an employee who refuses to agree to changes in his terms and conditions of employment consequent upon a re-organisation, tribunals should not confine themselves to the sole question cited in *Chubb Fire Security Ltd v Harper* (1983) of whether the employers had acted reasonably in deciding that the advantages to them of implementing the proposed changes outweighed any disadvantage which they should have contemplated that the employee may suffer. The task of weighing the advantages to the employer against the disadvantages to the employee is merely one factor which the tribunal has to take into account. Mere disadvantage to the employee does not mean the employer acted unreasonably. The test is whether the terms offered are, from the employer's point of view, ones which a reasonable employer could offer in the changed circumstances of the employer's business. In this case, the offer made by the employer was within the range of offers that were reasonable in all the circumstances; therefore, the decision to dismiss on a refusal of the offer was reasonable.

St John of God (Care Service) Ltd v Brooks (1992) EAT

The National Health Service funded the employer's care service. When funding was substantially reduced, the employer took the decision to employ the present staff on new, considerably less beneficial, contracts. After a period of consultation, the vast majority of the staff employed accepted the new terms and conditions. The applicant was dismissed for refusing to accept.

Held, by the EAT, that the question of whether the terms offered were those which a reasonable employer could offer (based on the decision in *Richmond Engineering*) was not the sole question to be considered. It was also necessary to examine the circumstances surrounding subsequent events after the offer by the employer was made. In this case, it was highly significant that other employees had accepted the offer. Furthermore, if there is a sound business reason for the re-organisation, the reasonableness of the employer's offer has to be looked at in that context.

Note

Also, on business re-organisations, see: *Hollister v NFU* (1979); *Kent County Council v Gilham* (1985); *Oakley v Labour Party* (1988); and *Catamaran Cruisers Ltd v Williams* (1994).

Note

Other examples of dismissal for 'some other substantial reason' include – *Dobie v Burns International Security Services (UK) Ltd* (1984) (dismissal at the behest of a third party); *Treganowan v Knee & Co* (1975) (dismissal due to employee's conflict with other workers); and *Kelman v Oram* (1983) (dismissal of publican's wife after dismissal of publican on other grounds).

Q What effect will the decisions of the EAT in *Haddon v Van Den Bergh* and *Wilson v Ethicon Ltd* have on determining the fairness of a dismissal in this area?

5.3 Time limits

Section 111(2) of the Employment Rights Act 1996

(1) A complaint may be presented to an industrial tribunal against an employer by any person that he was unfairly dismissed by the employer.

(2) Subject to sub-s (3), an industrial tribunal shall not consider a complaint under this section, unless it is presented to the tribunal:

  (a) before the end of the period of three months, beginning with the effective date of termination; or

(b) within such further period as the tribunal considers reasonable in a case where it is satisfied that it was not reasonably practicable for the complaint to be presented before the end of that period of three months.

(3) Where a dismissal is with notice, an industrial tribunal shall consider a complaint under this section if it is presented after the notice is given, but before the effective date of termination.

(4) ...

Palmer and Another v Southend-on-Sea Borough Council (1984) CA

The employees were dismissed after being convicted for stealing petrol. Their appeal against dismissal was unsuccessful, but it was intimated that, if their criminal appeals were successful, the employer would reconsider the position. Some time later, the Court of Appeal quashed their convictions, but the company refused to reinstate them. They then presented a claim for unfair dismissal that was now out of time. The tribunal refused the application, holding that, in the circumstances, it would have been reasonably practicable for the complaints to have been presented in time.

Held, by the Court of Appeal, that 'reasonably practicable' should not be construed so widely as to mean simply 'reasonable', nor should it be construed too narrowly as meaning 'reasonably capable physically of being done'. The question to consider is – was it reasonably feasible to present the complaint to the industrial tribunal within the relevant three months? The application of this test was, pre-eminently, an issue of fact for the tribunal to decide on a consideration of all the circumstances of the case. As the tribunal had not misunderstood the factual question for their decision, nor applied any test or principle wrong in law, there were no grounds for reviewing their finding that it had been reasonably practicable for the complaints to have been submitted within three months of the dismissals.

Note

The courts will also refuse to entertain a late application where an employee fails to put in an application in time because he or she is pursuing a domestic remedy, such as an internal appeal (see *Bodha v Hampshire Area Health Authority* (1982)).

Q   Can an individual make an application for unfair dismissal where he or she only becomes aware of the real grounds for the dismissal after the three month time limit has expired? See *Machine Tool Industry Association v Simpson* (1988) and *Marley (UK) Ltd v Anderson* (1994).

Jean Sorelle Ltd v Rybak (1991) EAT

After being dismissed, the employee first instructed a solicitor, who took no effective action. Later, she contacted a Citizen's Advice Bureau (CAB) and was informed that the time limit for her claim for unfair dismissal had now expired. However, when she contacted the Industrial Tribunal Office, she was informed, incorrectly, that this was not the case and that she still had time to present her application.

Held, by the EAT (following *Riley v Tesco Stores Ltd* (1980)), that a general principle had been established that failure by an advisor such as a solicitor, trade union officer or CAB officer to give the employee correct advice regarding the time limit is not a ground for a claim that it was 'not reasonably practicable' to apply in time. However, per Knox J: '... there is a clear factual difference between, on the one hand, advice obtained by a plaintiff from someone who is asked to advise the plaintiff in the prosecution of her claims against an employer, and, on the other hand, advice obtained by a plaintiff from an employee of the tribunal, which is charged in Parliament with the task of resolving the dispute between the parties.' In the present case, it was correct to treat advice from a tribunal employee as being in a different category from advice from a solicitor or a CAB and, therefore, the dismissed employee could hide behind this failure and show this was the reason for the delay.

London International College v Sen (1992) EAT

The facts were similar to the *Rybak* case, except the employee had consulted a solicitor as well as the Industrial Tribunal Office and both had provided incorrect advice. It was argued by the employer that, as soon as a solicitor is consulted, the general principle (enunciated above in *Rybak*) applies; consequently, the applicant should not now be permitted to contend that it was 'not reasonably practicable' to forward the application in time.

Held, by the EAT, that there is no rule that the mere fact of consulting a solicitor thereafter makes it reasonably practicable to present the application in time. It is a question of fact in every case. In this case, the substantial cause of failure to comply with the time limits was what was said by the tribunal employee, notwithstanding that the applicant had also been given erroneous advice by a solicitor. Therefore, the tribunal was entitled to conclude that it was not reasonably practicable for the plaintiff to present the application in time.

Note

On appeal from the EAT, the Court of Appeal in *Sen v International College* (1993) essentially agreed with the reasoning of the EAT and dismissed the employer's appeal.

Note

Where a claim is not presented in time due to the negligence of an advisor, the aggrieved employee may well be able to sue the advisor for the lost opportunity of securing a remedy for unfair dismissal.

St Basil's Centre v McCrossan (1991) EAT

The employee's claim had to be received by the Monday. He posted the claim on the previous Friday, but the application did not arrive at the tribunal until Tuesday. Evidence was accepted which showed that letters were normally received the day after posting. The employee argued that it was reasonable for him to expect what was posted on a Friday to arrive by the following Monday. The industrial tribunal agreed that, in these circumstances, it was not reasonably practicable for the complaint to be presented in time, and so considered the application on its merits.

Held, by the EAT, that, where an unfair dismissal application is posted within the three month time period, but arrives after that period has expired, the question to be determined is whether the plaintiff would reasonably expect the application to be delivered in time in the ordinary course of the post, which is a question of fact for the industrial tribunal to determine on the evidence. The EAT further went on to hold that, on this evidence, the tribunal was entitled to agree with the plaintiff that he could reasonably have expected delivery of the application before expiry of the three month period, and that, as it was, therefore, 'not reasonably practicable' for the complaint to be presented within the time limit, the tribunal was correct in accepting the late application.

Q   Do you think ignorance of the three month time limit or a genuine mistake as to the calculation of the time limit is a valid excuse in law sufficient to render it 'not reasonably practicable' to present a claim in time? See *Dedman v British Building and Engineering Appliances Ltd* (1974) and *Wall's Meat Co v Khan* (1979).

Capital Foods Retail Ltd v Corrigan (1993) IRLR

On being dismissed, the employee consulted a solicitor and a claim for unfair dismissal was sent to the industrial tribunal five weeks before the end of the time limit. Nothing happened for a number of months, by which time, the time limit had expired. On contacting his solicitor, the applicant was informed that there had been no acknowledgment from the tribunal that the application had been received, nor had the application been returned undelivered. A copy of the application was then sent with a covering letter explaining the unusual circumstances of the claim. The tribunal held that, in this situation, the claim was not time barred stating: '... there is, of course, a presumption that what is posted will be delivered.'

117

Held, by the EAT, that the tribunal had erred in accepting there was such a presumption, without expressly considering the question of whether reliance on such a presumption was reasonable in the circumstances. The unexplained failure of an application to reach the tribunal was not sufficient to satisfy the test, unless all reasonable steps were taken to see that the application had been duly received. *Per* Lord Coulsfield:

> It seems to us to be a matter of ordinary and prudent practice to employ some system of checking that replies which might reasonably be expected within certain periods have, in fact, been received, and that the conduct of business is taking its normal course. In the present case, it appears that the applicant's solicitor did not carry out any such check, but simply relied on the assumption that the application had been duly presented.

Note ───────────────────────────────

Also, on postal issues, see *Birmingham Midshires Building Society v Horton* (1991) and *Camden and Islington Community Services NHS Trust v Kennedy* (1996).

Schultz v Esso Petroleum Co Ltd (1999) CA

The employee, due to the pursuit of an internal appeal and then later due to illness, failed to present his application within the three month time limit. The tribunal held that, as he could have physically presented the claim before he became too ill, the time limit would not be extended.

Held, by the Court of Appeal, that the tribunal had misdirected itself on this issue. Just because the application could physically have been made does not mean that it was 'reasonably practicable' to present it. The better approach is to consider whether it could have been reasonably feasible, in the context of the circumstances, to present the application before the time limit expired. The relevant surrounding circumstances here were that the plaintiff was delaying the application whilst pursuing alternative remedies, and then was unable to present the application due to illness falling in the later, more critical weeks, leading up to the end of the limitation period.

Note ───────────────────────────────

London Underground v Noel (1999): an offer of re-employment, which is subsequently withdrawn, is not a circumstance that justifies an employee's failure to present an application within the three month time period from the date of the original dismissal.

6 Redundancy

6.1 Definition of redundancy

Section 139 of the Employment Rights Act 1996

(1) For the purposes of this Act, an employee who is dismissed shall be taken to be dismissed by reason of redundancy if the dismissal is wholly or mainly attributable to:

(a) the fact that his employer has ceased or intends to cease:

    (i) to carry on the business for the purposes of which the employee was employed by him; or

    (ii) to carry on that business in the place where the employee was so employed; or

(b) the fact that the requirements of that business:

    (i) for employees to carry out work of a particular kind; or

    (ii) for employees to carry out work of a particular kind in the place where the employee was employed by the employer,

have ceased or diminished or are expected to cease or diminish.

(2) For the purposes of sub-s (1), the business of the employer, together with the business or businesses of his associated employers, shall be treated as one (unless either of the conditions specified in paras (a) and (b) of that sub-section would be satisfied without so treating them).

6.1.1 The need for redundancy

Moon v Homeworthy Furniture (Northern) Ltd (1977) EAT

A factory was closed down and the whole workforce was made redundant. The employees claimed that there was not a genuine redundancy situation and they disputed the employer's contention that the factory was not economically viable.

Held, by the EAT, that it was not for the courts to become involved in a dispute over whether or not a redundancy situation was justified. The employees accepted that there was a cessation of work and, therefore, there was a redundancy within the meaning of what is now s 139(1)(a) of the Employment Rights Act 1996 (ERA). Kilner-Brown J said:

> The employees were and are seeking to use the industrial tribunal and the EAT as a platform for the ventilation of an industrial dispute. This appeal tribunal is unanimously of the opinion that, if that is what this matter is all about, then it must be stifled at birth ... we cannot tolerate any attempt by anybody to go behind the limits imposed on industrial tribunals.

6.1.2 Meaning of 'place where the employee was so employed'

O'Brien v Associated Fire Alarms Ltd (1968) CA

The applicants were employed in and around Liverpool and lived there also. Work in Liverpool diminished and they were ordered to work in Barrow, about 150 miles away. As there was no express term as to place of work, the issue was then whether a term could be implied in their contracts that they could be required to work anywhere in the north west of England. If so, they would not be entitled to a redundancy payment if they refused to work in Barrow.

Held, by the Court of Appeal, that, in these circumstances, it would be wrong to imply a term to this effect and, therefore, the applicants were redundant within the meaning of what is now s 139(1)(b)(ii) of the ERA 1996.

Per Salmon LJ:

> I would have thought that, as the material circumstances in which these contracts of employment were entered into are shrouded in mystery, it is permissible, if one is seeking to reconstruct the contract, to look at what happened while the men were being employed. The fact is that never during all the years in which they worked for the respondents were they ever asked to work anywhere except in the conurbation of Liverpool or those parts of Cheshire which they could reach from their homes so that they returned to their homes every night. This, of course, would be by no means conclusive about the terms of their employment if there were any evidence the other way, but it is all there is as to where they could be required to work. This indicates (and there is nothing to the contrary) that what they were doing during the year of their employment was all that they could be required to do in accordance with the terms of their employment. There is no evidence that the terms of their employment gave their employers the power to order them to do anything else ...

United Kingdom Atomic Energy Authority v Claydon (1974) NIRC

The applicant's contract permitted his employer to require him to work at any of the employer's establishments in Great Britain and overseas. He had worked for seven years in Suffolk, but was then asked to transfer to the Aldermaston plant. He refused and was dismissed.

Held, by the National Industrial Relations Court, that he was not redundant, as his contract enabled his employer to require him to move.

Bass Leisure Ltd v Thomas (1994) EAT

The applicant worked at a depot in Coventry and her employer, in accordance with a term in her contract, required her to work at another depot 20 miles away. She did not wish to do so and claimed that she was redundant.

Held, by the EAT, that she was redundant. The EAT applied a geographical, rather than a contractual test, unlike in the above two cases. In effect, the EAT asked the question 'where does the employee work?', and decided that the answer to this could not include a depot 20 miles from where she had previously worked. The employee's contract was useful in defining the normal place of work but was no longer decisive.

Q   Will the decision in *Bass Leisure v Thomas* benefit employees in the long run? Will the practical effect be to make it easier for employers to make employees redundant?

See, also, *High Table Ltd v Horst* (1997).

6.1.3 Requirements of the business for employees to carry out work of a particular kind

Hindle v Percival Boats Ltd (1969) CA

The applicant was employed as a boat builder and had built wooden boats. However, customers increasingly demanded fibre-glass vessels and the applicant was found to be too slow when it came to building these. He was therefore dismissed for being 'too good and too slow'. Was he redundant?

Held, by the Court of Appeal, that he was not redundant, because the requirements of the business had not altered.

Per Sachs LJ:

I would add that, provided the requirements of the business referred to in s 81(2)(b) [now s 139(1)(b)] remain constant, it does not matter whether the slowness of the employee which leads to the failure to 'pay for his keep' stems from the onset of years, from some physical cause, or from over-great addiction to what is sometimes termed perfectionism. Unfortunately for such addicts, perfectionism can produce a form of inefficiency in many walks of life – not merely in a workshop – however much one may praise the look of the product.

Vaux and Associated Breweries Ltd v Ward (1968) HC

A hotel was modernised and the employer decided to bring in younger and more glamorous bar staff. The applicant (Mrs Ward), who had been employed as a barmaid for 17 years, was dismissed, as it was felt that she would not fit in with the new image.

Held, by the High Court (QBD), that the applicant was not redundant, because the requirements of the business for work of the kind which the applicant was employed to do had not changed.

Parker LCJ referred to the reasons given by the industrial tribunal for holding that the applicant was not redundant, with which he agreed:

> The tribunal were of [the] opinion that the work to be carried out by a barmaid after Mrs Ward was dismissed was not different from that which she had carried out. She was engaged in serving behind the bar, either directly to customers or to waitresses to take to customers. Occasionally, if the waitress was not present, Mrs Ward would carry drinks to customers in the buffet. Seventy per cent of the drinks dispensed were beer ... The present barmaid serves behind the bar, occasionally going in front of the bar to serve customers.

North Riding Garages Ltd v Butterwick (1967) HC

The applicant had been employed at a garage as a workshop manager in charge of the repairs shop. In addition, he spent some time in actual mechanical work on the vehicles. However, the new owners wished him to do more work on the sales side of the business and to do more paperwork. They also introduced new methods, which the applicant found difficult to adapt to, and he was eventually dismissed.

Held, by the High Court (QBD), that he was not redundant, because the requirements of the business for work of a particular kind done by the applicant had not ceased or diminished.

Widgery J drew the following distinction:

> For the purposes of this Act, an employee who remains in the same kind of work is expected to adapt himself to new methods and techniques and cannot complain if his employer insists on higher standards of efficiency than those previously required; but, if new methods alter the nature of the work required to be done, it may follow that no requirement remains for employees to do work of the particular kind which has been superseded and that they are truly redundant ... If one looks at the primary facts disclosed by the evidence in this case, it is difficult to see what is the particular kind of work in which a requirement for employees has ceased or diminished. The vehicle workshop remained, as did the requirement for a workshop manager, and we do not understand the tribunal to have found that the volume of repair work had diminished to such an extent as

to make the respondent's dismissal wholly or mainly attributable to that fact. The only possible conclusion which appears to us to have been open to the tribunal on the evidence was that the respondent was dismissed because he could not do his job in accordance with the new methods and new standards required by the appellants.

Q   How different does a job have to be from the previous job in order for the employee to be redundant?

Chapman v Goonvean and Rostrowrack China Clay Co Ltd (1973) CA
The employer had provided free transport to employees who lived more than 30 miles away, but later withdrew this when some employees were made redundant and it was uneconomic to continue to provide it for the seven employees who remained. Some of these employees resigned and claimed redundancy.

Held, by the Court of Appeal, that they were not redundant. 'The requirements of the business – for the work of these seven men – continued just as before', *per* Lord Denning MR.

Johnson v Nottinghamshire Combined Police Authority (1974) CA
The applicants were employed as clerks and their hours of work were 9.30 am to 5.00 pm or 5.30 pm on a five day week. Their employer then asked them to work a shift system, under which one would work from 8.00 am to 3.00 pm on six days a week and the other would work from 1.00 pm to 8.00 pm on six days a week. The following week they would change over. The applicants resigned and claimed redundancy.

Held, by the Court of Appeal, that they were not redundant. Lord Denning MR said:

> A change in the hours of work is very different from a change in the place of employment. The statute expressly provides that, if the requirements for employees at 'the place' cease or diminish, there is a redundancy situation: see s 81(2)(b) [now s 139(1)(b) of the ERA 1996]. But it says nothing of the like effect as to 'hours' of work. If the employers require the same number of employees as before – for the same tasks as before – but require them at different hours, there is no redundancy situation. If the change in hours is unfair to a particular employee in the situation in which she finds herself, it might give rise to a claim for unfair dismissal under the Industrial Relations Act 1971, but it does not give rise to a redundancy payment.

Lesney Products & Co Ltd v Nolan (1977) CA
The applicants were employed as machine maintenance setters and worked on a three shift system of day, evening and night work. In order to cut costs, some workers were asked to work a double day shift on alternate weeks, instead of a day shift with long overtime and a night shift. This

reduced their opportunity to earn overtime and some of them claimed that they were redundant as a result of the changes.

Held, by the Court of Appeal, that they were not redundant. Lord Denning MR emphasised the rights of employers to re-organise their business:

> While I adhere to what I there said [that is, in *Johnson*, above], I think the phrase 'a redundancy situation' may be misleading. It is shorthand, and it is better always to check it by the statutory words. The dismissal must be attributable to 'the fact that the requirements of that business for employees to carry out work of a particular kind ... have ceased or diminished', etc.

> In applying that principle, it is important that nothing should be done to impair the ability of employers to re-organise their work force and their times and conditions of work so as to improve efficiency. They may re-organise it so as to reduce overtime and thus to save themselves money, but that does not give the man a right to redundancy payment. Overtime might be reduced, for instance, by taking on more men : but that would not give the existing staff a right to a redundancy payment. Also, when overtime is reduced by a re-organisation of working hours, that does not give rise to a right to a redundancy payment, so long as the work to be done is the same.

Robinson v British Island Airways Ltd (1977) CA

The applicant had been the flight operations manager and, as such, he was responsible to the general manger of operations and traffic (Mr Owen), who was himself responsible to the general manager. Under a re-organisation, Mr Owen's post was abolished, and replaced by the post of operations manager, and the applicant's post of flight operations manager was also abolished. The company required the holder of the new post of operations manager to have a pilot's licence; Mr Owen did not have one, but the applicant did. However, the applicant was not appointed to the new post and claimed unfair dismissal.

Held, by the Court of Appeal, that the applicant was redundant. Phillips J distinguished between the *Johnson* and the *Lesney* cases (above) on the grounds that, in those cases, the effect of a re-organisation was not to either change or diminish the requirements for work of a particular kind. However, here, it did:

> There is no doubt that the employee was dismissed. To what was his dismissal attributable? It seems to us that the work done by the flight operations manager was of a 'particular kind', and that the work done by the general manager operations and traffic was of a 'particular kind', and that each kind was different from the other. It seems to us that the work

done by the operations manager was of a 'particular kind' and of a kind different from that done by the general manager operations and traffic and different from that done by the flight operations manager. Thus, in our judgment, it can truly be said that the dismissal of the employee was attributable to that fact that the requirements of the business for employees to carry out work of a particular kind has ceased or diminished and that each was redundant.

Q   Contrast the approach taken by Phillips J in *Robinson* with those in the preceding three cases. To what extent do you consider, if at all, that the courts, in deciding whether an employee is redundant, have over-emphasised the managerial role/prerogative?

Cowen v Haden Ltd (1983) CA

The applicant was employed as a divisional contracts surveyor. His contract enabled his employer to require him to perform 'any and all duties which reasonably fell within the scope of his capabilities'. He was dismissed when his work as a divisional contracts surveyor ended.

Held, by the Court of Appeal, that the wide clause in his contract (set out above) was to be read in conjunction with his job as a divisional contracts surveyor, and was not to be read separately. Therefore, as his job had gone, he was redundant. Cumming Bruce LJ said:

> The effect of the words 'He will be required to undertake, at the direction of company, any and all duties which reasonably fall within the scope of his capabilities' was not to give the employers the right to transfer him from his job as regional surveyor to any job as a quantity surveyor in their organisation, but only to require him to perform any duties reasonably within the scope of his capabilities as regional surveyor.

Johnson v Peabody Trust (1996) EAT

The applicant was employed as a roofer but, in 1988, his contract of employment was varied, because there was less repair work and he was expected to undertake general building work as well as roofing. By 1993, his main work was general building, rather than roofing. He was subsequently laid off.

Held, by the EAT, that the applicant was redundant. He had been engaged 'to perform a particular, well recognised and well defined category of skilled trade', that is, as a roofer, and it was that 'basic contractual obligation' which decided whether he was redundant. As the roofing work had 'ceased or diminished', it followed that he was redundant.

Murray and Another v Foyle Meats Ltd (1999) HL

The respondents employed the appellants as 'meat plant operatives'. Although they normally worked in the slaughter hall, they could, under their contracts of employment, be required to work elsewhere and, occasionally, they did so. Employees who worked in other parts of the factory were employed on similar terms. Fewer employees were required in the hall due to falling business and the appellants were dismissed by reason of redundancy. They contended that their dismissals were unfair, because the words 'requirements for employees to carry out work of a particular kind' meant 'requirements for employees contractually bound to carry out work of a particular kind' and, because all employees were engaged on similar terms, no distinction could be made between those who worked in the slaughter hall and those who worked elsewhere in the factory. Accordingly, the appellants contended that it was wrong to only select for redundancy those engaged in the slaughter hall.

Held, by the House of Lords, that the appellants' contention was wrong and that the dismissals were by reason of redundancy. Lord Irvine LC, with whom the other Law Lords agreed, held that the contract test was the wrong one and overruled *Nelson v BBC* (1977). The function test, which asks whether the employer needs fewer employees to do the kind of work which the employee is actually doing, was also held to be wrong.

Lord Irvine LC held that the key word is 'attributable' and that both the 'contract test' and the 'function test' miss the point because, as he said, 'there is no reason in law why the dismissal of an employee should not be attributable to a diminution in the employer's need for employees, irrespective of the terms of his contract or the function which he performed'. *Per* Lord Irvine LC:

> The language of (the statutory definition of redundancy) is, in my view, simplicity itself. It asks two questions of fact. The first is whether one or other of various states of economic activity exists. In this case, the relevant one is whether the requirements of the business for employees to carry out work of a particular kind have diminished. The second one is whether the dismissal is attributable, wholly or mainly, to that state of affairs. This is a question of causation. In the present case, the tribunal found as a fact that the requirements of the business for employees to work in the slaughter hall had diminished. Secondly, they found that that state of affairs had led to the applicants being dismissed. That, in my opinion, is the end of the matter.

Note

This is one of the most significant cases in the law of redundancy, in that it settles a difficulty which had arisen since *Nelson v BBC*. In addition, Lord Clyde referred to the use of the contract test in *Cowen v*

Haden (see above), 'to which the Court of Appeal gave support' and, by implication, disapproved of the use of it in that case. Accordingly, the decision in *Cowen v Haden*, although probably correct on its facts, must be suspect in so far as it refers to a contract test. Moreover, the decision in *Murray* appears to have settled the issue concerning 'bumped redundancies', in that the House expressly approved of *Safeway Stores v Burrell* (1997). In this case, the EAT held that, where, for example, X is redundant and is given Y's job, then, in deciding whether Y is redundant, one needs to consider whether the requirements for Y's work had ceased or diminished. Finally, it is noteworthy that the approach in *Murray* was prefigured by that of the EAT in *Shawkat v Nottingham City Hospitals NHS Trust* (1999).

6.2 Right to claim a redundancy payment

6.2.1 Employees who cannot claim

The following employees cannot claim (all references are to sections of the ERA 1996):

(a) those aged under 20 (s 211(2)). Section 211(2) provides that the employee's period of continuous employment cannot begin earlier than his 18th birthday and that, with the rule that two years' continuous employment is needed, gives the age of 20;

(b) those who have reached normal retiring age or, if there is none, 65 (s 156);

(c) those with less than two years' continuous employment (s 155);

(d) those employed under a fixed term contract for two years or more who have renounced, in writing, their right to a redundancy payment (s 197(3));

(e) share fishermen (s 199(2));

(f) persons ordinarily working outside Great Britain unless, at the relevant time, they were working in Great Britain on the employer's instructions (s 196(6));

(g) Crown Servants and certain public officials (s 159);

(h) those employed as domestic servants by a near relative (as defined in s 161);

(i) classes of employees excluded by order of the Secretary of the State, in cases where a collective agreement covers the issue of redundancy (s 157);

(j) employees dismissed for misconduct (see 6.2.2, below);

(k) employees who refuse a suitable offer of alternative employment (see 6.3, below).

6.2.2 Employees dismissed for misconduct

Section 140(1) of the Employment Rights Act 1996 provides that, subject to sub-ss (2) and (3) (below), an employee shall not be entitled to a redundancy payment by reason of dismissal where his employer, being entitled to terminate his contract of employment without notice by reason of the employee's conduct, terminates it either:

(a) without notice; or

(b) by giving shorter notice than that which, in the absence of such conduct, the employer would be required to give to terminate the contract; or

(c) by giving notice (not being such shorter notice as mentioned in para (b), which includes, or is accompanied by, a statement that the employer would, by reason of the employee's conduct, be entitled to terminate the contract without notice.

Section 140(3) provides that, where the employer terminates the contract in accordance with s 140(1), that is, the employer dismisses for gross misconduct when the employee is already under notice for redundancy, the employee may apply to an industrial tribunal, which can award all or part of the redundancy payment.

Sanders v Ernest A Neale Ltd (1974) NIRC

Two employees were dismissed by reason of redundancy and the other employees went on strike in protest. They were dismissed, and later, the factory closed down.

Held, by the National Industrial Relations Court, that the employees who had been dismissed when on strike were not redundant. Donaldson P was very clear on the matter:

> In the present appeals, there was indeed a redundancy situation, but the tribunal found that it in no way caused the dismissals. The converse was true. It was the dismissals which caused the redundancy. The appellants were dismissed because they persistently refused to work normally. Their claim fails not because the redundancy was self-induced, but because it did not cause their dismissal.

Note

Despite this decision, the above statutory provisions remain obscure. Why are they needed? If an employee is dismissed for misconduct, then dismissal for redundancy does not arise. The view taken in the above case was that s 140(1) applies where the employee is dismissed for redundancy, but could have been dismissed for misconduct.

Section 140(2) provides that, if the employee's misconduct is the taking part in a strike during the 'obligatory period' of notice to terminate his or her contract, then dismissal for the 'misconduct' of going on strike will not disqualify a claim for a redundancy payment. However, in *Simmons v Hoover Ltd* (1977), the converse situation applied, that is, the employee first went on strike and was then issued with a redundancy notice. It was held that what is now s 140(2) did not apply and, therefore, the employee could not claim a redundancy payment.

6.3 Offer of alternative employment

6.3.1 The offer of alternative employment

If the employer makes the employee an offer, before the termination of his contract, to renew the contract or re-engage the employee on suitable alternative work, there are two possible consequences:

(a) if the employee accepts, then there is no dismissal, provided that there is a gap of less than four weeks between the contracts;

(b) if the employee does not accept, then, if his refusal to accept is unreasonable, he is disqualified from claiming a redundancy payment. (See ss 138, 142 and 146 of the ERA 1996.)

Two issues arise in these cases:

(a) was the alternative offer of employment suitable?;

(b) was the refusal of it by the employee reasonable?

These two questions overlap to some extent.

Taylor v Kent County Council (1969) HC

The applicant was made redundant as a headmaster and was offered a post as one of a pool of mobile teachers who would be sent to different schools when required. However, he would still receive the same salary entitlement as before.

Held, by the High Court (QBD), that the offer of alternative employment was unsuitable and he was entitled to refuse it. *Per* Lord Parker LCJ:

> One would think, speaking for myself, that for a headmaster of such experience, he would think an offer which, while guaranteeing him the same salary, reduced his status, was quite unsuitable. To go to quite a different sphere of activity, a director under a service agreement of a company is offered, on dismissal, a job as a navvy, and it is said: but we will guarantee you the same salary as you have been getting. I should have thought such an offer was plainly unsuitable ...

Spencer v Gloucestershire County Council (1985) CA

The applicants were school cleaners who were asked to accept fewer hours work as an economy measure. They refused, giving the reason that they could not do the job properly in the reduced number of hours.

Held, by the Court of Appeal, that their refusal was reasonable. Neill LJ said:

> Returning to the facts of the case, it seems to me that it cannot be right to say, as a general proposition, that it is not a good reason for an employee to refuse to do work, because he considers that the work he is being asked to do does not come up to a standard which he himself wishes to observe. It all depends on the facts of the case. There may well be cases where an employee wishes to apply a wholly unreasonable standard to the work, and say, 'I am only prepared to work to that standard'. But it seems to me that is eminently a matter for the Industrial Tribunal to evaluate in the particular circumstances.

Thomas Wragg & Sons Ltd v Wood (1976) EAT

The employee was aged 56 and had been given notice of redundancy on 24 October to take effect on 6 December. On the Monday following 24 October, he found another job and his employers offered him alternative employment on 5 December.

Held, by the EAT, that it was reasonable to refuse that offer. Lord MacDonald stated:

> The employee obviously acted with some diligence and was successful in obtaining other employment than with the employer. In our opinion, in doing so, he acted very sensibly and very reasonably. Faced at the end of this period of notice with the sudden offer of re-engagement by his employers, we consider that he did not act unreasonably in refusing that offer, having regard to the fact that he had already engaged himself in this other job.

Note ───────────────

See the following cases on offers of alternative employment: *Paton Calvert and Co Ltd v Westerside* (1979); *Standard Telephones v Yates* (1981); and *Hindes v Supersine Ltd* (1979).

6.3.2 Trial period

Section 138 of the ERA 1996 allows for a trial period where an employee's old contract is renewed and the employee is re-engaged under a new contract where there are differences (apart from *de minimis* ones) from the previous one. The trial period is for a minimum of four consecutive calendar weeks, but can be more by agreement. The effect of the trial period is that, if the employee leaves during it, he is not deemed to have accepted the new job. Instead, the tribunal must decide whether, in accordance with the rules and cases above, the new employment was suitable and the termination of that employment by the employee was unreasonable. (See s 138 of the ERA 1996.)

> **Note**
>
> Sections 147–54 of the ERA 1996 deal with the position of an employee who is laid off or is on short time and is made redundant.

6.4 Redundancy procedures

6.4.1 Procedures in relation to individuals

Section 105(1) of the ERA 1996 provides that an employee who is dismissed shall be regarded as unfairly dismissed if:

(a) the reason (or, if more than one, the principal reason) is that the employee is redundant; and

(b) it is shown that the circumstances constituting the redundancy applied equally to one or more employees in the same undertaking who held positions similar to that held by the employee and who have not been dismissed by the employer.

Section 98(4) of the ERA 1996 sets out the general rule regarding fairness of a dismissal, which applies to redundancy dismissals as well as to other dismissals. The determination of whether the dismissal is fair or unfair (having regard to the reason shown by the employer):

(a) depends on whether in the circumstances (including the size and administrative resources of the employer's undertaking) the employer asked reasonably or unreasonably in treating it (that is, the redundancy) as a sufficient reason for dismissing the employee; and

(b) shall be determined in accordance with equity and the substantial merits of the case.

6.4.2 Guidelines

Williams v Compair Maxam Ltd (1982) EAT

In this case, the EAT set out general guidelines for employers.

Per Browne Wilkinson J:

> ... there is a generally accepted view in industrial relations that, in cases where the employees are represented by an independent union recognised

by the employer, reasonable employers will seek to act in accordance with the following principles:

(1) The employer will seek to give as much warning as possible of impending redundancies so as to enable the union and employers who may be affected to take early steps to inform themselves of the relevant facts, consider possible alternative solutions and, if necessary, find alternative employment in the undertaking or elsewhere.

(2) The employer will consult the union as to the best means by which the desired management result can be achieved fairly and with as little hardship to the employees as possible. In particular, the employer will seek to agree with the union the criteria to be applied in selecting an employee to be made redundant. When a selection has been made, the employer will consider with the union whether the selection has been made in accordance with those criteria.

(3) Whether or not an agreement as to the criteria to be adopted has been agreed with the union, the employer will seek to establish criteria for selection which, so far as possible, do not depend solely upon the opinions of the person making the selection, but can be objectively checked against such things as attendance records, efficiency at the job, length of service.

(4) The employer will seek to ensure that the selection is made fairly in accordance with the criteria and will consider any representations the union may make as to such selection.

(5) The employer will seek to see whether, instead of dismissing an employee, he could offer him alternative employment.

The lay members stress that not all these factors are present in every case, since circumstances may prevent one or more of them being given effect to. But the lay members would expect these principles to be departed from only where some good reason is shown to justify each departure. The basic approach is that, in the unfortunate circumstances that necessarily attend redundancies, as much as is reasonably possible should be done to mitigate the impact on the workforce and to satisfy them that the selection has been made fairly and not on the basis of personal whim. That these are the broad principles currently adopted by reasonable employers is supported both by the practice of the industrial tribunals and, to an extent, by statute ...

Note

The significance of the decision of the House of Lords in *Polkey v AE Dayton Services Ltd* (1987) (see 5.2.3, above) in emphasising the importance of procedural fairness, which reinforced the importance of the above guidelines. See, also, Chapter 5.

6.4.3 Statutory provisions dealing with consultation with the relevant trade union

Section 188 of the Trade Union and Labour Relations (Consolidation) Act 1992

(As amended by the Collective Redundancies and Transfer of Undertakings (Protection of Employment) (Amendment) Regulations 1995 and the Collective Redundancies and Transfer of Undertakings (Protection of Employment) (Amendment) Regulations 1999.)

Section 188 Duty of employer to consult representatives

(1) Where an employee is proposing to dismiss as redundant 20 or more employees at one establishment within a period of 90 days or less, the employer shall consult about the dismissals all the persons who are appropriate representatives of any of the employees who may be affected by the proposed dismissals or may be affected by measures taken in connection with those dismissals.

(1A) The consultation shall begin in good time and, in any event:

    (a) where the employer is proposing to dismiss 100 or more employees as mentioned in sub-s (1), at least 90 days; and

    (b) otherwise, at least 30 days,

before the first of the dismissals takes effect.

(1B) For the purposes of this section, the appropriate representatives of any employees are:

    (a) if the employees are of a description in respect of which an independent trade union is recognised by their employer, representatives of the trade union, or

    (b) in any other case, whichever of the following employee representatives the employer chooses:

        (i) employee representatives appointed or elected by the affected employees otherwise than for the purposes of this section, who (having regard to the purposes for and the method by which they were appointed or elected) have authority from those employees to receive information and to be consulted about the proposed dismissals on their behalf;

        (ii) employee representatives elected by the affected employees, for the purposes of this section, in an election, satisfying the requirements of s 188A(1).

(2) The consultation shall include consultation about ways of:

    (a) avoiding the dismissals;

    (b) reducing the numbers of employees to be dismissed; and

(c) mitigating the consequences of the dismissals,

and shall be undertaken by the employer with a view to reaching agreement with the appropriate representatives.

(3) In determining how many employees an employer is proposing to dismiss as redundant, no account shall be taken of employees in respect of whose proposed dismissals consultation has already begun.

(4) For the purposes of the consultation, the employer shall disclose in writing to the [appropriate] representatives:

(a) the reasons for his proposals;

(b) the numbers and descriptions of employees whom it is proposed to dismiss as redundant;

(c) the total number of employees of any such description employed by the employer at the establishment in question;

(d) the proposed method of selecting the employees who may be dismissed;

(e) the proposed method of carrying out the dismissals, with due regard to any agreed procedure, including the period over which the dismissals are to take effect;

(f) the proposed method of calculating the amount of any redundancy payments to be made (otherwise than in compliance with an obligation imposed by or by virtue of any enactment) to employees who may be dismissed.

(5) That information shall be given to each of the appropriate representatives by being delivered to them, or sent by post to an address notified by them to the employer (in the case of representatives of a trade union), or sent by post to the union at the address of its head or main office.

(5A)The employer shall allow the appropriate representatives access to the affected employees and shall afford to those representatives such accommodation and other facilities as may be appropriate.

(7) If, in any case, there are special circumstances which render it not reasonably practicable for the employer to comply with a requirement of sub-s (1A), (2) or (4), the employer shall take all such steps towards compliance with that requirement as are reasonably practicable in those circumstances. Where the decision leading to the proposed dismissals is that of a person controlling the employer (directly or indirectly), a failure on the part of that person to provide information to the employer shall not constitute special circumstances rendering it not reasonably practicable for the employer to comply with such a requirement.

(7A)Where:

    (a) the employer has invited any of the employees who may be dismissed to elect employee representatives; and

    (b) the invitation was issued long enough before the time when the consultation is required by sub-s (1A)(a) or (b) to begin to allow them to elect representatives by that time,

the employer shall be treated as complying with the requirements in relation to those employees if he complies with those requirements as soon as is reasonably practicable after the election of the representatives.

(7B) If, after the employer has invited affected employees to elect representatives, the affected employees fail to do so within a reasonable time, he shall give to each affected employee the information set out in sub-s (4).

(8) This section does not confer any rights on a trade union, a representative or an employee except as provided by ss 189 to 192, below.

Note ──

The 1999 Regulations insert a new s 188A into the Act, containing detailed provisions for the election of employee representatives.

6.4.4 When should consultation begin?

Section 188(1) refers to a situation where the employer is proposing to dismiss. However, the Redundancy Consultation Directive 75/129/EEC states that consultation must begin when the employer is 'contemplating redundancies'. In *APAC v Kirvin Ltd* (1978), it was held that the word 'proposing' meant that consultation need only begin when the employer has formed a definite view that redundancies are needed. But, in *R v British Coal Corp ex p Vardy* (1993), Glidewell LJ said that:

> ... [under the] Directive, consultation is to begin as soon as the employer contemplates redundancies, whereas under the Act, it only needs to begin when he proposes to dismiss as redundant an employee. The verb 'proposes' in its ordinary usage relates to a state of mind which is much more certain and further along the decision making process than the verb 'contemplate'; in other words, the Directive envisages consultation at an early stage when the employer is first envisaging the possibility that he may have to make employees redundant.

Note ──

(1)   In *Griffin v South West Water Services Ltd* (1995), Blackburne J disagreed with Glidewell LJ's view on this point.

(2)   In *Governing Body of the Northern Ireland Hotel and Catering College v NATFHE* (1995), it was held that the duty to consult the relevant union applied even where none of that union's members were being made redundant.

6.4.5 Special circumstances defence

Clarkes of Hove Ltd v Bakers Union (1978) CA

The issue was whether the special circumstances defence (now in s 188(7)) applied, in that the employer was relieved of his obligation to consult. In this case, the employer had been in financial difficulty and, instead of initiating the consultation procedure, it sought a buyer for some of its shops in order to raise capital to enable it to continue trading. When a potential buyer pulled out, it then made all of its employees redundant.

Held, by the Court of Appeal, that insolvency was not a special circumstance so as to remove the need for an employer to consult.

Per Geoffrey Lane LJ:

> It seems to me that the way in which the phrase was interpreted by the industrial tribunal is correct. What they said, in effect, was this – that insolvency is, on its own, neither here nor there. It may be a special circumstance, it may not be a special circumstance. It will depend entirely on the cause of the insolvency whether the circumstances can be described as special or not. If, for example, sudden disaster strikes a company, making it necessary to close the concern, then plainly, that would be a matter which was capable of being a special circumstance and that is so whether the disaster is physical or financial. If the insolvency, however, were merely due to a gradual run down of the company, as it was in this case, then those are the facts on which the industrial tribunal can come to the conclusion that the circumstances were not special. In other words, to be special, the event must be something out of the ordinary, something uncommon, and that is the meaning of the words 'special' in the context of this Act.

Note

Where an employer fails to consult, then a protective award may be sought by the relevant trade union, employee representatives or in any other case, where there is no consultation machinery, by the employees themselves. An industrial tribunal may then make a protective award which is up to 30–90 days' pay, depending on whether the number dismissed is over 20 or over 100 (s 190 of the Trade Union and Labour Relations (Consolidation) Act 1992).

7 Continuity of Employment and Transfer of Undertakings

7.1 Continuity of employment

7.1.1 Employment Rights Act 1996

Section 210

(1) References in any provision of this Act to a period of continuous employment are (unless provision is expressly made to the contrary) to a period computed in accordance with this chapter (ss 210–19).

(2) In any provision of this Act which refers to a period of continuous employment expressed in months or years:

(a) a month means a calendar month; and

(b) a year means a year of 12 calendar months.

(3) In computing an employee's period of continuous employment for the purposes of any provision of this Act, any question:

(a) whether the employee's employment is of a kind counting towards a period of continuous employment; or

(b) whether periods (consecutive or otherwise) are to be treated as forming a single period of continuous employment,

shall be determined week by week, but where it is necessary to compute the length of an employee's period of employment, it shall be computed in months and years of 12 months in accordance with s 211.

(4) Subject to ss 215 to 217, a week which does not count in computing the length of a period of continuous employment breaks continuity of employment.

(5) A person's employment during any period shall, unless the contrary is shown, be presumed to have been continuous.

Note ───

Section 210(5) provides that, where there is a dispute about continuity of employment with an employer, there is a presumption of continuity which it is for the employer to rebut. However, this presumption does not apply where the employee has been employed by different employers (*Secretary of State for Employment v Cohen* (1987)).

Section 211

(1) An employee's period of continuous employment for the purposes of any provision of this Act:

  (a) (subject to sub-ss (2) and (3)) begins with the day on which the employee starts work; and

  (b) ends with the day by reference to which the length of the employee's period of continuous employment is to be ascertained for the purposes of the provision.

(2) For the purposes of ss 155 and 161(2), an employee's period of continuous employment shall be treated as beginning on the employee's 18th birthday if that is later than the day on which the employee starts work.

(3) If an employee's period of continuous employment includes one or more periods which (by virtue of s 215, 216 or 217), while not counting in computing the length of the period do not break continuity of employment, the beginning of the period shall be treated as postponed by the number of days falling within that intervening period, or the aggregate number of days falling within those periods, calculated in accordance with the section in question.

Note

Section 211(1)(a) provides that the employee's period of continuous employment begins with the day on which the employee starts work. In *General of the Salvation Army v Dewsbury* (1984), the employee's contract began on 1 May, but she actually began work on 4 May. The EAT held that the phrase 'day on which the employee starts work' means the day on which the contract of employment begins and not the day on which the employee actually begins to perform his/her contractual duties.

Section 212

(1) Any week during the whole or part of which an employee's relations with his employer are governed by a contract of employment counts in computing the employee's period of employment.

(2) Any week (not within sub-s (1)) during an employee's period of absence from work occasioned wholly or partly by pregnancy or childbirth, after which the employee returns to work in accordance

with s 79, or in pursuance of an offer described in s 96(3), counts in computing the employee's period of employment.

(3) Subject to sub-s (4), any week (not within sub-s (1)) during the whole or part of which an employee is:

(a) incapable of work in consequence of sickness or injury;

(b) absent from work on account of a temporary cessation of work;

(c) absent from work in circumstances such that, by arrangement or custom, he is regarded as continuing in the employment of his employer for any purpose; or

(d) absent from work wholly or partly because of pregnancy or childbirth,

counts in computing the employee's period of employment.

(4) Not more than 26 weeks count under sub-s (3)(a) or (subject to sub-s (2)) sub-s (3)(d) between any periods falling under sub-s (1).

7.1.2 Temporary cessation of work (s 212(3)(b))

Fitzgerald v Hall Russell & Co Ltd (1969) HL

Held, by the House of Lords, that the above phrase means a cessation of the employee's work; there is no requirement that the employer's business should have ceased. The court held that one should look at each case with the benefit of hindsight, if necessary, to see if the cessation was temporary. The fact that the parties considered at the time that the cessation would be temporary was important, but the fact that they did not do so would not mean that cessation could not be temporary.

Ford v Warwickshire County Council (1983) HL

The applicant was a teacher who had been employed under a series of eight fixed term contracts, each for the academic year from September to July.

Held, by the House of Lords, that the break each year from July to September was a temporary cessation of work which did not, therefore, break continuity of employment. Lord Diplock said that:

... the whole scheme of the Act appears to me to show that it is in the sense of 'transient', that is, lasting only for a relatively short time, that the word 'temporary' is used ...

Note

Lord Diplock's approach appears, from one part of his speech, to be similar to that of the House of Lords in *Fitzgerald v Hall Russell*, that is, a broad approach is required in these cases. However, at a later point in his speech, Lord Diplock suggested that, in some cases, one should compare the length of the gap with the length of the periods of work on either side of it. *Per* Lord Diplock:

> It also follows from what I have said that successive periods of seasonal employment of other kinds under fixed term contracts, such as employment in agriculture during harvest-time or in hotel work during the summer season, will only qualify as continuous employment if the length of the period between two successive seasonal contracts is so short in comparison with the length of the season during which the employee is employed as properly to be regarded by the industrial tribunal as no more than a temporary cessation of work in the sense that I have indicated.

Flack v Kodak Ltd (1986) CA

The applicant had been employed for irregular periods of time in the photo-finishing department of Kodak, her work patterns varying according to seasonal demand.

Held, by the Court of Appeal, that Lord Diplock's 'mathematical' approach (above) was not appropriate to irregular work patterns. Woolf LJ said:

> What is a short time in one employment is not necessarily a short time in another employment. In deciding what is relatively a short time in a particular employment, it is now clearly established that it is necessary to look at the period of dismissal with hindsight – looking backwards as to the circumstances from the date of the final dismissal. In doing this, the period of dismissal relative to the period of employment is of the greatest importance. However, it is the whole period of employment which is relevant. In the case of irregular employment, if the periods of employment either side of the dismissal are only looked at, a most misleading comparison would be drawn.

Note

See, also, *Bentley Engineering Co Ltd v Crown* (1976) and *Berwick Salmon Fisheries Co Ltd v Rutherford* (1991).

Q   Which of the different approaches in the above cases to the question of whether there is a temporary cessation of work do you consider to be preferable?

7.1.3 'Where by arrangement or custom, the employment is regarded as continuing' (s 212(3)(c))

In *Ford v Warwickshire County Council* (above), the House of Lords held that, in order for this provision to apply, there must be no subsisting contract. In the earlier case of *Lloyds Bank Ltd v Secretary of State for*

Employment (1979), it was held that an employee who worked one week on and one week off had continuity preserved by what is now s 212(3)(c) of the Employment Rights Act 1996 (ERA), but this is now doubtful in the light of *Ford*.

Booth and Others v United States of America (1999) EAT

The applicants had been employed under a series of fixed term contracts for a total period which was in excess of two years, but with a gap of about two weeks between each contract. At the end of each contract, they were informed in writing that the contract had terminated and they were paid any outstanding pay and other benefits. They claimed that they had continuity of employment under s 212(3)(c) (see above).

Held, by the EAT, that they did not, because there was no arrangement that employment was continuing, especially as it was clear that the employer did not intend this.

Note, also:

(a) *Sweeney v J & S Henderson (Concessions) Ltd* (1999). The EAT held that continuity was not broken where the employee left employment on the Saturday, but returned on the following Friday. Section 235 defines 'week' as a week ending with a Saturday and, therefore, the employee was employed during part of the week. The reason for the break was irrelevant;

(b) *Collison v BBC* (1998). The EAT held that a compromise agreement relating to a dismissal, which was stated to be in full and final settlement of all claims arising, did not prevent the employee from relying on service prior to that date in computing continuity of employment.

7.1.4   Continuity of employment and receipt of a redundancy payment

Lassman and Others v Secretary of State for Trade and Industry (1999) EAT
The EAT considered the effect of s 214 of the ERA 1996, which provides that continuity of employment is broken where 'a redundancy payment has previously been paid to the employee'. In this case, employees were dismissed in the belief that they were redundant, but it was then accepted that there had been a transfer within the Transfer of Undertakings (Protection of Employment) Regulations (TUPE) 1981. Section 214(2)(a) refers to a redundancy payment in respect of a dismissal, but here, there had been no dismissal and, therefore, continuity was not affected.

7.1.5 Continuity of employment and strikes and lock-outs

Section 216

(1) A week does not count under s 212 if, during the week, or any part of the week, the employee takes part in a strike.

(2) The continuity of an employee's period of employment is not broken by a week, which does not count under this Chapter (whether or not by virtue only of sub-s (1)) if, during the week, or any part of the week, the employee takes part in a strike; and the number of days which, for the purposes of s 211(3), fall within the intervening period is the number of days between the last working day before the strike and the day on which work was resumed.

(3) The continuity of an employee's period of employment is not broken by a week if, during the week, or any part of the week, the employee is absent from work because of a lock-out by the employer; and the number of days which, for the purposes of s 211(3), fall within the intervening period is the number of days between the last working day before the lock-out and the day on which work was resumed.

Note

In *Clarke Chapman-John Thompson Ltd v Walters* (1972), it was held that, where there is a gap between the end of the strike and when the employee actually returns to work, then this is likely to be regarded as a temporary cessation of work.

7.1.6 Change of employer

Section 218 deals with the situation where the trade or business or undertaking is itself transferred. Section 218(2) provides that continuity is preserved, but this begs the question of what is meant by 'trade, business or undertaking'.

Woodhouse v Peter Brotherhood Ltd (1972) CA

The applicant had worked for Crossleys at its plant, which produced diesel engines. Crossleys sold the plant to Peter Brotherhood, who used it to manufacture spinning machines, compressors and steam turbines. There was no transfer of goodwill. The applicant continued to work at the plant for the new employers.

Held, by the Court of Appeal, that there was no transfer of the business, but only of the physical assets, and so continuity of employment was broken. *Per* Lord Denning MR:

If anyone had been asked prior to August 1965, 'What business is being carried on in the factory at Sandiacre?', his answer would have been, 'The manufacture of spinning machines, compressors and steam turbines'. If he had been asked 'Is it the same business?', he would have said 'No. The manufacture of diesel engines has now gone to Manchester. All that is being done at Sandiacre is the manufacture of spinning machines, etc'. True, the same men are employed using the same tools, but the business is different.

Note

See, also, *Melon v Hector Powe Ltd* (1980), where there was also held to be only a transfer of assets, and *Lloyd v Brassey* (1969), where it was held that the sale of the land on which farming took place constituted the transfer of the business of the farm.

Section 218 also provides that continuity is preserved where:

(a) by statute one corporate body is replaced by another (s 218(3));

(b) where the employers, not being a corporation, die and the personal representatives carry on the business (s 218(4));

(c) where the employer is a partnership, personal representatives or trustees and there is a change in their composition (s 218(5));

(d) where the employee is taken into the employment of another who is an associated employer of the first employer (s 218(6));

(e) where the employee is employed by the governors of a school which is maintained by the local education authority, and is then employed directly by the local education authority or vice versa;

(f) where a person employed by a health service employer is then employed by another health service employer.

7.2 Transfer of undertakings

7.2.1 Common law position

Nokes v Doncaster Amalgamated Colleries Ltd (1940) HL

An order was made under s 129 of the Companies Act 1939 for the amalgamation of two companies.

Held, by the House of Lords, that the contracts of employment were not transferred. Lord Atkin emphasised the right of the employee to choose whether to serve in the new company:

> ... the servant was left with his inalienable right to choose whether he would serve his new master, or not.

7.2.2 Transfer of Undertakings (Protection of Employment) Regulations 1981

Note ──
The Regulations were made so as to implement the provisions of the Acquired Rights Directive (77/187/EEC).

7.2.3 Relevant transfer

2(1) In these Regulations:

> ... 'relevant transfer' means a transfer to which these Regulations apply, and 'undertaking' includes any trade or business.

Dr Sophie Redmond Stichting v Bartol (1992) ECJ

The applicant was a Dutch organisation, which was non-commercial. The object was to provide services to drug addicts. The local authority grant was taken away from the applicant and given to another organisation, the Sigma Foundation, which took over the work, clients and premises of the applicant. Sigma wished to keep on some, but not all, of the workers employed by the applicant. The issue was whether the Acquired Rights Directive applied to non-commercial organisations.

Held, by the ECJ, that, in principle, it did:

> It should be recalled that, in its judgment of 7 February 1985, *Abels* (p 469, points 11–13), the Court held that the scope of the provision of the Directive at issue cannot be appraised solely on the basis of a textual interpretation, because of the differences between the various language versions of that provision and because of the divergences between the national legislation defining the concept of a contractual transfer.

> In consequence, the Court gave a sufficiently broad interpretation to that concept to give effect to the purpose of the Directive, which is to ensure that the rights of employees are protected in the event of a transfer of their undertaking, and held that that Directive was applicable wherever, in the context of contractual relations, there is a change in the legal or natural person who is responsible for carrying on the business and who incurs the obligations of an employer towards employees of the undertaking (see, most recently, the judgment of 15 June 1988, *Bork International* (1989)).

Note ──
As a result of the *Bartol* case, the UK Government amended the Regulations by s 33(2) of the Trade Union and Employment Rights Act 1993, because the Regulations had previously stated that the term 'undertaking' 'does not include any undertaking or part of an undertaking which is not in the nature of a commercial venture'.

Relevant transfer

3(1) Subject to the provisions of these Regulations, these Regulations apply to a transfer from one person to another of an undertaking situated immediately before the transfer in the UK or part of one which is so situated.

(2) Subject as aforesaid, these Regulations so apply whether the transfer is effected by sale or by some other disposition or by operation of law.

(3) Subject as aforesaid, these Regulations so apply, notwithstanding:

(a) that the transfer is governed or effected by the law of a country or territory outside the UK;

(b) that persons employed in the undertaking or part transferred ordinarily work outside the UK;

(c) that the employment of any of those persons is governed by any such law.

(4) It is hereby declared that a transfer of an undertaking or part of one:

(a) may be effected by a series of two or more transactions; and

(b) may take place whether or not any property is transferred to the transferee by the transferor.

Premier Motors (Medway) Ltd v Total Oil Great Britain Ltd (1984) CA

The business was sold by the employer, but the purchaser decided not to continue that business and, therefore, not to employ its employees. For a month after the sale was completed, the vendors continued to run the business under a licence from the purchasers but, thereafter, the contracts of employment of the applicants were terminated.

Held, by the Court of Appeal, that the business was transferred, and it made no difference that the purchasers did not intend to continue to run the business.

Note

The approach in this case adopts the test used in cases involving continuity of employment for employment protection rights (see *Woodhouse v Peter Brotherhood Ltd*, 7.1.6, above); it distinguishes between the transfer of a business as a going concern (where continuity is preserved) and a mere transfer of assets (where it is not), although the fact that assets have been transferred is, of course, significant.

Spijkers v Gebroeders Benedik Abbatoir CV (1986) ECJ

Held, by the ECJ, that it was necessary to decide whether there was a transfer of an 'economic entity' which 'retains its identity', and this will depend on a variety of factors.

This case broadly supports the approach taken by the UK courts (see above), but the law here is far from settled and will be considered in later cases under 7.3, below.

7.2.4 Effect of a transfer on contracts of employment

5(1) Except where objection is made under para (4A) below, a relevant transfer shall not operate so as to terminate the contract of employment of any person employed by the transferor in the undertaking or part transferred but any such contract which would otherwise have been terminated by the transfer shall have effect after the transfer as if originally made between the person so employed and the transferee.

(2) Without prejudice to para (1) above, but subject to para (4A) below, on the completion of a relevant transfer:

(a) all the transferor's rights, powers, duties and liabilities under or in connection with any such contract, shall be transferred by virtue of this Regulation to the transferee; and

(b) anything done before the transfer is completed by or in relation to the transferor in respect of that contract or a person employed in that undertaking or part shall be deemed to have been done by or in relation to the transferee.

(3) Any reference in para (1) or (2) above to a person employed in an undertaking or part of one transferred by a relevant transfer is a reference to a person so employed immediately before the transfer, including, where the transfer is effected by a series of two or more transactions, a person so employed immediately before any of those transactions.

(4) Paragraph (2) above shall not transfer or otherwise affect the liability of any person to be prosecuted for, convicted of and sentenced for any offence.

(4A) Paragraphs (1) and (2) above shall not operate to transfer his contract of employment and the rights, powers, duties and liabilities under or in connection with it if the employee informs the transferor or the transferee that he objects to becoming employed by the transferee.

(4B) Where an employee so objects, the transfer of the undertaking or part in which he is employed shall operate so as to terminate his contract of employment with the transferor, but he shall not be treated, for any purpose, as having been dismissed by the transferor.

(5) Paragraphs (1) and (4A) above are without prejudice to any right of an employee arising apart from these Regulations to terminate his contract of employment without notice, if a substantial change is made

in his working conditions to his detriment; but no such right shall arise by reason only that, under that paragraph, the identity of his employer changes unless the employer shows that, in all the circumstances, the change is a significant change and is to his detriment.

Note ───

The effect of reg 5 is that the contract of employment operates after the transfer as if it had been made originally between the employee and the transferee of the business. It is necessary to read reg 5 along with reg 8(1), the effect of which is to make any dismissal of an employee on the transfer of an undertaking automatically unfair, if the reason or principal reason for the dismissal was the transfer or a reason connected with it. However, a defence is provided by reg 8(2). This provides that, where an economic, technical or organisational reason entailing changes in the workforce of either the transferor or the transferee before or after a relevant transfer is the reason or principal reason for dismissing an employee, then the dismissal is deemed to be for a 'substantial reason' (s 98(1) of the ERA 1996). The onus is then, as in other unfair dismissal cases, on the employer to show that he acted reasonably in dismissing the employee (s 98(4)).

Cowell v Quilter Goodison Co Ltd and QC Management Services Ltd (1989) CA

The applicant was an equity partner in a firm, but when the business was transferred, he was then employed by the transferee.

Held, by the Court of Appeal, that he was not an employee before the transfer, because (*per* Lord Donaldson MR) an equity partner is someone who 'provides services under a contract for services'.

Note ───

This case is of interest in illustrating the definition of an employee under these Regulations. An employee is defined as including not only a servant or apprentice, but anyone who *works* for another in any other capacity, except an independent contractor under a contract for services. This was not wide enough to include the applicant in this case.

Katsikas v Konstantinidis (1993) ECJ

The applicant was employed as a cook in a restaurant, but when the restaurant was sold, the applicant refused to work for the new owner and was therefore dismissed by his employer, the previous owner.

Held, by the ECJ, that the Acquired Rights Directive did not prevent an employee objecting to his contract of employment being automatically transferred. In fact, if the Directive:

... allows an employee to remain in employment with a new employer, on the same conditions as those agreed with the transferor, it cannot be interpreted as obliging the employee to continue his employment relationship with the transferee.

This was because such an obligation would undermine the fundamental rights of the employee, who must be free to choose his employer and cannot be obliged to work for an employer that he has not freely chosen.

It follows from that that the provisions of Art 3(1) of the Directive do not prevent an employee from objecting to the transfer of his contract of employment or of his employment relationship and, therefore, not benefiting from the protection provided to him by the Directive.

Note
As a result of this case, paras 4A and 4B were inserted (see above) but, if an employee does object to a transfer, then he will have no rights against either the transferor or transferee.

Sunley Turriff Holdings Ltd v Thomson (1995) EAT

The employee was the company secretary and chief accountant of X Co and its subsidiary, Y Co. His contract of employment was with X Co, but he did work which was related to Y Co. Both companies went into receivership, and Y Co, the subsidiary, was sold to Z Co.

Held, by the EAT, that the employee's contract was transferred, as he was employed in that part of the undertaking which was transferred to Z Co. Therefore, he was able to claim unfair dismissal against Z Co, because he had not been taken on by it.

Note
The EAT applied the test laid down by the ECJ in *Botzen v Rotterdamsche Droogdok Maatschappij BV* (1985), which held that, where part of an undertaking is transferred, as here, it is a question of fact 'as to which part of the business or undertaking the employee was assigned'. The industrial tribunal in *Sunley* had pointed out that in a case such as this, one needed to 'lift the veil of incorporation' and had found that Y Co was no more than 'a shell company'; therefore, the employee had, in reality, worked for one single undertaking before the transfer.

Michael Peters Ltd v Farnfield (1995) EAT

The employee concerned was the Chief Executive of Michael Peters Group plc, which was the holding company for a group of 25 subsidiary design consultancy companies. Four of these were sold to X Co, and the Chief Executive of the group company claimed that his contract of employment had been transferred to X Co.

Held, by the EAT, that his contract had not been transferred, because his contract was with the parent company and that was not the transferor of the undertaking. In effect, the EAT was unwilling to pierce the corporate veil.

Note ───────

See, also, *Duncan Web Offset (Maidstone) Ltd v Cooper* (1995), where the EAT said that industrial tribunals must look carefully to see that the Transfer of Undertakings Regulations were not being evaded by devices such as the use of subsidiary companies.

Askew v Governing Body of Clifton Middle School and Others (1999) CA

The appellant worked as a teacher at a school, which ceased to be maintained by the local education authority, and was made redundant. He applied to work at the school which replaced his old school, but his application was not successful. He claimed that he had been unfairly dismissed, because TUPE applied.

Held, by the Court of Appeal, that TUPE did not apply, because there was no transfer of employer. He was not employed by the governing body of his old school, but by the local education authority, and the local education authority had not made a relevant transfer.

Bernadone v Pall Mall Services Group Ltd and Others (1999) HC

It was held that, on the transfer of an undertaking where TUPE applied, tortious liability was transferred, because the duty of care owed by employers to employees arose from an implied term in the contract of employment. Therefore, in this case, liability to an employee injured at work was transferred.

Allen and Others v Amalgamated Construction Co Ltd (1999) ECJ

It was held by the ECJ that the Acquired Rights Directive could apply to transfers between subsidiary companies in a group, provided that they were distinct legal persons with separate employment relationships with their employees, even though the companies had the same ownership and management, and were engaged in the same work.

7.2.5 At what point must the employee have been employed by the transferor in order to be able to claim that the Regulations apply to him?

Litster v Forth Dry Dock and Engineering Co Ltd (1989) HL

The 12 applicants had all been employees of the transferor company and were dismissed an hour before the transfer. The applicants were not engaged by the transferee employer.

Held, by the House of Lords, that the applicants could claim under reg 8(1), even though at the very moment of the transfer, they were not employed. *Per* Lord Oliver:

> Having regard to the manifest purpose of the Regulations, I do not, for my part, feel inhibited from making such an implication in the instant case. The provision in reg 8(1), that a dismissal by reason of a transfer is to be treated as an unfair ground for dismissal, is merely a different way of saying that the transfer is not to 'constitute a ground for dismissal' as contemplated by Art 4 of the Directive, and there is no good reason for denying to it the same effect as that attributed to that Article. In effect, this involves reading reg 5(3) as if there were inserted after the words 'immediately before the transfer' the words 'or would have been so employed if he had not been unfairly dismissed in the circumstances described in reg 8(1)'. For my part, I would make such an implication which is entirely consistent with the general scheme of the Regulations and which is necessary if they are effectively to fulfil the purpose for which they were made, of giving effect to the provisions of the Directive. This does not involve any disapproval of the reasoning of the Court of Appeal in *Spence's* case (1986), which, on the facts there found by the industrial tribunal, did not involve a dismissal attracting the consequences provided in reg 8(1).

Note

In *Secretary of State for Employment v Spence* (1986) (referred to by Lord Oliver, above), the Court of Appeal had held that reg 5 (and thereafter reg 8 also) only applies to employees employed at the actual moment of the transfer. However, although *Litster* has now overruled this, *Spence*, on its facts, was a case where the dismissal was justified under reg 8(2), below. In *Litster*, the House of Lords was following the decision of the ECJ in *P Bork International (In Liquidation) v Foreningen of Arbejdsledere i Danmark* (1989). See, also, *Brooke Lane Finance Co v Bradley* (1988).

7.2.6 Contracts in restraint of trade and reg 5

Morris Angel Ltd v Hollande (1993) CA
The employee was managing director of a holding company and its subsidiary companies. His contract contained a restraint of trade clause, preventing him, for one year after leaving the company's employment, from soliciting the customers of the companies. The holding company was then transferred and the applicant was dismissed by the transferee company.

Held, by the Court of Appeal, that the restraint of trade clause applied so that the transferee company could enforce the clause if the employee did business with anyone who, in the year before the transfer, had done business with the holding company (that is, the transferor company) and did not apply if he did business with anyone who had done business with the transferee company. This was because reg 5(1) states that the contract 'shall have effect after the transfer as if originally made between the person so employed and the transferee', that is, the transferee is treated as the employer with whom the employee made the contract containing the restraint of trade clause.

Credit Suisse First Boston (Europe) Ltd v Lister (1998) CA

The defendant was employed by the transferor of a business, and his contract of employment contained a non-solicitation clause. He agreed with the transferee of the business that, on termination of his employment, he would not engage in competitive activity as well as solicitation. He was paid £2,000 for agreeing to this clause. Subsequently, he left the transferee's employment and worked in breach of this clause.

Held, by the Court of Appeal, that the restraint of trade clause was unenforceable by virtue of reg 5(1) of TUPE (see above), which provides that the contract shall have effect 'as if originally made between the transferor and the transferee'. The ECJ in *Foreningen af Arbejdsledere i Danmark v Daddy's Dance Hall* (1998) had held that, as Moore-Bick J put it in the High Court: '... the agreement is ineffective in so far as it purports to impose on the employee an obligation to which he was not previously subject.' The fact that the employee received a benefit (£2,000) for agreeing to the alteration so that the agreement also included competitive activity was irrelevant, because the court held that it was wrong to conduct a kind of balancing exercise to see if, on the whole, the employee was, as a result of the transfer, in a worse position than before.

7.2.7 Dismissal resulting from an economic, technical or organisational reason entailing changes in the workforce (reg 8(2))

Berriman v Delabole Slate Ltd (1985) CA

The applicant was employed as a quarry man in a business which was transferred. The transferee company wished to bring the applicant's contract of employment into line with the contracts of their own employees and, as a result, they reduced the amount of guaranteed pay that the applicant received. He claimed constructive dismissal.

Held, by the Court of Appeal, that the defence (known as the ETO defence) in reg 8(2) did not apply. *Per* Brown-Wilkinson J:

> Then, in order to come within reg 8(2), it has to be shown that *that* reason is an economic, technical or organisational reason entailing changes in the workforce. The reason itself (that is, to produce standardisation in pay) does not involve any change either in the number or the functions of the workforce. The most that can be said is that such organisational reason *may* (not must) lead to the dismissal of those employees who do not fall into line, coupled with the filling of the vacancies thereby caused by new employees prepared to accept the conditions of service. In our judgment, that is not enough … the phrase 'economic, technical or organisational reason entailing changes in the workforce', in our judgment, requires that the change in the workforce is part of the economic, technical or organisational reason. The employers' plan must be to achieve changes in the workforce. It must be an objective of the plan, not just a possible consequence of it.

Note

See *Crawford v Swinton Insurance Brokers Ltd* (1990), where the transfer and its resulting re-organisation led to changes to the jobs of transferred employees, and it was held that reg 8(2) did apply, because there were actual changes in the workforce. See, also, *McGrath v Rank Leisure Ltd* (1985).

Whitehouse v Chas A Blatchford & Sons Ltd (1999) CA

The transferee of a business, which supplied appliances to a hospital, had successfully bid for a contract, but the bid was made conditional on a reduction in staffing costs, which was to be achieved by making one of 13 technicians redundant. The appellant was the employee selected and he claimed that his dismissal was in breach of TUPE.

Held, by the Court of Appeal, that the ETO (economic, technical or organisational reason) defence applied. The dismissal was not solely because of the transfer, although had it been, it would have been unfair. The situation was not the same as where the seller of a business dismisses employees solely in order to get a better price for it. Instead, the reason for the dismissal related to the future conduct of the business and the need to reduce running costs in the light of a reduction in funding from the health authority.

7.3 The Transfer of Undertakings Regulations and 'contracting-out'

7.3.1 Introduction

The issue in many of the cases below has been whether labour by itself can qualify as the undertaking, so that when labour is contracted out, the Regulations apply. The ECJ has, in recent years, given a number of rulings in this area and the law is not yet entirely clear.

Spijkers v Gebroeders Benedik Abbatoir CV (1986) ECJ

... the decisive criterion for establishing whether there is a transfer for the purposes of the directive is whether the business in question retains its identity.

Consequently, a transfer of an undertaking, business or part of a business does not occur merely because its assets are disposed of. Instead, it is necessary to consider, in a case such as the present, whether the business was disposed of as a going concern, as would be indicated, *inter alia*, by the fact that its operation was actually continued or resumed by the new employer, with the same or similar activities.

In order to determine whether those conditions are met, it is necessary to consider all the facts characterising the transaction in question, including the type of undertaking or business, whether or not the business's tangible assets, such as buildings and movable property, are transferred, the value of its intangible assets at the time of the transfer, whether or not the majority of its employees are taken over by the new employer, whether or not its customers are transferred and the degree of similarity between the activities carried on before and after the transfer and the period, if any, for which those activities were suspended. It should be noted, however, that all those circumstances are merely single factors in the overall assessment which must be made and cannot therefore be considered in isolation.

Note ───────────────────────────────────────

What is especially significant in the present context is that the ECJ referred to whether 'the majority of its employees (that is, of the former business) are taken on, along with the other factors.

Rask and Christensen v ISS Kantineservice A/S (1993) ECJ

Four canteens owned by Phillips were contracted out. Under the contract, ISS (the transferee) agreed to take over all the staff previously employed by Phillips, and to do so on the same conditions of employment. ISS agreed to be responsible for the day to day running of the canteen and Phillips placed the physical assets needed for running the canteen at the disposal of ISS, although these remained in the ownership of Phillips.

Held, by the ECJ, that there had been a transfer of the business of running canteen services, even though the only assets actually transferred were the contracts of employment.

Schmidt v Spar- und Leihkasse der früheren Ämter Bordesholm (1994) ECJ

Mrs Schmidt was employed as the only cleaner in a branch of a bank in Germany. The bank then contracted out of the cleaning and the contractor (that is, the transferee of the business) offered to employ Mrs Schmidt, but at a wage which she claimed was less than her previous wage.

Held, by the ECJ, that there was a transfer of the business and it made no difference that only one employee was transferred:

> The fact that, in its case law, the Court includes the transfer of such assets among the various factors to be taken into account by a national court to enable it, when assessing a complex transaction as a whole, to decide whether an undertaking has in fact been transferred, does not support the conclusion that the absence of these factors precludes the existence of a transfer. The safeguarding of employees' rights, which constitutes the subject matter of the Directive, as is clear from its actual title, cannot depend exclusively on consideration of a factor which the Court has, in any event, already held not to be decisive on its own (judgment in *Spijkers v Benedik*: 24/85 [1986] ECR 1119, para 12).

> According to the case law of the Court (see the judgment in *Spijkers*, cited above, at para 11, and the judgment in *Dr Sophie Redmond Stichting v Bartol*, Case C-29/91 [1992] IRLR 366, para 23), the decisive criterion for establishing whether there is a transfer for the purposes of the Directive is whether the business in question retains its identity. According to the case law, the retention of that identity is indicated *inter alia* by the actual continuation or resumption by the new employer of the same or similar activities. Thus, in this case ... the similarity in the cleaning work performed before and after the transfers – which is reflected, moreover, in the offer to re-engage the employee in question – is typical of an operation which comes with the scope of the Directive and which gives the employee whose activity has been transferred the protection afforded to him by that Directive.

Dines and Others v Initial Health Care Services and Another (1994) CA

Initial Health Care Services had provided cleaning services to hospitals, but when their contract ran out, the new contract was awarded to Pall Mall Services, who offered employment to all those previously employed by Initial Services. Pall Mall Services introduced their own equipment, stock and supplies.

Held, by the Court of Appeal, that there was a transfer of the undertaking. Neill LJ stated:

The European cases demonstrate that the fact that another company takes over the provision of certain services as a result of competitive tendering does not mean that the first business or undertaking necessarily comes to an end ... a transfer may take place in two phases.

Note

This case is of interest in that the EAT, before the ruling by the ECJ in *Schmidt*, had held that there was no transfer, because the business of the first contractors had ceased, and the fact that the same workforce was employed did not give rise to a transfer. The Court of Appeal gave judgment after the decision in *Schmidt*.

Ledernes Hovedorganisation (acting for Rygaard) v Dansk Arbejdsgiverforening (acting for Stro Molle Akustik A/S) (1996) ECJ

The main building contractors agreed that work which had been subcontracted to firm X would be completed by firm Y. Y refunded to X the cost of materials supplied and took on responsibility for two of X's apprentices.

Held, by the ECJ, that no transfer of the undertaking had taken place, because the authorities cited above presuppose that the transfer relates to a stable economic entity whose activity is not limited to performing one specific works contract.

That is not the case of an undertaking which transfers to another undertaking one of its building works, with a view to the completion of that work. Such a transfer could come within the terms of the directive only if it included the transfer of a body of assets, enabling the activities or certain activities of the transferor undertaking to be carried on in a stable way.

That is not so where, as here, the transferor undertaking merely makes available to the new contractor certain workers and material for carrying out the works in question.

Note

This case clearly showed a difference of emphasis from that in *Schmidt*, but could be confined to its own facts, that is, the requirement of a 'stable economic entity' should only apply, as in *Rygaard*, where a one-off contract was transferred, and not generally. In *BSG Property Services v Tuck* (1996), Mummery J, in the EAT, held that the principle in *Rygaard* should only apply to activities under a short term one-off contract. In this case, Tuck and 13 others worked for a local authority as housing maintenance personnel. The local authority then contracted out this service to BSG, which did not employ Tuck or any of the other applicants. It was held that there had been a transfer to BSG, who were liable to the applicants for unfair dismissal. If *Rygaard* had applied, it is difficult to see how there could have been a transfer, because no 'stable economic entity' was transferred. See, also, *Merckx and Neuhuys v Ford Motor Co Belgium* (1996).

Suzen v Zehnacker Gebaudereingung GmbH Krankenhausservice (1997) ECJ

Mrs Suzen worked for a company which had a contract to clean a school. When this contract ended, and the contract was awarded to another company, Mrs Suzen's employers dismissed her. She sought a declaration that her contract had been transferred to the contractor.

Held, by the ECJ, that it had not. The reasoning of the ECJ is in line with that of *Rygaard* and shows a retreat from *Schmidt*:

... the mere fact that the service provided by the old and the new awardees of the contract is similar does not therefore support the conclusion that an economic entity has been transferred. An entity cannot be reduced to the activity entrusted to it. Its identity also emerges from other factors, such as it workforce, its management staff, the way in which its work is organised, its operating methods or indeed, where appropriate, the operational resources available to it.

The mere loss of a service contract to a competitor cannot, therefore, by itself, indicate the existence of a transfer within the meaning of the Directive. In those circumstances, the service undertaking previously entrusted with the contract does not, on losing a customer, thereby cease fully to exist, and the business or part of a business belonging to it cannot be considered to have been transferred to the new awardee of the contract.

Note

Two other UK cases dealing with contracting out:

(a) *Kenny v South London Manchester College* (1993), where prison education had been contacted out to a local authority but, on re-tendering, it was then contracted out to a local college.

Michael Ogden QC (sitting as a deputy High Court judge) took a straightforward view:

The prisoners and young offenders who attend, say, a carpentry class next Thursday will, save for those released from the institution, be likely in the main to be those who attended the same class in the same classroom the day before, and will doubtless be using exactly the same tools and machinery.

(b) *Wren v Eastbourne Borough Council* (1993): when a local authority contracted out its street cleaning and refuse collection services to a private company, there was held to be a transfer. (One important distinction between *Wren* and *Dines* (above) is that *Dines* concerned a subsequent re-tendering exercise.)

Q   Do you consider that the decisions above in *Kenny* and *Wren* would now be different in the light of the change of approach by the ECJ in *Suzen*?

Francisco Hernandez Vidal SA v Gomez Perez and Others (1999) ECJ

Sanchez Hidalgo and Others v Asociacion de Servicios Aser and Sociedad Cooperativa Minerva (1999) ECJ

The ECJ considered the applicability of the Acquired Rights Directive in cases of contracting out of services. The ECJ emphasised that the question is whether an 'economic activity' has been transferred 'as indicated by the fact that its operation is actually continued or resumed'. Accordingly, the emphasis in *Suzen* on whether a major part of the workforce is taken over is not present in this judgment. The ECJ, and other courts, have been concerned that, in order to take advantage of *Suzen* and argue that no transfer has taken place, an employer might simply refuse to take over the workforce, as happened in the case below.

ECM (Vehicle Delivery Service) Ltd v Cox and Others (1999) CA

Axial Ltd employed the respondents as drivers and yardmen. Axial Ltd had a contract with VAG Ltd to deliver cars imported into the UK, but Axial Ltd then lost the contract to ECM, who were the appellants. The respondents claimed that there was a relevant transfer within the meaning of TUPE.

Held, by the Court of Appeal, that there was a relevant transfer. The decision is noteworthy for an attempt by the Court to reconcile the decisions in *Suzen* and *Schmidt*. Mummery LJ said that, 'The importance of *Suzen* had, I think, been overstated', and he held that it was still necessary to carry out a factual appraisal of the kind detailed in *Spijkers* (above) and which had occurred in this case also. Moreover, he said that the vital question was whether 'the undertaking has continued and retained its identity in different hands'.

In this particular case, none of the employees had been taken on by ECM, because they were claiming unfair dismissal on the basis that TUPE applied, and ECM obviously did not want to prejudice their position that TUPE did not apply. The Court of Appeal held that the failure to take on any of the employees was irrelevant, because one needed to have regard to why they were not taken on. The ECJ in *Suzen* had said that 'the mere fact that the service provided by the old and new awardees of a contract is similar does not support the conclusion that an economic entity has been transferred'. The Court of Appeal in *ECM* is not disputing this but is, in effect, going behind it to the earlier rulings in *Spijkers* and *Schmidt*.

7.3.2 Variation of contractual rights consequent upon a transfer

Wilson and Others v St Helens Borough Council; British Fuels Ltd v Meade and Baxendale (1998) HL

Both of these appeals concerned the question of whether dismissals of employees prior to the transfer of an undertaking were nullities so that, when the undertaking was transferred, the dismissals could be disregarded and employees could retain the benefit of the terms and conditions of their previous employment, despite the fact that they had now been engaged by the transferor employer on different terms.

In *Wilson*, the appellants were employed at a community home run by the county council, which was then taken over by the borough council. The appellants were made redundant. They were re-employed by the borough council, but on different terms and conditions, in particular, at a reduced salary. In *Baxendale*, the appellants were employed by National Fuel Distributors, which then merged with British Fuels Group. Once again, they were dismissed on the grounds of redundancy and re-employed by the new group, known as British Fuels Ltd, but again, on different terms and conditions, including a reduced salary.

Held, by the House of Lords, that the dismissals of the employees were not nullities and were instead legally effective. Lord Slynn, with whose opinion the others agreed, pointed out that, although neither the transferor nor transferee can use the transfer as a justification for dismissal; if a dismissal actually occurs, then it is effective, even though it may be unfair, because the employee cannot compel the employer to re-employ him. Accordingly, employees who are re-employed will have a new contract of employment which can, of course, differ from the previous one.

The issue is then precisely what variations in terms and conditions consequent on a transfer are effective. Lord Slynn said that a variation, which is 'due to the transfer and to no other reason', is invalid, and that a variation may be due to the transfer even if it comes after the transfer. However, he said that 'there must, or at least may, come a time when the link with the transfer is broken or can be treated as no longer effective'. One could say that this decision raises more questions than it answers.

7.4 Transfers of undertakings and consultation

Regulation 10 of the Transfer of Undertakings Regulations provides that, where there is a relevant transfer, then there is a duty to inform and consult 'appropriate representatives'. The Collective Redundancies and Transfers of Undertakings (Protection of Employment) (Amendment) Regulations 1995, as amended by the Collective Redundancy and Transfer of Undertakings (Protection of Employment) (Amendment) Regulations 1999, provide that this means:

(a) employee representatives appointed or elected by the employees in question; or

(b) representatives of an independent trade union recognised by the employer as representing those employees.

> Note
>
> The 1999 Regulations provide that employers must consult representatives of recognised trade unions and, only if no trade union is recognised can employee representatives be consulted. Employee representatives can be either existing employee representatives or representatives specially elected for the purpose. The 1999 Regulations contain detailed provision for the election of employee representatives. If employees fail to elect representatives, then the employer must give directly to employees the information which he would have given to the representatives (see reg 9).

Regulation 10 provides that the employer must provide the following information to the representatives:

(a) when the relevant transfer is to take place and the reasons for it;

(b) the legal, economic and social implications for the affected employees;

(c) the measures which he envisages he will take in relation to those employees affected by the transfer;

(d) if the employer is the transferor, the measures which the transferee envisages he will be taking.

This information must be given to the 'appropriate representatives ... long enough before a relevant transfer to enable consultations to take place'. Where the employer envisages that he will be 'taking measures' in relation to the transfer, he must enter into consultations with the 'appropriate representatives', with a view to seeking their agreement to measures to be taken and must consider any representations made, and also reply to them giving reasons if any representations are rejected.

Regulation 11 provides that the 'appropriate representatives' or any affected employee may present a complaint to an industrial tribunal that there has been a failure to consult. The employer may put forward the 'special circumstances' defence (as in a failure to consult about impending redundancies) and affected employees may be awarded a maximum of four weeks' pay.

Q   Do you consider that the level of compensation for a failure to consult here should be raised to the same level as that for a failure to consult about impending redundancies?

8 Equal Pay

8.1 Equal Pay Act 1970

Section 1 Requirement of equal treatment for men and women in the same employment

(1) If the terms of a contract under which a woman is employed at an establishment in Great Britain do not include (directly or by reference to a collective agreement or otherwise) an equality clause, they shall be deemed to include one.

(2) An equality clause is a provision which relates to terms (whether concerned with pay or not) of a contract under which a woman is employed (the 'woman's contract'), and has the effect that:

    (a) where the woman is employed on like work with a man in the same employment:

        (i) if (apart from the equality clause) any term of the woman's contract is or becomes less favourable to the woman than a term of a similar kind in the contract under which that man is employed, that term of the woman's contract shall be treated as so modified as not to be less favourable; and

        (ii) if (apart from the equality clause) at any time the woman's contract does not include a term corresponding to a term benefiting that man included in the contract under which he is employed, the woman's contract shall be treated as including such a term.

    (b) Where the woman is employed on work rated as equivalent with that of a man in the same employment:

        (i) if (apart from the equality clause) any term of the woman's contract determined by the rating of the work is or becomes less favourable to the woman than a term of a similar kind in the contract under which the man is employed, that term of the woman's contract shall be treated as so modified as not to be less favourable; and

(ii) if (apart from the equality clause) at any time, the woman's contract does not include a term corresponding to a term benefiting that man included in the contract under which he is employed and determined by the rating of the work, the woman's contract shall be treated as including such a term.

(c) Where a woman is employed on work which, not being work in relation to which para (a) or (b) above applies, is, in terms of the demands made on her (for instance, under such headings as effort, skill and decision), of equal value to that of a man in the same employment:

(i) if (apart from the equality clause) any term of the woman's contract is or becomes less favourable to the woman than a term of a similar kind in the contract under which that man is employed, that term of the woman's contract shall be treated as so modified as not to be less favourable; and

(ii) if (apart from the equality clause) at any time, the woman's contract does not include a term corresponding to a term benefiting that man included in the contract under which he is employed, the woman's contract shall be treated as including such a term.

(4) A woman is to be regarded as employed on like work with men if, but only if, her work and theirs is of the same or a broadly similar nature, and the differences (if any) between the things she does and the things they do are not of practical importance in relation to terms and conditions of employment; and, accordingly, in comparing her work with theirs, regard shall be had to the frequency or otherwise with which any such differences occur in practice, as well as to the nature and extent of the differences.

Note

The three ways in which equal pay can be claimed:

(a) like work (s 1(2)(a));

(b) work rated as equivalent (s 1(2)(b));

(c) work of equal value (s 1(2)(c));

Note, also, that, although the Act refers to a woman, it applies equally to a man.

8.2 European Community law

8.2.1 Article 141 of the Treaty of Rome

Each Member State shall during the first stage and subsequently maintain the application of the principle that men and women should receive equal pay for equal work.

For the purposes of this Article, 'pay' means the ordinary basic or minimum wage or salary and any other consideration, whether in cash or in kind, which the worker receives, directly or indirectly, in respect of his employment from his employer.

Equal pay without discrimination based on sex means:

(a) that pay for the same work at piece rates shall be calculated on the basis of the same unit of measurement;

(b) that pay for the same work at time rates shall be the same for the same job.

8.2.2 The Equal Pay Directive (Council Directive 75/117/EEC)

Article 1

The principle of equal pay for men and women outlined in Art 119 [now Art 141] of the Treaty, hereinafter called 'principle of equal pay', means, for the same work or for work to which equal value is attributed, the elimination of all discrimination on grounds of sex with regard to all aspects and conditions of remuneration.

In particular, where a job classification system is used for determining pay, it must be based on the same criteria for both men and women and so drawn up as to exclude any discrimination on grounds of sex.

Article 2

Member States shall introduce into their national legal system such measures as are necessary to enable all employees who consider themselves wronged by failure to apply the principle of equal pay to pursue their claims by judicial process after possible recourse to other competent authorities.

Article 3

Member States shall abolish all discrimination between men and women arising from laws, regulations or administrative provisions which is contrary to the principle of equal pay.

Article 4

Member States shall take the necessary measures to ensure that provisions appearing in collective agreements, wage scales, wage agreements or individual contracts of employment which are contrary to the principle of equal pay shall be, or may be declared, null and void, or may be amended.

Article 5

Member States shall take the necessary measures to protect employees against dismissal by the employer as a reaction to a complaint within the undertaking or to any legal proceedings aimed at enforcing compliance with the principle of equal pay.

Article 6

Member States shall, in accordance with their national circumstances and legal systems, take the measures necessary to ensure that the principle of equal pay is applied. They shall see that effective means are available to take care that this principle is observed.

Note

Article 141 is directly enforceable in Member States and takes precedence over domestic law. (So far as the UK is concerned, this is by virtue of s 2 of the European Communities Act 1972.) Directive 75/117/EEC, however, as with all EC Directives, is only directly enforceable against a State employer or an emanation of it (see *Marshall v Southampton and South West Hampshire Area Health Authority* (1986), 9.8.1, below). However, as Directive 75/117/EEC does not establish any new principles, but instead clarifies Art 141, in practice, it can be said that it does have direct effect, in that it is used in the interpretation of Art 141 (see, also, 8.3.3, below).

Macarthys Ltd v Smith (1980) ECJ

X, a man, was employed as manager of one of the stockrooms of the employer's warehouses. He was paid about £60 a week. He left in October 1975, and the employee claiming equal pay was appointed four months later. She was paid £50 a week for duties which were virtually the same as those of X. She claimed equal pay with him.

Held, by the Court of Appeal, that the Equal Pay Act 1970 did not permit a comparison with a previous male employee, but it referred the matter to the ECJ for a determination of whether Art 141 applied. The ECJ held that Art 141 was not confined to situations where men and women were contemporaneously doing equal work. The ECJ stated that:

> In such a situation, the decisive test lies in establishing whether there is a difference in treatment between a man and woman performing 'equal work' within the meaning of Art 141. The scope of that concept, which is

entirely qualitative in character, in that it is exclusively concerned with the nature of the services in question, may not be restricted by the introduction of a requirement of contemporaneity

It must be acknowledged, however, that, as the EAT properly recognised, it cannot be ruled out that a difference in pay between two workers occupying the same post, but at different periods in time, may be explained by the operation of factors which are unconnected with any discrimination on grounds of sex. That is a question of fact which it is for the court or tribunal to decide ... the principle that men and woman should receive equal pay for equal work, enshrined in Art 119 [now Art 141] of the EEC Treaty, is not confined to situations in which men and woman are contemporaneously doing equal work for the same employer.

Note
This case was one of the very first decisions of the ECJ to affect UK employment law. Note that the effect was not to overrule the Equal Pay Act, but to broaden its scope. See, also, *Diocese of Hallam v Connaughton* (1996).

8.3 Meaning of 'like work', 'work rated as equivalent' and 'work of equal value'

8.3.1 Like work

Shields v E Coomes Holdings Ltd (1978) CA
Miss Shields was employed as a counter hand by the appellant in its bookmaker's shop and was paid 92 p an hour. A male counterhand was employed at the same shop at a rate of £1.06 an hour. Although the work done by the man and by Miss Shields was virtually the same, the man was there partly to deter potential troublemakers. However, there was no evidence that the man was especially trained in order to do this part of the job, nor that he had ever done it.

Held, by the Court of Appeal, that, on the application of s 1(4) of the Equal Pay Act 1970, the differences between the work of Miss Shields and the man were not of practical importance in relation to terms and conditions of employment. One must not compare the contractual obligations of the man and the woman (an error into which the industrial tribunal in this case had fallen), but instead compare the functions which the man and the woman actually perform.

Capper Pass Ltd v Lawton (1976) EAT
Mrs Lawton was employed as a cook, preparing meals for directors of the company and their guests.

Held, by the EAT, that she was employed on like work with two assistant chefs in the kitchen serving the factory canteen. Any differences in work done were not of practical importance in relation to terms and conditions of employment. Phillips J set out some useful guidance on how to approach making a comparison:

> It seems to us that, in most cases, the enquiry will fall into two stages. First, is the work of the same, or, if not, 'of a broadly similar' nature? This question can be answered by a general consideration of the type of work involved, and of the skill and knowledge required to do it. It seems to us to be implicit in the words of sub-s (4) that it can be answered without a minute examination of the detail of the differences between the work done by the man and the work done by the woman. But, secondly, if on such an examination, the answer is that the work is of a broadly similar nature, it is then necessary to go to consider the detail and to enquire whether the differences between the work being compared are of 'practical importance in relation to terms and conditions of employment'. In answering that question, the Industrial Tribunal will be guided by the concluding words of the sub-section. But again, it seems to us, trivial differences, or differences not likely in the real world to be reflected in the terms and conditions of employment, ought to be disregarded. In other words, once it is determined that work is of a broadly similar nature, it should be regarded as being like work, unless the differences are plainly of a kind which the industrial tribunal in its experience would expect to find reflected in the terms and conditions of employment.

Note

Dugdale v Krafts Foods Ltd (1976), which held that the time at which work is done is not by itself relevant. However, Phillips J pointed out in *National Coal Board v Sherwin* (1978) that this does not mean that men and woman cannot be paid extra for working at night or at weekends, or at other inconvenient times. If the additional remuneration is justified by the inconvenience of the time at which it is done, the claim (for equality) will not succeed.

Thomas v National Coal Board (1987) EAT

Woman canteen assistants claimed that they were employed on like work with a man who had been employed on permanent night work as a canteen assistant and had been paid at a higher rate.

Held, by the EAT, that the fact he was alone on permanent night duty 'added responsibility which was a difference of practical importance' (*per* Sir Ralph Kilner Brown); thus, the industrial tribunal had been entitled to find that the man and the woman were not employed on 'like work'.

Q   Contrast *Thomas v National Coal Board* with *Shields v Coomes*.

Note ───
See, also, on the question of what constitutes 'like work': *Eaton Ltd v Nuttall* (1977); *Calder and Another v Rowntree Mackintosh Confectionery Ltd* (1993); and *Maidment v Cooper & Co (Birmingham) Ltd* (1978).
───

8.3.2 Work rated as equivalent

A claim under this head depends on there being a valid job evaluation scheme. Where such a scheme exists, an applicant may claim that her work has been rated as equivalent under it. On the other hand, an applicant may challenge a job evaluation scheme on the ground that it does not fulfil the criteria set out in s 1(5) of the Equal Pay Act 1970.

This provides that:

> A woman is to be regarded as employed on work rated as equivalent with that of any men if, but only if, her job and their job have been given an equal value, in terms of the demand made on a worker under various headings (for instance effort, skill, decision), on a study undertaken with a view to evaluating in those terms the jobs to be done by all or any of the employees in an undertaking or a group of undertakings, or would have been given an equal value, but for the evaluation being made on a system setting different values for men and women on the same demand under any heading.

Bromley and Others v H & J Quick Ltd (1988) CA
Women clerical workers brought an 'equal value' claim (see 8.3.3, below), in which they compared their work to that done by male managers. A job evaluation scheme had been carried out, which had given different values to the jobs done by the women as compared to those done by the men. In the Court of Appeal, Dillon LJ emphasised that a job evaluation scheme, in order to satisfy the requirements of s 1(5) of the Equal Pay Act 1970, must be both non-discriminatory and also analytical. Analytical meant that the jobs of each worker 'must have been valued in terms of the demand made on the worker under the various headings' (as required by s 1(5) above). That had not been done in this case.

Note ───
Section 1(5) only gives examples of headings which may be used. The ACAS Guide No 1 gives a different list of factors: skills, responsibility, physical and mental requirements and working conditions.
See, also, *Arnold v Beecham Group Ltd* (1982) (a job evaluation scheme can be relied on as soon as it has been accepted as valid by all parties, even though it has not yet been formally implemented).
───

8.3.3 Work of equal value

Note

This head was introduced into the Equal Pay Act 1970 by s 1 of the Equal Pay (Amendment) Regulations 1983 (SI 1983/1794), following the decision of the ECJ in *Commission of the European Communities v United Kingdom* (1982) that the existing equal pay laws did not comply with the Equal Pay Directive in failing to allow a claim based on work of equal value.

Hayward v Cammell Laird Shipbuilders Ltd (1988) HL

Mrs Hayward was employed as a canteen cook and claimed that her work was of equal value with that of male painters, thermal insulation engineers and joiners employed by the company. Her claim succeeded, but the courts then had to decide what she was actually entitled to. Was her entitlement to:

(a) the same basic rate of pay as her male comparator;

(b) a comparison of all the terms of her contract (including elements such as meal breaks, sickness benefits and holidays)?

Under approach (b), she would be no better off as a result of her claim because, when all the terms of the contract were taken into account, she was better off than her male comparators. For example, she had a paid meal break, but they did not. The House of Lords, reversing the Court of Appeal, held that approach (a) was correct. The approach was contractual. A woman who can point to a term of her contract which is less favourable that that of a man is entitled to have that term made not less favourable as a term of her contract, under the equality clause in s 1(1) of the Equal Pay Act. Lord Goff said:

What does sub-s (ii) [of ss 1–3 of the Equal Pay Act] in each case provide? It provides that, if the woman's contract does not include a term corresponding to a term benefiting the male comparator included in his contract, her contract shall be treated as including such a term. Next, what does such a provision mean? If I look at the words used, and give them their natural and ordinary meaning, they mean quite simply that one looks at the man's contract and at the woman's contract, and if one finds in the man's contract a term benefiting him which is not included in the woman's contract, then that term is treated as included in hers. It is obvious that this approach cannot be reconciled with the approach favoured by the Court of Appeal, because it does not require, or indeed permit, the court to look at the overall contractual position of each party, or even to look at their overall position as regards one particular matter, for example, 'pay' in the wide sense adopted by the Court of Appeal. To achieve that result, it would be necessary, in sub-s (ii), to construe the word 'term' as referring to the totality of the relevant contractual provisions relating to a particular subject matter, for example, 'pay' or, alternatively, to construe the words 'benefiting that man' as importing the necessity of a comparison in relation to the totality of the relevant contractual provisions concerning a particular subject matter, and then, for a conclusion to be reached that, on balance, the man has thereby benefited. [Lord Goff then indicated that he could not approve the approach favoured by the Court of Appeal.]

Note

For the interpretation placed by the ECJ on the word 'pay', see 8.6, below.

Pickstone and Others v Freemans plc (1988) HL

Mrs Pickstone was employed as a warehouse operative and claimed that her work was of equal value with that of a man employed as a 'checker warehouse operative', who was paid £4.22 a week more than her. However, one man was employed in the same establishment as a warehouse operative doing exactly the same work as Mrs Pickstone.

Held, by the House of Lords, that her claim could still be brought. Section 1(2)(c) of the Equal Pay Act 1970 required that in order to bring an 'equal value' claim, the chosen comparator must not be doing 'like' work or 'work rated as equivalent'. It did not mean that a claim was precluded because other men were on 'like work' or 'work rated as equivalent'. Lord Keith of Kinkel said:

The question is whether the exclusionary words in para (c) [s 1(2)(c), see 8.1, above] are intended to have effect whenever the employers are able to point to some man who is employed by them on like work with the woman plaintiff within the meaning of para (a) or work rated as equivalent with hers within the meaning of para (b), or whether they are intended to have effect only where the particular man with whom she seeks comparison is employed on such work. In my opinion, the latter is the correct answer. The opposite result would leave a large gap in the equal work provision, enabling an employer to evade it by employing one token man on the same work as a group of potential woman plaintiffs who were deliberately paid less than a group of men employed on work of equal value with that of the woman. This would mean that the United Kingdom had failed yet again fully to implement its obligations under Art 119 [now Art 141] of the Treaty and the Equal Pay Directive, and had not given full effect to the decision of the European Court in *Commission of the European Communities v United Kingdom* (1982). It is plain that Parliament cannot possibly have intended such a failure.

Note

The procedure under the Industrial Tribunals (Rule of Procedure) Regulations 1985 for making an equal value claim has been severely criticised for its complexity and, in particular, for the separation of two issues:

(a) any claim by a respondent that the work was not of equal value; and

(b) any claim that the variation was due to a material difference other than sex.

Only if the applicant succeeded on these points would the industrial tribunal refer the case to an independent expert for a report. In practice, it often takes a considerable time for the expert to prepare the report. However, the Sex Discrimination and Equal Pay (Miscellaneous Amendments) Regulations 1996 now allow industrial tribunals to deal with all the issues together as in a normal case, and each party may, as in other types of cases, appoint experts. This should enable the procedure to be considerably shortened.

Wood v William Ball Ltd (1999) EAT

Held, by the EAT, that it was not for a tribunal to decide if work is of equal value. The parties must be given the opportunity to adduce their own evidence.

8.4 Genuine material differences

Section 1(3) of the Equal Pay Act 1970

(3) An equality clause shall not operate in relation to a variation between the woman's contract and the man's contract if the employer proves that the variation is genuinely due to a material factor which is not the difference of sex and that factor:

(a) in the case of an equality clause falling within sub-s (2)(a) or (b) above, must be a material difference between the woman's case and the man's; and

(b) in the case of an equality clause falling within sub-s 2(c) above, may be such a material difference.

Calder and Another v Rowntree Mackintosh Confectionery Ltd (1993) CA

The applicant was employed part time as a machine operator in a packing department, and worked an all female 'twilight shift' (5.30 pm to 10.30 pm). She claimed equal pay with a man employed as a machine operator in another packing department, who worked on a predominantly male rotating shift. This meant working from 8.00 am to 4.00 pm one week, and 4.00 pm to midnight the other week. He received a 20% shift premium.

Held, by the Court of Appeal, that the variation in pay was genuinely due to the fact that the man worked on a rotating shift. The applicant had argued that the shift premium reflected two factors: the inconvenience in having to work a rotating shift and the requirement to work unsocial hours, and that this latter requirement applied to her also. Therefore, she argued she was entitled to some additional compensation. However, the Court of Appeal disagreed. *Per* Balcombe LJ:

> The fact that some indeterminate part of the shift premium represented compensation for working unsocial hours does not necessarily preclude a finding that the payment of the shift premium was genuinely due to working rotating shifts.

> Essentially, the appellant's complaint is not discrimination on the grounds of sex – it is of unfairness; that workers (including woman) on the rotating shift receive compensation which includes an element for working unsocial hours, whereas those on the twilight turn, who also work unsocial hours, receive no sufficient compensation. But, as Geoffrey Lane LJ said in *National Vulcan Engineering Insurance Group Ltd v Wade* (1978):

>> It is not for the tribunal to examine the employer's system with the object of seeing whether it is operating efficiently or even fairly. The only inquiry is whether it is genuine – that is to say, designed to differentiate between employees on some basis other than the basis of sex.

Note ───

NAAFI v Varley (1977) is a good example of the genuine material difference defence.

───

Jenkins v Kingsgate (Clothing Productions) Limited (No 2) (1981) EAT

The applicant worked part time as a machinist. All male machinists (except one) were employed full time and were paid at a higher rate than the applicant, who claimed equal pay with the men on the basis of 'like work'.

Held, by the EAT (following a reference to the ECJ), that the payment of differential wages to part time workers, as compared to full time, could only be a genuine material difference if the payment of a lower rate for part time workers was intended to achieve an objective unrelated to sex. There could be discrimination if the differences of pay between full and part time workers were 'in reality, merely an indirect way of reducing the level of pay of part time workers on the ground that the group of workers is composed exclusively or predominantly of women'.

Note ───

The case was one of the first to introduce the concept of indirect discrimination into equal pay law, but there remained a doubt about whether this concept applied under Art 141. The *Bilka* case (below) showed that it could.

Handels-OG Kontorfunktionaerernes Foribund i Danmark v Dansk Arbejdsgiverforening (acting for Danfoss) (1989) ECJ

Held, by the ECJ, that, under the Equal Pay Directive, where an employer operates a system of individual supplements applied to basic pay, which is implemented so that a woman cannot identify the reason for a difference in pay between her and a man doing the same work (lack of transparency), then, if a woman establishes that, in relation to a relatively large number of employees, the average pay of a woman is less than that for men, then the burden of proof is on the employer to show that this is not so.

> Note
>
> The object of the ruling is to encourage employers to seek 'transparency', and to enable a woman to work out why she has been awarded a particular rate of pay as compared with a man. Compare the above case with the earlier Court of Appeal decision in *National Vulcan Engineering Group Ltd v Wade* (1978) and also that of the later judgment of the ECJ in *Nimz v Freie und Hansestadt Hamburge* (1991).

Bilka-Kaufhaus GmbH v Weber von Hartz (1986) ECJ

A department store in Germany operated an occupational pension scheme, under which part time employees were eligible for pensions only if they had worked full time for at least 15 years over a total period of 20 years. The applicant had worked for the store for 15 years, but some of the time had been part time.

Held, by the ECJ, that an occupational scheme which excludes part time employees will infringe Art 141 where the exclusion affects a far greater proportion of women than men, unless the employer can show that the exclusion of part time employees is objectively justified on grounds unrelated to sex. The store had put forward, as a justification for excluding part time workers, the reason that it wished to discourage part time work, because it said that, in general, part time workers refuse to work in the late afternoon and on Saturdays. The ECJ held that it was open to the national court to find that the measures chosen by the store:

> ... correspond to a real need on the part of the undertaking, and are appropriate with a view to achieving the objectives pursued and are necessary to that end ...

Strathclyde Regional Council v Wallace and Others (1998) HL

The nine respondents, who were teachers, performed the duties of principal teachers, but they had neither been appointed to that position, nor did they receive the salary of such a teacher. They were among a group of 134 unpromoted teachers in the same position, 81 of whom were men and 53 women. They claimed equal pay with a male comparator who had been appointed as a principal teacher and who, therefore, received the salary of one.

Held, by the House of Lords, that where, as here, the disparity in pay has nothing to do with gender, then it is not for the employer to establish in a s 1(3) defence that the reasons for the disparity in pay justified the disparity. There is only a burden on the employer to justify a difference in pay where the employer 'is relying on a factor which is sexually discriminatory' (*per* Lord Browne-Wilkinson). He pointed out that the object of the respondents was 'to achieve equal pay for like work regardless of sex, not to eliminate any inequalities due to sex discrimination'. This, he pointed out, was not the object of the Act. 'The purpose of s 1 of the Equal Pay Act 1970 is to eliminate sex discrimination in pay not to achieve fair wages.'

Note

This case is of great significance in clarifying the question of when an employer has to justify a difference in pay under the 'genuine material difference' defence in s 1(3) of the Equal Pay Act 1970. Lord Browne-Wilkinson held, *obiter,* that even where there is a sexually discriminatory practice (unlike in the present case), it is still open to the employer to justify it under s 1(3) by applying the test in the *Bilka* case (above). The *Bilka* case introduced the concept of indirect discrimination into Art 141 and thus, in effect, into the Equal Pay Act. This was developed further in the next two cases.

R v Secretary of State for Employment ex p Equal Opportunities Commission and Another (1994) HL

The Equal Opportunities Commission argued that the thresholds of claiming unfair dismissal and redundancy (employees working for at least 16 hours a week) indirectly discriminated against women employees, because nearly 90% of employees excluded from claiming were women.

Held, by the House of Lords, that, in principle, these thresholds were indirectly discriminatory. It was open to the Secretary of State to show, by reference to objective factors, that these thresholds had the beneficial social policy aim of bringing about an increase in the amount of part time work but, on the facts, he had failed to show this.

Note

See, also, *R v Secretary of State for Employment ex p Seymour Smith* (1995), 9.2.1, below.

Enderby v Frenchay Health Authority (1993) CA

The applicant was a speech therapist and claimed that she was employed on work of equal value to that done by male principal grade pharmacists and clinical psychologists employed on the NHS, who were paid substantially more than her. The employer argued that the difference in pay was due to different collective bargaining agreements for the two groups of women and, as these were not discriminatory, they amounted to a genuine material factor justifying a difference in pay.

Held, by the Court of Appeal (following a reference to the ECJ), that:

> ... where significant statistics disclose an appreciable difference in pay between two jobs of equal value, one of which is carried out almost exclusively by women and the other predominantly by men, Art 119 [now Art 141] of the Treaty requires the employer to show that that difference is based on objectively justified factors unrelated to any discrimination on grounds of sex. The fact that the rates of pay at issue are decided by collective bargaining processes conducted separately for each of the two professional groups concerned, without any discriminatory effect within each group, does not preclude a finding of *prima facie* discrimination, where the results of those processes show that two groups with the same employer and the same trade union are treated differently. If the employer could rely on the absence of discrimination within each of the collective bargaining processes taken separately as sufficient justification for the difference in pay, he could, as the German Government pointed out, easily circumvent the principle of equal pay by using separate bargaining processes ...

> Accordingly, the fact that the respective rates of pay of two jobs of equal value, one carried out almost exclusively by women and the other predominantly by men, were arrived at by collective bargaining processes which, although carried out by the same parties, are distinct and, taken separately, have in themselves no discriminatory effect, is not sufficient objective justification for the difference in pay between those two jobs.

Accordingly, indirect discrimination will be presumed where there is significant statistical evidence that a predominantly female group of workers are being paid less than a group of predominantly male workers, although the work done by both groups is of equal value. The employer must then discharge the onus of showing that the difference is objectively justified.

Evesham v North Hertfordshire Health Authority and Secretary of State for Health (1999) EAT

This case followed from the decision in *Enderby*, because the appellant was one of the speech therapists involved in that case. Having won her claim that her work was of equal value to that of a clinical psychologist, she then, in this litigation, claimed that she should be placed on the pay scale for the post of her comparator at a level appropriate to her years of service as a speech therapist.

Held, by the EAT, that this was the wrong approach and that, instead, she should mirror her comparator on the incremental pay scale and, therefore, enter it at the lowest level, which was where he was. To hold otherwise would mean that she would receive pay in excess of that received by her comparator, although she had established that her work was of equal value to his. This would be wrong.

Clay Cross (Quarry Services) Ltd v Fletcher (1979) CA
A woman sales clerk was employed on the same rate of pay as a male sales clerk, who had been engaged at a later date. The employer's defence was that of 'market forces'; that is, the male clerk had been the only suitable applicant for the post and he had refused to accept it unless he was paid the same wages as in his previous post.

Held, by the Court of Appeal, that it was not open to an employer to use this defence, Denning MR said that:

> ... the employer cannot avoid his obligations under the Act by saying 'I paid him more because he asked for more' or 'I paid her less because she was willing to work for less'.

Rainey v Greater Glasgow Health Board (1987) HL
The applicant, a female prosthetist, claimed equal pay with a male prosthetist who had been paid considerably more than her because he was one of a group hired to join the NHS from the private sector when the prosthetic service was set up for the first time in the NHS in Scotland. It had been found necessary to pay the group at a higher rate to match their private sector salaries because of the difficulties of recruiting from within the NHS. The applicant, by contrast, had joined the NHS immediately after completion of her training.

Held, by the House of Lords, that the difference in pay was justified, because there was an objective justification for putting the man into a higher scale on entry, given the difficulty in recruitment. Lord Keith observed that:

> In my opinion, these statements [in *Fletcher* (above)] are unduly restrictive of the proper interpretation of s 1(3). The difference must be 'material', which I would construe as meaning 'significant and relevant', and it must be between 'her case and his'. Consideration of a person's case must necessarily involve consideration of all the circumstances of that case. These may well go beyond which is not very happily described as 'the personal equation', that is, the personal qualities by way of skill, experience or training which the individual brings to the job. Some

circumstances may on examination prove to be not significant or not relevant, but others may do so, though not relating to the personal qualities of the employer. In particular, where there is no question of intentional sex discrimination, whether direct or indirect (and there is none here), a difference which is connected with economic factors affecting the efficient carrying on of the employer's business or other activity may well be relevant.

The House of Lords adopted the test in the *Bilka* case (see above) for deciding whether there were any objectively justified grounds for the variation in pay – that is, did the measures taken correspond to a real need on the part of the employer, and were they appropriate and necessary to achieving that end?

Note

This case can also be seen as an example of red-circling. See *Snoxell v Vauxhall Motors Ltd* (below).

Enderby v Frenchay Health Authority (1993) ECJ

Another issue in this case was whether the market forces defence applied.

Held, by the ECJ, that, in principle, it is open to an employer to demonstrate 'an objectively justified economic ground' for a difference in pay based on market forces but, if so, it is for the national court to determine how much of the difference in pay is attributable to that reason. An employer will not necessarily be able to justify the whole of the difference in pay on the basis of market forces.

Ratcliffe v North Yorkshire County Council (1995) HL

The council had, following the introduction of compulsory competitive tendering, established a direct service organisation (DSO) for the provision of school meals. However, after it became apparent that the DSO could not compete with commercial bodies, staff employed at the DSO were forced to take a pay cut. These staff were almost all female and their workload was rated as of equal value with other workers employed by the council (road sweepers, leisure attendants and refuse collectors), who were almost exclusively men. The result of the pay cut was to reduce their pay to below that of their male comparators.

Held, by the House of Lords, that the material factor which led to the difference in pay was due to the difference of sex (that is, the almost exclusively female group, as compared with almost exclusively male group) and was therefore unlawful.

Q   Is it possible to distinguish the above case from *Rainey v Greater Glasgow Health Board*?

Note

In *Ratcliffe*, the House of Lords held that the requirement that a difference in pay must be objectively justified (see *Bilka*, above) applies in both direct and indirect discrimination in cases of equal pay, but in practice, it would be most unusual for a court to find that a case of direct discrimination was objectively justified.

Barry v Midland Bank plc (1999) HL

The appellant was employed by the respondents full time for 11 years and then, following maternity leave, she worked part time until her employment was terminated, when she took voluntary severance pay. She claimed that the voluntary severance payment scheme discriminated against her because, although her severance pay was based on length of service (both full and part time), it was only based on the final pay that she was earning at the date of termination. As, in her case, this was her pay when she was working part time, she argued that the failure to take into account her period of full time work had a disproportionate impact on women as compared with men because, as a greater number of women than men worked part time, then their severance pay would be calculated in the same way as hers.

Held, by the House of Lords, that her claim failed, because the severance pay scheme did not have a discriminatory effect. Lord Slynn said that: '... all employees, men and women, full and part time, of all ages, receive a payment based on final salary.' Even if the scheme was restructured, 'there would be losers as well as winners' (*per* Lord Nicholls). Moreover, the primary objective of the scheme was to provide compensation for loss of a job and 'loss of a job entails loss of the actual salary being paid' (*per* Lord Nicholls). It was not remuneration for past service.

Snoxell v Vauxhall Motors (1977) EAT

The company, until 1971, had separate grades for men and women for the same jobs. It then introduced an amended structure for both men and women. One of the male grades had, in the past, been given too high a status, and so it was assimilated to a lower grade, but those men already at the grade were red-circled, that is, their pay was protected at the higher rate. No women were in the red-circled grades.

Held, by the EAT, that, in deciding cases of this type, one must look at the original reason why the difference in pay arose; one must look back beyond the decision to red-circle. In this case, the original reason for the difference in pay was discriminatory, because women had not been allowed to enter the grade on which the men were. Therefore, the women's claim to equal pay succeeded.

Note ───
There have been cases where red-circling has succeeded as a defence. See *Charles Early and Marriott (Witney) Ltd v Smith and Ball* (1977) and compare with *Benveniste v University of Southampton* (1989).

Q   Do you consider that, in principle, red-circling can ever be justified as a defence to a claim for equal pay?

8.5   Area of comparison

Section 1 of the Equal Pay Act 1970 applies where men and women are employed by the same employer or by an associated employer.

Section 1(6) deals with the meaning of the terms 'employed' and 'associated employer', and also with the position where men and women are employed by the same employer, but at different establishments:

(6) Subject to the following sub-sections, for the purpose of this section:

(a) 'employed' means employed under a contract of service or of apprenticeship or a contract personally to execute any work or labour, and related expressions shall be construed accordingly; ...

(c) two employers are to be treated as associated if one is a company of which the other (directly or indirectly) has control or, if both are companies of which a third person (directly or indirectly) has control, and men shall be treated as in the same employment with a woman if they are men employed by her employer or any associated employer at the same establishment or at establishments in Great Britain which include that one and at which common terms and conditions of employment are observed, either generally or for employees of the relevant classes.

Leverton v Clwyd County Council (1989) HL
The applicant was employed as a nursery nurse and brought a claim that her work was of equal value with that of a male clerical worker who worked in a different establishment to hers. The issue was whether 'common terms and conditions of employment were observed'. The employer argued that they were not, because there were differing entitlements to the amount of holiday as between the nursery workers and their comparators, and their hours of work were different. However, all the relevant employees were covered by the same collective agreement, the terms of which were contained in the 'Purple Book'.

Held, by the House of Lords, that there were common terms and conditions. The differences in pay and hours of work were irrelevant, because one was not comparing the terms and conditions of the applicant and her comparators. Instead, s 1(6) required the terms and conditions at the establishment to be the same and/or at least broadly similar; here, they were, because all relevant employees were covered by the same collective agreement.

Note

The applicant's claim failed, however, because the difference in hours worked and holiday entitlement was a genuine material difference (s 1(3)).

British Coal Corp v Smith (1996) HL

The applicants were 1,286 women employed as canteen workers or cleaners at 47 different establishments. They brought an equal value claim and named 150 male comparators who were employed as clerical workers or surface mine workers at 14 different establishments.

Held, by the House of Lords, that the applicants were in the same employment as their comparators because, for the purpose of s 1(6), a comparison between terms and conditions needed to be on a broad basis. Lord Slynn observed that:

The real question is what the legislation was seeking to achieve. Was it seeking to exclude a woman's claim unless, subject to *de minimis* exceptions, there was complete identity of terms and conditions for the comparator at his establishment and those which applied or would apply to a similar male worker at her establishment? Or was the legislation seeking to establish that the terms and conditions of the relevant class were sufficiently similar for a fair comparison to be made, subject always to the employer's right to establish a 'material difference' defence under s 1(3) of the Act?

If it was the former, then the woman would fail at the first hurdle if there was any difference (other than a *de minimis* one) between the terms and conditions of the men at the various establishments, since she could not then show that the men were in the same employment as she was. The issue as to whether the differences were material so as to justify different treatment would then never arise.

I do not consider that this can have been intended.

Note

The difference between the *British Coal Corp* and the *Leverton* cases was, as pointed out by Lord Slynn, that in *Leverton*, the crucial question was 'between whose terms and conditions should the comparison be made?' Here, the identity of the comparators had been settled; instead, the question was 'whether there was a sufficient identity between the respective terms and conditions for them to be common'.

Lawrence and Others v Regent Office Care Ltd and Others (1999) EAT
This case followed on from the *Ratcliffe* case (see 8.4, above) because, after that decision, the provision of school meals was put out to tender and the appellants, who had been employed by North Yorkshire County Council, now became employed by outside contractors. The appellants brought an equal pay claim, seeking to compare themselves with current employees of the county council.

Held, by the EAT, that their claim failed, because it was necessary for the appellant and the comparator to be 'in a loose and non-technical sense in the same establishment or service' (*per* Morrison P); this was not the case here.

Note

This case is of interest in that it was argued that s 1(6) of the Equal Pay Act 1970 could not apply, because the private contractor and the county council were obviously not associated employers. Nevertheless, the EAT considered whether the provisions of Art 141 could be invoked so as to disapply s 1(6) on the ground that it offended Community law. Although the EAT decided that Art 141 should not be given 'a much wider interpretation', the test used by Morrison P is certainly wider than that in s 1(6), and this area may well see future developments. Watch this space!

8.6 Meaning of 'pay' for the purpose of the Equal Pay Act 1970

Barber v Guardian Royal Exchange Assurance Group (1990) ECJ
The male applicant had been made redundant at the age of 52 and would not, under the company's occupational pension scheme, be entitled to a pension until the age of 55, whereas a woman in these circumstances would be entitled to a pension at 50.

Held, by the ECJ, that benefits which are paid under a private, contracted-out pension scheme are within the definition of 'pay' in Art 141 and, therefore, there was a clear case of infringement of the Equal Pay Act 1970.

The following points also emerge from this decision:

(1)   It extended the term 'pay' to benefits paid on redundancy, including both redundancy payments and also *ex gratia* payments.

(2)   It does not apply to State pensions or to pensions paid under statutory authority: *Griffin v London Pension Fund Authority* (1993).

(3)   It continues the trend of decisions of the ECJ to broaden the scope of the term 'pay'. See *Garland v British Rail Engineering* (1982), which held that concessionary travel given to employees after retirement was 'pay', and therefore came within Art 141.

(4)   In *Roberts v Birds Eye Walls Ltd* (1994), the ECJ held that it was not a breach of Art 141 for an employer to reduce the amount of the bridging pension which a women employee received to take account of the fact that she will receive a State pension at the age of 60, whereas a man will only do so at 65. Accordingly, the man will not suffer the reduction in his bridging pension, because he will not receive his State pension till five years later.

(5)   The ECJ in *Barber* held that this decision was not to operate retrospectively and, therefore, Art 141 could not be relied upon to claim any entitlement to a pension with effect from any date before 17 May 1990, being the date of the ruling in *Barber*. The only exceptions to the rule are those who have already initiated legal proceedings, or raised an equivalent claim under national law, before that date.

Note

However, in *Gillespie v Northern Health and Social Services Board* (1996), it was held that the Equal Pay Act does not apply to maternity pay. The applicant argued that she should be entitled to full pay whilst on maternity leave because, if the only reason why she did not receive full pay was because she was on maternity leave, that must be direct discrimination against her on the grounds of sex.

The ECJ, however, held that women who are on maternity leave are in a special position, which is not comparable with that of a man or woman at work.

Abdoulaye and Others v Regie Nationale des Usines Renault (1999)

The ECJ held that the fact a woman had received a maternity bonus, whereas a man had not received a paternity bonus, was not a breach of the Equal Treatment Directive, because the man and woman were not in comparable situations.

Q   How do you consider that the decision in *Gillespie* can be justified?

8.7   Remedies

A claim for equal pay may be brought before an employment tribunal, which may declare that the applicant's contract contains an equality clause.

Levez v TH Jennings (Harlow Pools) Ltd (No 2); Hicking v Basford Group (1999) EAT

The EAT held that the provisions in s 2(5) of the Equal Pay Act 1970, which imposed a two year limitation on arrears of pay in claims made under the Act, was unlawful as being in breach of the principle of equivalence in European Community law. This principle requires that the rule which is in issue should be applied without distinction where the purpose of the rule and the cause of action are similar. In this situation, the EAT held that there was a breach of this principle, because claims for arrears of pay for up to six years are permitted where there has been an unlawful deduction from wages and, more crucially in this case, the six year period applied in claims under the Race Relations Act 1976, which applies where the claim is that there has been racial discrimination in relation to, *inter alia*, terms of employment. In effect, the Equal Pay Act 1970 is the counterpart of the provisions in relation to sex and race discrimination, and so the principle of equivalence is breached.

9 Discrimination

9.1 Direct discrimination

9.1.1 Sex Discrimination Act 1975

Section 1 Sex discrimination against women

(1) A person discriminates against a woman in any circumstances relevant for the purposes of any provision of this Act if:

(a) on the grounds of her sex, he treats her less favourably than he treats or would treat a man ...

Section 2 Sex discrimination against men

(1) Section 1 and the provisions of Pts I and II relating to sex discrimination against women are to be read as applying equally to the treatment of men ...

Section 3 Discrimination against married persons

(1) A person discriminates against a married person of either sex for the purposes of any provision of Pt II if:

(a) on the grounds of his or her marital status, he treats that person less favourably than he treats or would treat an unmarried person of the same sex ...

James v Eastleigh Borough Council (1990) HL

A married couple, Mr and Mrs James were both aged 61. On reaching pensionable age at 60, Mrs James received free admission to the local authority swimming pool. This benefit was denied to Mr James, who had not yet reached the male pensionable age of 65. It was alleged that this was direct discrimination against Mr James solely on grounds of sex. In the judgment of the Court of Appeal, the applicant's less favourable treatment was not 'on the grounds of [his] sex', as in determining discrimination, the subjective reason for the defendant's actions, rather than the causative effect of that action, was of paramount importance.

Held, by a majority of the House of Lords (rejecting the above argument of the Court of Appeal), that discrimination is 'on grounds of sex' if the sex of the plaintiff is a substantial cause of the less favourable treatment. To determine this, the *'but for'* test should be applied – discrimination arises if the applicant would have received the same treatment as a person of the opposite sex *but for* his or her sex. Thus, on the basis of an affirmative answer to the question – would the applicant, a man of 61, have received the same treatment as his wife, *but for* his sex – Mr James had been unlawfully discriminated against.

Note
Even where a gender based criterion (such as pregnancy) only affects members of one sex and not the other (so making a comparison with the other sex impossible), action taken against an employee on the basis of this criterion can still amount to direct discrimination (see 9.8, below).

Porcelli v Strathclyde Regional Council (1986)
The plaintiff was a laboratory technician, who was subjected to a campaign of verbal and physical sexual harassment by two male colleagues in an attempt to force her to seek a transfer to other employment. The defendant argued that the treatment was meted out to her not because she was a woman *per se*, but because she was personally disliked by these fellow employees.

Held, by the Court of Session, that the sexual harassment was clearly adopted against the plaintiff because she was a woman, which would not have been adopted against an equally disliked man. In these circumstances, the applicant had been treated 'less favourably' (on the grounds of her sex) than a man would have been treated.

Note
For further examples, see: *Snowball v Gardner Merchant* (1987); *Bracebridge Engineering Ltd v Darby* (1990); *Stewart v Cleveland Guest (Engineering) Ltd* (1994); *Insitu Cleaning Co Ltd v Heads* (1995); *Reed & Bull Information Systems Ltd v Stedman* (1999); *Leicester University v A* (1999); *AM v WC and SPV* (1999).

Q   Do you think the Protection from Harassment Act 1997 (which is intended to deal with 'stalkers') could also be utilised to protect women from harassment at work?

Note
In 1991, the EC Commission issued a Recommendation (91/131/EEC) on the Protection of the Dignity of Women and Men at Work endorsed by the EC Council. This does not impose direct legal obligations, but invites Member States to develop and implement policies to prevent

and combat sexual harassment at work, and to ensure that adequate procedures are readily available to deal with incidents of harassment.

Q   In practical terms, what steps can employers take to prevent harassment at work?

Burrett v West Birmingham Health Authority (1994) EAT

A nurse challenged a requirement that female members of staff had to wear a nurse's cap, which she regarded as undignified and demeaning, when male nurses, who wore a different uniform, did not. The tribunal rejected her claim that this was less favourable treatment on the grounds of sex.

Held, by the EAT, following *Schmidt v Austicks Bookshop Ltd* (1978), that where uniform requirements are imposed on both sexes, discrimination is not established just because these requirements are different; nor is it established merely by the employee's own subjective belief that she is being less favourably treated.

Note ———————————————————————————

On appearance and dress codes, see *Smith v Safeway plc* (1996).

Skyrail Oceanic Ltd v Coleman (1981) CA

Due to a possible conflict of interest at work, the defendant decided that either the applicant or her husband had to be dismissed. As the applicant's husband was automatically regarded by the defendant as the 'breadwinner' of the family, she was dismissed.

Held, by the Court of Appeal, that this action was based on a general stereotypical assumption that men are more likely than women to be the primary supporters of their spouses and children, and was, therefore, inherently discriminatory.

Note ———————————————————————————

Also on discriminatory stereotypes, see *Hurley v Mustoe* (1981) and *Horsey v Dyfed County Council* (1982).

9.1.2   Race Relations Act 1976

Section 1   Racial discrimination

(1) A person discriminates against another in any circumstances relevant for the purposes of any provision of this Act if:

   (a) on racial grounds, he treats that other less favourably than he treats or would treat other persons; ...

Section 3   Meaning of 'racial grounds' ...

(1) In this Act, unless the context otherwise requires:

'racial grounds' means any of the following grounds, namely colour, race, nationality or ethnic or national origins ...

Mandla v Lee (1983) HL

An orthodox Sikh boy, required by the rules of his religion to wear a turban, was refused admission to school on the grounds that wearing a turban would breach the school's rules on uniform. Before the court could determine whether he had been discriminated against on racial grounds, it was necessary to ascertain whether he was a member of a 'racial or ethnic group' within the meaning of the Act.

Held, by the House of Lords, that Sikhs were members of an ethnic group, as the term 'ethnic' should be interpreted widely. *Per* Lord Fraser of Tullybelton:

For a group to constitute an ethnic group for the purposes of the Race Relations Act, it must regard itself, and be regarded by others, as a distinct community by virtue of certain characteristics. It is essential that there is:

(1) a long shared history, of which the group is conscious as distinguishing it from other groups, and the memory of which keeps it alive;

(2) a cultural tradition of its own, including family and social customs and manners, often, but not necessarily, associated with religious observance. In addition, there are other relevant characteristics, one or more of which will commonly be found and will help to distinguish the group from the secondary community;

(3) either a common geographical origin, or descent from a small number of common ancestors;

(4) a common language, not necessarily peculiar to the group;

(5) a common literature peculiar to the group;

(6) a common religion different from that of the neighbouring groups or from the general community surrounding it;

(7) a sense of being a minority or being an oppressed or a dominant group within a larger community.

Note

Also on racial/ethnic groups, see: *Seide v Gillette Industries* (1980) (Jews); *CRE v Dutton* (1989) (gipsies); *Gwynedd County Council v Jones* (1986) (Welsh); *Dawkins v Department of the Environment* (1993) (Rastafarians); and *Northern Joint Police Board v Power* (1997) (English).

Owen and Briggs v James (1982) CA

The applicant was a black female who was twice rejected for a job as a secretary with the defendant's organisation. The successful white candidate had inferior skills and qualifications. On appointment, the interviewer told the successful candidate 'why take on coloured girls when English girls are available?'. The defendant argued that, even if there had been racial prejudice, it was only one of several reasons why the applicant was not offered employment.

Held, by the Court of Appeal, that race need not be the only cause of the detriment, so long it was an important factor. On the evidence submitted, it was clear that, by refusing or deliberately omitting to offer the applicant employment, the defendants had treated the applicant less favourably than they had treated other persons of a different race.

Note ——————————————————————————————

Also, as an example of direct race discrimination, see *Weathersfield v Sargent* (1999), where the white complainant had resigned after being given an unlawful instruction to discriminate against blacks and Asians. The Court of Appeal held that an employee is unfavourably treated on 'racial grounds' if they are required to carry out a racially discriminatory policy, even though the instruction concerns others of a different racial group from the complainant. Thus, the words 'racial grounds' are capable of covering any action based on race.

Where employees allege they are being paid less than their colleagues of a different race for similar work, they may take an action for direct discrimination on the grounds they have suffered 'less favourable treatment' – see *Wakeman v Quick Corp* (1999) (where similar allegations are made due to sex discrimination, claims are based on the Equal Pay Act 1970 and associated EEC Articles and directives).

9.2 Indirect discrimination

9.2.1 Sex Discrimination Act 1975

Section 1   Sex discrimination against women

(1) A person discriminates against a women in any circumstances relevant for the purposes of any provision of this Act if:

(a) ...

(b) he applies to her a requirement or condition which he applies or would apply equally to a man, but:

(i)   which is such that the proportion of women who can comply with it is considerably smaller than the proportion of men who can comply with it; and

(ii) which he cannot show to be justifiable irrespective of the sex of the person to whom it is applied; and

(iii) which is to her detriment, because she cannot comply with it.

Price v Civil Service Commission (1978) EAT

To be eligible for recruitment into the civil service executive officer grade, all applicants had to be between the ages of 17–28. Mrs Price was a 35 year old mother, whose application was thus subsequently rejected.

Held, by the EAT, that, when applying s 1(b) of the Act, there is not always a need for the parties to submit detailed statistics to ascertain whether a requirement has a disproportionate effect on women; rather, a common sense approach to the issue may be taken. Consequently, the court accepted the applicant's 'common sense' argument that this age requirement was discriminatory, as fewer women than men could comply with it, since a larger number of women of that age group than men will be having, or bringing up, children.

Home Office v Holmes (1984) EAT

The applicant was an executive officer employed by the Immigration and Nationality Department of the Home Office. All employees on her grade were required to work full time. After a period of maternity leave, the plaintiff requested that she be allowed to return to work on a part time basis. The Home Office rejected her request.

Held, by the EAT, that: (I) the obligation on the plaintiff to work full time amounted to a 'requirement' or 'condition' for the purposes of the statute, as it was an essential term of her contract; (II) this was to her 'detriment' since, unless she went on working full time, she would be dismissed; (III) the employers had not been able to justify the requirement merely by the proposition that full time work was the common and accepted form of employment; (IV) as the proportion of women who could, in practical terms (due to their responsibilities in raising children), comply with the requirement to work full time was smaller than the proportion of men who could comply, the applicant had been indirectly discriminated against on the grounds of her sex.

Pearse v Bradford Metropolitan Council (1988) EAT

One requirement of eligibility to apply for the post of senior lecturer at Bradford college was that the applicant was a full time member of staff. The applicant claimed this requirement was indirectly discriminatory, as the proportion of women (21%) who could comply was significantly smaller than the proportion of men who could comply (46%).

Held, by the EAT, that the applicant had chosen the wrong pool for the comparison. As further qualifications were required for the post, the proper pool of comparison to ascertain whether the requirement of being employed full time had a disproportionate impact on women were those of both sexes with these additional qualifications.

Note

On the correct 'pool' for comparison, see, also, *Meer v London Borough of Tower Hamlets* (1988); *Jones v University of Manchester* (1993); and *London Underground Ltd v Edwards* (1998).

R v Secretary of State for Employment ex p Seymour Smith (1995) CA

The applicants challenged the qualifying period for claiming unfair dismissal, which had been increased in 1985 from one year to two years. They argued it was indirectly discriminatory towards women, as there were fewer women in the labour force who could comply with this requirement necessary in order to enjoy protection against unfair dismissal. The defendants argued, *inter alia,* that the increase in the threshold period was undertaken to encourage 'labour flexibility' and increase employment opportunities; it was therefore 'justified'.

Held, by the Court of Appeal, that: (I) for a presumption of indirect discrimination to arise, there must be a considerable difference in the number or percentage of one sex in the advantaged or disadvantaged group as against the other sex; (II) on the statistical evidence, for every 100 men who could meet the condition (of two years qualifying employment), only 88 women could; (III) this was a considerable distinction between the sexes; (IV) for the discriminatory legislation to be 'objectively justified', it must meet the aim of the social policy with effective measurable outcomes. There was no evidence that this was the case; (V) consequently, the adverse impact the qualifying qualifications had on women consisted of indirect sex discrimination and was incompatible with domestic legislation and the principle of equal treatment enshrined in the Equal Treatment Directive.

Note

This decision was appealed to the House of Lords, who sent the case, for a determination of this issue, to the ECJ. The ECJ failed to fully answer the question as to whether the two years' continuous service requirement was discriminatory. However, the issue is more of an academic question now that, since 1 June 1999, employment tribunals can hear claims of unfair dismissal by employees with one year of continuous service.

Meade-Hill v British Council (1995) CA

The applicant was employed as a manager for the defendant in London. Her contract of employment included a mobility clause, which stipulated that she could be expected to 'serve in such parts in the UK ... as the Council may in its discretion require ...'. Due to a re-organisation of head office, the defendant made it known that the applicant was expected to transfer to Manchester. The applicant issued proceedings in the county court for a declaration (pursuant to s 77 of the Sex Discrimination Act 1975) that the mobility clause was unenforceable on the grounds that it was indirectly discriminatory, as a greater proportion of women than men from the relevant pool were secondary earners and, therefore, less able or willing to move house.

Held, by the Court of Appeal (with Stuart Smith LJ dissenting), that the inclusion of this mobility clause into a contract of employment amounted to unlawful sex discrimination, since a higher proportion of women than men were secondary earners, so that, accordingly, a higher proportion of women than men would find it impossible to comply with the 'requirement' to move their workplace and home.

Q   In *Hampson v Department of Education and Science* (1989), the Court of Appeal held that, in determining whether a discriminatory condition is 'justifiable', an objective balance needs to be struck between the discriminatory effect of the condition and the reasonable needs of the party who applies the condition. With this judgment in mind, are there any circumstances where a flexibility or mobility clause would be 'justifiable' under the Act?

Coker and Osamor v The Lord Chancellor (1999)

The applicants were denied the opportunity to apply for the post of 'Special Advisor' to the Lord Chancellor, as it was not advertised and went to an individual known to the Lord Chancellor. They claimed they had been directly and indirectly discriminated against on grounds of sex (first applicant) and sex and race (second applicant).

Held, by the employment tribunal, that the first applicant (but not the second, due to her inability to meet the fundamental requirements) had been discriminated against by this process and had suffered a 'detriment' by being unable to apply for the position. The Lord Chancellor had imposed a 'requirement or condition' that the successful candidate must be personally known to him. This had a disproportionate impact as between men and women, as there were more men than women who were eligible for the position in the light of this criteria – appointment on the basis of personal knowledge. Where the overriding need is to appoint someone on merit (as here), this requirement could not be justified.

9.2.2 Race Relations Act 1976

Section 1   Racial discrimination

(1) A person discriminates against another in any circumstances relevant for the purposes of any provisions of this Act if:

(a) ...

(b) he applies to that other a requirement or condition which he applies or would apply equally to persons not of the same racial group as that other, but:

(i) which is such that the proportion of persons of the same racial group as that other who can comply with it is considerably smaller than the proportion of persons not of that racial group who can comply with it; and

(ii) which he cannot show to be justifiable irrespective of the colour, race, nationality or ethnic or national origins of the person to whom it is applied; and

(iii) which is to the detriment of that other because he cannot comply with it.

(2) It is hereby declared that, for the purposes of this Act, segregating a person from other persons on racial grounds is treating him less favourably than they are treated.

Section 3   Meaning of racial group

(1) In this Act, unless the context otherwise requires:

'racial group' means a group of persons defined by reference to colour, race, nationality or ethnic or national origins, and references to a person's racial group refer to any racial group into which he falls.

Perera v Civil Service Commission (1982) EAT

Perera was an executive officer in the civil service who had been born in Sri Lanka and emigrated to the UK as an adult. On a number of occasions, he had failed promotion boards, despite possessing several accountancy and legal qualifications. During proceedings alleging race discrimination, it was found that it was a civil service practice that an upper age limit of 32 was applied for promotions from Perera's grade.

Held, by the EAT, that the age limit was a requirement or condition that had an indirectly discriminatory effect, as a substantial number of black people who emigrated to Britain did so as adults; thus, a considerably smaller percentage of blacks than whites could comply with that age requirement.

Discrimination in employment

9.3.1 Race Relations Act 1976

Section 4 Discrimination against applicants and employees

(1) It is unlawful for a person, in relation to employment by him at an establishment in Great Britain, to discriminate against another:

(a) in the arrangements he makes for the purpose of determining who should be offered that employment; or

(b) in the terms on which he offers him that employment; or

(c) by refusing or deliberately omitting to offer him that employment.

(2) It is unlawful for a person, in the case of a person employed by him at an establishment in Great Britain, to discriminate against that employee:

(a) in the terms of employment which he affords him; or

(b) in the way he affords him access to opportunities for promotion, transfer or training, or to any other benefits, facilities or services, or by refusing or deliberately omitting to afford him access to them; or

(c) by dismissing him, or subjecting him to any other detriment.

De Souza v Automobile Association (1986) CA

The applicant, of Indian descent, had overheard one of her managers refer to her as 'the wog'. She contended that this was a racial insult, which constituted 'a detriment' within the meaning of s 4(2)(c) of the Race Relations Act 1976.

Held, by the Court of Appeal, that the expression 'some other detriment' should be given a wide meaning and so was not limited to where the applicant suffered tangible harm such as demotion or dismissal. It included situations where a worker is subject to a disadvantage because racial slurs have created a hostile working environment. However, it would have to be shown by the applicant that it had been intended for her to hear the abusive comment and that, having heard it, a reasonable employee in the plaintiff's position would have felt disadvantaged at work.

Q Should injury to feelings *per se* be considered an adequate detriment for the purposes of the legislation?

Eke v Commissioners of Customs and Excise (1981) EAT

The applicant was employed as an executive officer. Throughout his career, he was denied promotion. In one of his promotion reports, it was recorded that the applicant was the subject of racial prejudice by his colleagues, which may have affected the views of his superiors. At no time did his employers institute an investigation of the alleged prejudice.

Held, by the EAT, that the defendant's refusal to investigate complaints of unfair treatment may amount to a refusal of access to 'any other benefits, facilities or services' within the meaning of s 4(2)(b), so long as the refusal to investigate is itself on 'racial grounds'.

Note ───

Section 6 of the Sex Discrimination Act 1975 (repeating the terminology of s 4 of the Race Relations Act 1976) also provides that it is unlawful for an employer to discriminate against a woman on the grounds of her sex in employment (see *Saunders v Richmond Upon Thames Borough Council* (1977)).

9.4   Exceptions

9.4.1   Race Relations Act 1976

Section 5   Exceptions for genuine occupational qualifications

(1) In relation to racial discrimination:

(a) s 4(1)(a) or (c) does not apply to any employment where being of a particular racial group is a genuine occupational qualification for the job; and

(b) s 4(2)(b) does not apply to opportunities for promotion or transfer to, or training for, such employment.

(2) Being of a particular racial group is a genuine occupational qualification for a job only where:

(a) the job involves participation in a dramatic performance or other entertainment in a capacity for which a person of that racial group is required for reasons of authenticity; or

(b) the job involves participation as an artist's or photographic model in the production of a work of art, visual image or sequence of visual images for which a person of that racial group is required for reasons of authenticity; or

(c) the job involves working in a place where food or drink is provided to and consumed by members of the public or a section of the public in a particular setting for which, in that job, a person of that racial group is required for reasons of authenticity; or

(d) the holder of the job provides persons of that racial group with personal services promoting their welfare, and those services can most effectively be provided by a person of that racial group.

Tottenham Green Under Fives Centre v Marshall (1989) EAT

A children's day care centre, financed by the London Borough of Haringey, had a policy of maintaining an ethnic balance amongst staff and children. In pursuance of this policy, on an Afro-Caribbean worker leaving, the recruitment advert specified that the post was open only to persons of the same race. Mr Marshall was rejected by the defendant because of his ethnic origin. The defendant argued that s 5(2)(d) applied, as the holder of the post would be required to provide personal services, such as reading and talking to the children in dialect.

Held, by the EAT, that being of Afro-Caribbean origin was a genuine occupational qualification for the post of nursery worker within s 5(2)(d). *Per* Wood J:

> ... whether services can most effectively be provided by a person of that racial group is an issue for the tribunal that needs to carry out a delicate balancing exercise, bearing in mind the need to guard against discrimination and the desirability of promoting racial integration ... if a responsible employer makes a conscious decision to commit an act of discrimination founded upon a genuinely and reasonably held belief that a genuine occupational requirement will best promote the welfare of the recipient, considerable weight should be given to that decision when reaching a conclusion whether or not the defence succeeds.

London Borough of Lambeth v CRE (1990) CA

The council advertised two posts in its housing department, stating that the posts were open only to Afro-Caribbean and Asian candidates. The council argued that the exception (of genuine occupational qualification) contained in s 5(2)(d) applied, as over half of the council tenants were of Afro-Caribbean or Asian racial origin, and that housing services could be more sensitively and effectively promoted to these groups by black employees.

Held, by the Court of Appeal, that, although the local authority housing department provide 'services' that benefit the recipients, it could not be said that these services were 'personal' within the ordinary plain meaning of the word. 'Personal' indicates that the services are provided at an individual face to face level and that the identity of the giver and recipient of the services is of importance. Although the particular posts advertised did require knowledge of, and sensitivity to, ethnic minorities, the method adopted to achieve this was unlawful.

Note ───

Section 7 of the Sex Discrimination Act 1975 also permits discrimination where the sex (as opposed to the race) of the applicant is a genuine occupational qualification for the post. Genuine occupational qualifications under the Sex Discrimination Act include where the nature of the job calls for a man for reasons of physiology (but excluding physical strength or stamina); authenticity in dramatic performances; to preserve decency or privacy; where the holder of the job provides personal services promoting welfare and education and these services can most effectively be provided by a man, and where the job involves duties outside the UK and a women could not effectively perform the duties concerned, due to the laws and customs of that country. See, further, *Sisley v Britannia Security Systems* (1983), *Etam plc v Rowan* (1989) and *Lasertop Ltd v Webster* (1997).

9.5 Vicarious liability and liability for the actions of a third party

9.5.1 Race Relations Act 1976

Section 32 Liability of employers and principals
(1) Anything done by a person in the course of his employment shall be treated for the purposes of this Act as done by his employer as well as by him, whether or not it was done with the employer's knowledge or approval.

(2) Anything done by a person as agent for another person with the authority (whether express or implied, and whether precedent or subsequent) of that other person shall be treated for the purposes of this Act as done by that other person as well as by him.

(3) In proceedings brought under this Act against any person in respect of an act alleged to have been done by an employee of his, it shall be a defence for that person to prove that he took such steps as were reasonably practicable to prevent the employee from doing that act, or from doing in the course of employment acts of that description.

Note
A similar provision is contained in s 41 of the Sex Discrimination Act 1975. On this, see *Waters v Commissioner of Police of the Metropolis* (1997); *Chief Constable of Lincolnshire v Stubbs* (1999); and *ST v North Yorkshire County Council* (1999).

Jones v Tower Boot Co Ltd (1997) CA
The applicant had suffered severe racial abuse at the hands of fellow employees and had also been subjected to racially motivated assaults, including being branded with a hot screwdriver and whipped. The EAT held, following *Irving v Post Office* (1987), that the perpetrators were not

engaged in this activity in the 'course of employment', but were classically engaged on a 'frolic of their own' and, consequently, the employer was not liable for the discriminatory harassment.

Held, by the Court of Appeal, that the common law test of employer's vicarious liability applied in the the law of tort was now inappropriate in determining liability under the Race Relations Act 1976. *Per* Waite LJ:

> It would be particularly wrong to allow racial harassment on the scale that was suffered by the complainant in this case at the hands of his workmates – treatment that was wounding both emotionally and physically – to slip through the net of employer responsibility by applying to it a common law principle evolved in another area of the law to deal with vicarious responsibility for wrongdoing of a wholly different kind. To do so would seriously undermine the statutory scheme of the Discrimination Acts and flout the purposes which they were passed to achieve ... [otherwise] the more heinous the act of discrimination, the less likely it would be that the employer would be liable.

Waite LJ continued by stressing that an employer was liable for all actions by employees, whether or not committed with the employer's knowledge or approval, unless the employer was able to satisfy the 'reasonable steps' defence contained in s 32(3).

Q   Would the existence of an equal opportunities policy at the workplace be sufficient to satisfy the 'reasonable steps' defence?

Burton v De Vere Hotels (1996) EAT

The plaintiff was engaged as a waitress at the defendant's hotel. During the after dinner speech of a third party, the plaintiff was distressed and upset by racially motivated 'jokes' and comments directed at herself and colleagues. The plaintiff argued that the employer was responsible for placing her in a discriminatory environment created by the conduct of the third party invited onto the employer's premises.

Held, by the EAT, that the general principle is that an employer 'subjects' an employee to the 'detriment' of racial harassment within the meaning of s 4(2)(c), 'if he causes or permits the racial harassment to occur in circumstances in which he can control whether it happens or not'. An industrial tribunal should ask itself whether:

> ... [the employer,] by the application of good employment practices, could have prevented the harassment or reduced the extent of it[?] If there is such a finding, then the employer has subjected the employee to the harassment.

In these circumstances, the employer was responsible for the actions of the third party invited on to his premises, as he was in a position to take steps to stop the harassment from continuing.

Note

On the reasonable steps defence, see *Balgobin v London Borough of Tower Hamlets* (1987).

Sidhu v Aerospace Composite Technology Ltd (1999)

Mr Sidhu was the victim of a racially motivated assault by another employee at a day outing organised by the employer. After an investigation, both Mr Sidhu (who had taken action to defend himself) and the other employee were dismissed.

Held, by the EAT, that the employer was liable for the racial assault, as the incident was still 'in the course of employment' for the purposes of s 32(1) of the Race Relations Act, even though it took place outside of the employer's premises. Furthermore, the employer had discriminated against the applicant by taking a deliberate decision to ignore the fact that the assault was racially motivated when investigating the matter, and by taking the decision that the applicant should be dismissed due to his own involvement in the incident.

9.6   Procedure and proof

R v Birmingham City Council ex p EOC (1989) HL

Birmingham City Council operated single sex grammar schools. As there were more places available for boys than girls, the council set a higher pass mark for girls than boys in the grammar school entrance examination. It was argued that this was a discriminatory act, notwithstanding the submission that the council had no discriminatory motive or intention.

Held, by the House of Lords, that, although the intention or motive of the defendant to discriminate is strong evidence of discrimination and relevant as an aid to the applicant in discharging their burden of proof, it is not a necessary condition for liability *per se*. *Per* Lord Goff:

> The intention or motive of the defendant to discriminate, though it may be relevant so far as remedies (or proof) are concerned ... is not a necessary condition to liability; it is perfectly possible to envisage cases where the defendant had no such motive, and yet did in fact discriminate on the ground of sex.

O'Neill v Governors of St Thomas More School (1996) EAT

The applicant was an unmarried teacher of religious education at a Roman Catholic school, who became pregnant following a relationship with a Roman Catholic priest and was subsequently dismissed. The industrial tribunal found that this did not amount to sex discrimination, as one of the important motives for the dismissal was that the pregnancy resulted from with a priest (rather than a layperson), which had seriously ~putation as a teacher of religious education.

Held, by the EAT, that the tribunal had misapplied the law. The tribunal should have applied an objective test, ignoring the subjective motive for the dismissal. So long as the pregnancy 'precipitated and permeated the decision to dismiss', then this, as the cause of the dismissal, was, *prima facie*, unlawful discrimination.

Note
On intention and motive, see, also, *Nagarajan v London Regional Transport* (1999).

West Midlands Transport Executive v Singh (1988) CA

The applicant was a ticket inspector employed by the defendants. He alleged racial discrimination in the process of selection for promotion when he failed to be promoted after 13 vacancies for senior inspector fell vacant. The employers denied racial discrimination and referred to their equal opportunities policy, adopted in 1983. The applicant requested discovery of statistics relating to the application of this policy, from which to establish evidence of racial discrimination in the past, and to thereby draw an inference of discrimination in the present case.

Held, by the Court of Appeal, that a tribunal is entitled to order discovery of documents that record the sex or racial breakdown of the workforce and the qualifications of job applicants and to order the discovery of statistics of the numbers of white and non-white persons who had applied for similar posts in the past. This information was relevant to the complaint, as it may establish a pattern in the treatment of a particular group relevant to this case and enables a tribunal to scrutinise the employer's contention that they operate an effective equal opportunities policy and so do not discriminate.

King v Great Britain China Centre (1991) CA

The applicant was born in China, but educated in England. She had applied for the post of deputy director of the Centre, a Government sponsored organisation. The advert for the post specified that applicants must have excellent knowledge of China and be a fluent Chinese speaker. She was not shortlisted for the post. All the candidates were white UK graduates. The employer failed to provide an adequate explanation as to why the applicant had not been called for interview.

Held, by the Court of Appeal, that this amounted to sufficient evidence that the applicant had been unlawfully discriminated against on the grounds of her race. The Court of Appeal laid down the following guidelines on the question of the drawing of an inference of discrimination to discharge the applicant's burden of proof. *Per* Neil LJ:

(1) It is for the applicant who complains of racial discrimination to make out his or her case. Thus, if the applicant does not prove the case on the balance of probabilities, he or she will fail.

(2) It is important to bear in mind that it is unusual to find direct evidence of racial discrimination. Few employers will be prepared to admit to such discrimination even to themselves. In some cases, the discrimination will not be ill intentioned but merely based on an assumption that 'he or she would not have fitted in'.

(3) The outcome of the case will therefore usually depend on what inferences it is proper to draw from the primary facts found by the tribunal. These inferences can include, in appropriate circumstances, any inferences that it is just and equitable to draw in accordance with s 65(2)(b) of the Act of 1976 from an evasive or equivocal reply to a questionnaire.

(4) Though there will be some cases where, for example, the non-selection of the applicant for a post or for promotion is clearly not on racial grounds, a finding of discrimination and a finding of a difference in race will often point to the possibility of racial discrimination. In such circumstances, the tribunal will look to the employer for an explanation. If no explanation is then put forward, or if the tribunal considers the explanation to be inadequate or unsatisfactory, it will be legitimate for the tribunal to infer that the discrimination was on racial grounds. This is not a matter of law but ... 'almost common sense'.

(5) It is unnecessary and unhelpful to introduce the concept of a shifting evidential burden of proof. At the conclusion of all the evidence, the tribunal should make findings as to the primary facts and draw such inferences as they consider proper from those facts. They should then reach a conclusion on the balance of probabilities, bearing in mind both the difficulties which face a person who complains of unlawful discrimination and the fact that it is for the complainant to prove his or her case.

Qureshi v London Borough of Newham (1991) CA

Qureshi was an Asian teacher of physics. He applied and was shortlisted for the post of head of science. He was unsuccessful in his application. During the selection process, the borough's equal opportunities procedures were not followed. The tribunal upheld the applicant's assertion that he had been unlawfully discriminated against due to the defendant's failure to follow selection procedures.

Held, by the Court of Appeal, that a failure on the part of an employer to take proper steps to counter racial discrimination by failing to comply with their own equal opportunities policy can be evidence from which unlawful prejudice may be inferred. However, this cannot be implied here, as these failures were not deliberate and were more the product of incompetence than racial prejudice.

Chapman v Simon (1994) CA

The applicant, a black teacher, was engaged in a protracted dispute with her head teacher over a previous dispute that the applicant had had with a colleague. The applicant was reported by the head teacher to the local education authority and formally disciplined. It was argued that this was racially discriminatory, as a white teacher would not have been treated in a similar manner; an informal resolution of the dispute would have been attempted first. The industrial tribunal found for the applicant on the grounds that 'subconsciously or unconsciously', the headteacher had been affected and influenced in her actions by the colour of the applicant.

Held, by the Court of Appeal, that: (I) in order to make an inference of racial discrimination, it is essential to make findings of primary fact from which it is legitimate to make that inference. This had not been the case here, where an unsupported conclusion of subconscious prejudice had been made; (II) the jurisdiction of the tribunal is limited to adjudicating on actual complaints made by the applicant. If those complaints are not made out, it is not for the tribunal to find other acts of discrimination unrelated to the original complaint.

Note ───────────────────────────────────────

See, also, on inference of discrimination: *Chattopadhyay v Headmaster of Holloway School* (1981); *Noone v North West Thames Regional Health Authority* (1988); *Baker v Cornwall County Council* (1990); *Leicester University Students' Union v Mahomed* (1995); *Glasgow City Council v Zafar* (1998); and *Robson v Commissioners of Inland Revenue* (1998).

9.7 Remedies

9.7.1 Race Relations Act 1976

Section 54

(1) Where an industrial tribunal finds that a complaint is well founded, the tribunal shall make such as the following as it considers just and equitable:

(a) ...

(b) an order requiring the respondent to pay to the complainant compensation of an amount corresponding to any damages he could have been ordered by a county court or by a sheriff court to pay to the complainant if the complaint had fallen to be dealt with under s 57.

Section 56

(1) A claim by any person that another person:

(a) has committed an act of discrimination against the claimant which is unlawful by virtue of Pt 3; ...

may be made the subject of civil proceedings in like manner as any other claim in tort or (in Scotland) in reparation for breach of statutory duty ...

(3) As respects an unlawful act of discrimination falling within s 1(1)(b), no award of damages shall be made if the respondent proves that the requirement or condition in question was not applied with the intention of treating the claimant unfavourably on racial grounds

(4) For the avoidance of doubt, it is hereby declared that damages in respect of an unlawful act of discrimination may include compensation for injury to feelings, whether or not they include compensation under any other head.

HM Prison Service v Johnson (1997) EAT

A black prison officer had been subjected to a racist campaign by fellow prison officers, designed to humiliate him in order to force his resignation. The industrial tribunal granted an award of £28,000, of which £21,000 was for injury to feelings.

Held, by the EAT, that the award for injury to feelings was not excessive when compared to the size of damages obtained by plaintiffs suing for injury to reputation in the tort of defamation. The EAT further provided guidelines for industrial tribunals to follow on the question of compensation for injury to feelings in race discrimination cases:

(1) Awards for injury to feelings are purely compensatory. They should not be inflated in order to punish the tortfeasor.

(2) However, awards should not be so low that they would diminish respect for the legislation which clearly condemns discrimination.

(3) Awards should bear some similarity to the range of awards in personal injury cases.

(4) In exercising their discretion in assessing a sum, tribunals should remind themselves of the value in everyday life of the sum they have in mind. This may be done by reference to purchasing power or by reference to earnings.

Although the statutory ceiling of £11,000 damages for race discrimination was lifted in 1994 (see the Race Relations (Remedies) Act), it is still the case that, where unintentional indirect discrimination occurs, no damages are recoverable. However, it is the employer who must satisfy the burden of establishing that the requirement or condition was not applied with the intention of treating the applicant less favourably (see *JH Walker v Hussain* (1996)). Furthermore, in *De Souza v London Borough of Lambeth* (1999), the Court of Appeal held that the Race Relations (Remedies) Act only applied to cases initiated after that Act came into force. Thus, Mr De Souza, was unable to enforce the award of £358,288 handed down by the EAT in 1997, as the original tribunal complaint was made in 1990.

Note ——————————————————————

Until 1993, compensation levels for sex discrimination were also limited to £11,000. As a consequence of the decision of the the ECJ in *Marshall v Southampton and South West Hampshire Health Authority (No 2)* – that a limitation on compensation was contrary to Art 6 of the Equal Treatment Directive – the Sex Discrimination and Equal Pay (Remedies) Regulations 1993 formally removed the ceiling on compensation for sex discrimination. As a consequence, numerous claims have been made, resulting in compensation payments in excess of the old limits. See, further, *Ministry of Defence v Cannock* (1994) and *Orlando v Didcot Power Station Sports and Social Club* (1996).

9.8 Discrimination and European Community law

9.8.1 The Equal Treatment Directive (76/207/EEC)

Article 1

1 The purpose of this Directive is to put into effect in the Member States the principle of equal treatment for men and women as regards access to employment, including promotion, and to vocational training and as regards working conditions and ... social security. This principle is hereinafter referred to as 'the principle of equal treatment'.

...

Article 2

1 For the purposes of the following provisions, the principle of equal treatment shall mean that there shall be no discrimination whatsoever

on grounds of sex, either directly or indirectly, by reference in particular to marital or family status.

Article 3

1 Application of the principle of equal treatment means that there shall be no discrimination whatsoever on grounds of sex in the conditions, including selection criteria, for access to all jobs or posts, whatever the sector or branch of activity, and to all levels of the occupational hierarchy.

Article 4

...

Article 5

1 Application of the principle of equal treatment with regard to working conditions including the conditions governing dismissal, means that men and women shall be guaranteed the same conditions without discrimination on grounds of sex ...

Note

This Directive is wider than UK domestic law, as it does not seek to limit protection by requiring a comparative approach to the position of a man, and the exceptions to it are more limited than those contained in the Sex Discrimination Act. Consequently, plaintiffs have attempted to either apply this directive directly (see *Marshall*, below) or have argued that the provisions of domestic law on discrimination ought to be interpreted in the light of the Directive (see *Webb*, below).

Marshall v Southampton and South West Hampshire Area Health Authority (1986) ECJ

The defendant health authority, in pursuance of their retirement policy, dismissed the plaintiff, Marshall, as she had reached the normal State retirement age of 60. She would not have been dismissed if she had been a man, as men did not have to retire until they reached the age of 65. Marshall framed her claim under Community law, as the Sex Discrimination Act 1975 (at the time) permitted discrimination on grounds of sex arising from a provision in relation to retirement. The Court of Appeal applied to the ECJ for a ruling as to whether Marshall's dismissal was an act of discrimination prohibited by the directive and, if so, whether or not the directive could be relied upon in these circumstances, in a national court or tribunal.

Held, by the ECJ, that: (I) a dismissal of a women solely because she had reached the State retirement age (which is different for men), contravened Art 5(1) of the Directive; (II) this matter did not fall within any of the exclusions provided by the Directive, nor did the social security Directive, which permits discrimination in the area of pensions affect this determination; (III) where the national provision does not conform with the requirements of the Directive, the Directive could be relied upon by individuals against any State employer or any emanation of the State, such as, in this case, a health authority.

Note ───

The meaning of the expression 'emanation of the State' is discussed further by the European Court of Justice and by the House of Lords in *Foster v British Gas* (1990).

Webb v EMO Air Cargo (UK) Ltd (1994) ECJ

The plaintiff was an employee who was trained by the defendant company to take over the duties of an employee temporarily on maternity leave. When it became known that the plaintiff was herself pregnant, and therefore unable to cover for the absent employee, she was dismissed. Section 5(3) of the Sex Discrimination Act requires that any comparison of the cases of persons of different sex must be such that the relevant circumstances in the one case are the same, or not materially different in the other. If circumstances are materially different, there can be no complaint of sex discrimination. It was thus argued by the defendant that either: (i) there was no male equivalent of a pregnant woman, making the comparison required by s 5(3) impossible (as was decided in *Turley v Allders Department Stores Ltd* (1980)); or (ii) if a comparison could be made, with the hypothetical sick man who is absent for a similar length of time (see *Hayes v Malleable Working Men's Club* (1985)), then, as the defendant would have treated a sick man in exactly the same way, by dismissing him, there was no discernible discrimination in this case.

The EAT and the Court of Appeal both agreed with the latter argument and so dismissed the plaintiff's appeal from the industrial tribunal. The House of Lords referred the matter of whether this dismissal violated Art 2(1) of the Equal Treatment Directive to the ECJ for a preliminary ruling.

Held, by the ECJ (applying their judgment in *Hertz* (1991) and *Dekker v VJV Centrum* (1991)), that:

... in circumstances such as those of Mrs Webb, termination of a contract for an indefinite period on grounds of the women's pregnancy cannot be justified by the fact that she is prevented, on a purely temporary basis, from performing the work for which she has been engaged. There can be no question of comparing the situation of a woman who finds herself incapable, by reason of pregnancy discovered very shortly after the conclusion of the employment contract, of performing the task for which she was recruited, with that of a man similarly incapable for medical or other reasons ... pregnancy is not in any way comparable with a pathological condition, and is even less so with unavailability for work on non-medical grounds, both of which are situations that may justify the dismissal of a woman without discriminating on the grounds of sex.

Note
UK courts have accepted the argument that they are under an obligation to interpret the domestic law, as far as possible, in the light of the wording and purpose of the relevant piece of European law (see *Marleasing SA v La Comercial Internacional de Alimentacion* (1992) and *Litster v Forth Dry Dock Ltd* (1989)). In *Webb v EMO Air Cargo Ltd (No 2)* (1995), the House of Lords attempted to reconcile the domestic law on discrimination with the ECJ's guidance on the Equal Treatment Directive. They held that, where pregnancy is a relevant circumstance in the treatment of a woman, then that amounts to a gender based criterion, which is automatically to be viewed as sex discrimination, as *but for* her sex, the women would not have been subjected to that treatment. *Per* Lord Keith:

... in a case where a woman is engaged for an indefinite period, the fact that the reason why she will be temporarily unavailable for work at a time when to her knowledge her services will be particularly required is pregnancy, is a circumstance relevant to her case, being a circumstance which would not be present in the case of the hypothetical man.

Q   Do you agree with Lord Keith's further observation (in *Webb*) that, if an employer were to be liable for unlawful sex discrimination for a dismissal where the employment was only to be for a temporary period, that 'would be likely to be perceived as unfair to employers and as tending to bring the law on sex discrimination into disrepute'? Are there any provisions in the Equal Treatment Directive to justify Lord Keith's belief (and that of the other Law Lords) that this exception exists?

Note
On the issue of the non-renewal of a fixed term contract on grounds of pregnancy, see *Caruana v Manchester Airport plc* (1996).

Brown v Rentokill Ltd (1998) ECJ
The applicant was absent from work from the beginning of her pregnancy, due to a variety of pregnancy-related illnesses. In accordance with the employer's rules, she was dismissed, as she had exceeded 26 weeks of sickness absence. It was argued by the defendant employer that the ECJ's decision in *Webb* on the Equal Treatment Directive did not apply here, as the relevant circumstance that lead to her dismissal was her illness – the

precise reason for the illness was not relevant. There was a distinction between dismissal due to illness caused by pregnancy and dismissal due to pregnancy *per se*. The Court of Session held (applying *dicta* of the ECJ in *Hertz* (1991) that, where sickness arises after maternity leave, there is no reason to treat this any differently from general illness) that there had been no discrimination. The plaintiff had been treated in the same way as a man would have been treated in comparable circumstances.

Held, by the ECJ, that dismissal of a woman at any time during her pregnancy for absences due to incapacity for work, caused by an illness resulting from that pregnancy, is direct discrimination on grounds of sex, contrary to the EC Equal Treatment Directive.

Note ──────────────
See, also, *Lewis Woolf Ltd v Corfield* (1997) and *Thibault* (1998).

Note ──────────────
In *Abbey National v Formoso* (1999), it was held by the EAT, following the ECJ's decision in *Brown*, that an employee had suffered a detriment and so was discriminated against on grounds of her sex where she was dismissed following a disciplinary hearing which she was incapable of attending, due to a pregnancy-related illness.

Rees v Apollo Watch Repairs (1996) EAT

To cover for the applicant's maternity leave, the employers engaged a third party as a replacement. As they subsequently found the replacement to be a more efficient worker, the applicant was dismissed. The employer argued that the cause of dismissal was the efficiency of the replacement, not the pregnancy of the applicant. The tribunal concluded that, since a man in comparable circumstances would also have been dismissed, there was no unlawful discrimination.

Held, by the EAT, that the tribunal had applied the wrong test by comparing her position with a hypothetical man. What was relevant was the underlying and effective cause of the dismissal. Pregnancy was the predominant cause; if the applicant had not been absent on maternity leave, she would not have been dismissed. This clearly, therefore, constituted discrimination on the grounds of sex.

Note ──────────────
Where an employee is on maternity leave but is unable to return to work on the due date due to pregnancy-related illness, a dismissal in these circumstances would be unfair (see s 99, below) and discriminatory – *Caledonia Bureau of Investment and Property v Caffrey* (1998) and *Halfpenny v Ige Medical Systems Ltd* (1999).

Note

There are further domestic and European provisions protecting the position of pregnant women. The Pregnant Workers Directive 92/85/EEC requires women to be protected from dismissal 'during the period from the beginning of their pregnancy to the end of the maternity leave ... save in exceptional circumstances not connected with their condition ...'. In order to comply with this Directive, s 99 of the Employment Rights Act 1996 provides that it is automatically unfair to dismiss a female employee for a reason connected to their pregnancy, childbirth or maternity leave. The compensation provisions under this Act are, however, less generous than under the Sex Discrimination Act. On the issue of discriminatory pay on grounds of pregnancy, note the application of Art 119 and the Equal Pay Directive in *Kuickly Shrive* (1999).

9.9 Discrimination on grounds of sexual orientation

R v Ministry of Defence ex p Smith (1996) CA

The applicant was a serving member of the armed forces, who had been administratively discharged pursuant to the Ministry of Defence policy that homosexuality was incompatible with service in the armed forces. In proceedings for a judicial review of the decision, the applicant argued it was contrary to Art 8 of the European Convention on Human Rights and Art 2 of the Equal Treatment Directive (76/207/EEC).

Held, by the Court of Appeal, that: (I) the expression 'sex' within Directive 76/207 does not include sexual orientation, but was limited to gender discrimination. Therefore, the Ministry's policy prohibiting homosexuals from serving in the armed services could not be challenged as a breach of the Equal Treatment Directive; (II) since the UK's obligation under Art 8 of the European Convention is not enforceable by domestic courts, it is not apposite for the court to enter into examination of the question of whether the ban represents a breach of this Article.

P v S and Cornwall County Council (1996) ECJ

The applicant was employed as a male general manager of an educational unit by the local authority. When the applicant informed the defendant that she intended to have a gender reassignment, she was given three months notice of dismissal. The industrial tribunal considered that, although the Sex Discrimination Act did not apply to these circumstances, the Equal Treatment Directive, with its wider form of wording, may be applicable. Accordingly, it referred the issue of whether a person dismissed because of transsexuality can rely on the Equal Treatment Directive, to the ECJ.

Held, by the ECJ, that the principle of equal treatment for men and women means that there should be 'no discrimination whatsoever on grounds of sex' and is the expression of the principle of equality which is one of the fundamental principles of community law:

> Accordingly, the scope of the Directive cannot be confined simply to discrimination based on the fact that a person is one or the other sex. In view of its purpose and the nature of the rights which it seeks to safeguard, the scope of the Directive is also such as to apply to discrimination arising, as in this case, from the gender reassignment of the person concerned ... therefore, dismissal of a transsexual for a reason related to gender reassignment must be regarded as contrary to Art 5(1) of the Directive.

Note ——————————————————————————

The EAT in *Chessington World of Adventures v Reed* (1997) applied the reasoning of the ECJ in *P v S and Cornwall County Council* (1996) to find that discrimination for a reason related to gender reassignment is sex discrimination contrary to the Sex Discrimination Act 1975, as the Sex Discrimination Act must be interpreted in a manner consistent with the purpose of the Directive.

R v Secretary of State for Defence ex p Perkins (1997) HC

The applicant was a Royal Navy medical assistant who was discharged by the Navy for his known homosexual orientation. He challenged this established policy of the Ministry of Defence by bringing judicial review proceedings, seeking a reference to the ECJ that discrimination based on sexual orientation was contrary to the Equal Treatment Directive 76/207/EEC.

Held, by the High Court, that, in the light of the opinion of the Advocate General and the decision of the ECJ in *P v S and Cornwall County Council* (1996) that asserted the fundamental principle of equality, it was likely that the Equal Treatment Directive did protect those of homosexual orientation. Thus, as there was an arguable case that the application of the Directive was not restricted to gender discrimination, the question of whether the protection of the Equal Treatment Directive includes discrimination on grounds of sexual orientation should be referred to the ECJ for a preliminary ruling.

Note ——————————————————————————

See, also, *Grant v South West Trains Ltd* (1998). The applicant was a lesbian who was denied travel concessions for her female partner granted to other employees who had partners of the opposite sex. The ECJ held that there had been no breach of Art 119 (on equal pay), or of the Equal Pay Directive, as European Community law does not cover discrimination based on sexual orientation.

9.10 Disability Discrimination Act 1995

Section 1   Meaning of 'disability' and 'disabled person'

(1) Subject to the provisions of Sched 1, a person has a disability for the purposes of this Act if he has a physical or mental impairment which has a substantial and long term adverse effect on his ability to carry out normal day to day activities.

(2) In this Act, 'disabled person' means a person who has a disability.

Note ————————————————————————————————

By Sched 1, para 1(1), a 'mental impairment' includes clinically recognised mental illness, but excludes certain personality disorders and an addiction to alcohol, nicotine or 'any other substances'. Also, see the Disability Discrimination (Meaning of Disability) Regulations 1996 (SI 1996/1455); the Secretary of State's Guidance on sub-s (1) and Sched 1, para 4(1) of the Act. They all further elaborate on matters to be taken into account in determining whether an impairment 'has a substantial and long term adverse effect on his ability to carry out normal day to day activities'. For example, under Sched 1, para 4(1), an impairment affects the ability of a person to carry out 'normal day to day activities' only if it affects the following – mobility, manual dexterity, physical co-ordination, continence, ability to lift, speech, hearing or eyesight, memory or ability to concentrate and perception of the risk of physical danger. Some impairments will automatically be treated as an impairment for the purposes of the section, for example, severe disfigurement, progressive diseases, conditions that require regular medication, use of prosthesis, etc. Recent cases have established that ME (myalgic encephalomyelitis) is a disability: *O'Neill v Simm & Co Ltd* (1998), as is MS (multiple sclerosis): *Buxton v Equinox Design Ltd* (1999)).

Goodwin v The Patent Office (1999)

The applicant, who was a paranoid schizophrenic, was dismissed from his post after complaints by other staff about his disturbing behaviour.

Held, by the EAT, that the applicant was a 'disabled person' within the meaning of the Disability Discrimination Act. The statutory definition of disability requires an applicant to show that they have an impairment which has a substantial and long term adverse effect on their abilities to carry out normal day to day activities. As the applicant could hardly carry out an ordinary conversation with work colleagues, this was evidence that his ability to concentrate and communicate was substantially impaired. Thus, his capacity to function at work on a day to day basis had been significantly and sufficiently adversely affected by his disability, for the purposes of satisfying s 1.

Note ───
On the application of the definition of 'disability' within the Act, see, also, *Vicary v British Telecommunications plc* (1999).

Section 2   Past disabilities

(1) The provisions of this Part ... apply in relation to a person who has had a disability as they apply in relation to a person who has that disability.

(2) Those provisions are subject to the modifications made by Sched 2 ...

Note ───
By Sched 2, para 5, the definition of 'disabled person' includes someone who has had a qualifying disability in the past, so long as the effects lasted 12 months or more after the first occurrence. On the construction of s 2 and Sched 2, see *Greenwood v British Airways plc* (1999).

Section 4   Discrimination against applicants and employees

(1) It is unlawful for an employer to discriminate against a disabled person –

(a) in the arrangements which he makes for the purpose of determining to whom he should offer employment;

(b) in the terms on which he offers that person employment; or

(c) by refusing to offer, or deliberately not offering, him employment.

(2) It is unlawful for an employer to discriminate against a disabled person whom he employs:

(a) in the terms of employment which he affords him;

(b) in the opportunities which he affords him for promotion, a transfer, training or receiving any other benefit; or

(c) by refusing to afford him, or deliberately not affording him, any such opportunity; or

(d) by dismissing him, or subjecting him to any other detriment

(3)–(6) ...

Note ───
A Code of Practice has been issued advising employers how to avoid discriminating against disabled staff. This Code provides general guidance and may be taken into account by an employment tribunal or court when deliberating on breaches of the Act.

Section 5   Meaning of 'discrimination'

(1) For the purposes of this Part, an employer discriminates against a disabled person if:

    (a) for a reason which relates to the disabled person's disability, he treats him less favourably than he treats or would treat others to whom that reason does not or would not apply; and

    (b) he cannot show that the treatment in question is justified.

(2) ... an employer also discriminates against a disabled person if:

    (a) he fails to comply with a s 6 duty imposed on him in relation to the disabled person; and

    (b) he cannot show that his failure to comply with that duty is justified.

Note ———

Discriminatory treatment is only justified if 'the reason for it is both material to the circumstances of the particular case and substantial' (s 5(3)(4)). The Code of Practice gives examples where justification is not available as a defence, such as where the disabled person was discriminated against because of generalised assumptions about his or her abilities, or because of adverse reactions from fellow employees or customers.

Clark v TDG Ltd (1999) CA

The applicant suffered a back injury at work. The medical prognosis was that, although the injury should improve over a 12 month time period, it was not possible to say when the applicant would be able to return to work. On receipt of the report, the applicant was dismissed. The employment tribunal and the EAT had both reached the conclusion that the applicant had not been discriminated against, as he had been treated no differently from a person who was off work for the same amount of time, albeit for a different reason.

Held, by the Court of Appeal, that the applicant had been treated less favourably (for a reason which related to his disability) than others to whom that reason did not apply when he was dismissed on grounds of his absence due to disability. The test of less favourable treatment does not turn on a like for like comparison of the treatment of the disabled person and of another in similar circumstances. As the Disability Discrimination Act does not contain an express provision to this effect, it is not appropriate to make the type of comparison as is undertaken under the Sex Discrimination or Race Relations Acts.

Baynton v Saurus General Engineers Ltd (1999) EAT

The applicant was dismissed due to his long term injury. The employment tribunal found that the dismissal was justified, in that the applicant could not do his job and there was no suitable alternative work.

Held, by the EAT, that in applying the test of justification under s 5(3), the tribunal must carry out a balancing exercise between the interests of the disabled employee and the interests of the employer. With this in mind, this dismissal was not 'justified', as the tribunal had failed to engage in this balancing exercise and had not taken into account all the relevant factors, such as the effect of the failure of the employers to warn the applicant that he was at the risk of dismissal, or to ascertain the up to date medical position before dismissal.

Section 6   Duty of employer to make adjustments

(1) Where:

(a) any arrangements made by or on behalf of an employer; or

(b) any physical feature of premises occupied by the employer,

place the disabled person concerned at a substantial disadvantage in comparison with persons who are not disabled, it is the duty of the employer to take such steps as it is reasonable, in all the circumstances of the case, for him to have to take, in order to prevent the arrangements or feature having that effect.

Note ──

This requirement applies to: (i) arrangements for determining who should be offered employment; (ii) the terms on which employment is offered; and (iii) conditions on which employment, promotion, transfer, training or other benefits are offered, provided that the employer knew or should have known that the person is or was disabled (s 6(2), (5)). Section 6(3) provides examples of steps which an employer may have to take in order to comply with sub-s (1), such as, *inter alia*, making adjustments to premises, allocating some of the disabled person's duties to others, transferring the disabled person, altering the disabled person's working hours, acquiring or modifying equipment, providing a supervisor.

Section 6(4) deals with the issue of determining when it is reasonable to expect employers to take a particular step in order to comply with sub-s (1). The following must be taken into account:

(a) the extent to which the adjustment would prevent the disabled person being put at a disadvantage;

(b) the extent to which it is practicable for the employer to make the adjustment;

(c) the financial and other costs;

(d) the extent to which making the adjustment would disrupt the employer's activities;

(e) the size of the employer's financial and other resources (including the size of the workforce); and

(f) the availability to the employer of financial or other assistance in making the adjustment (for example, from the disabled person or from an outside organisation).

Tarling v Wisdom Toothbrushes Ltd (1997)
The applicant, who suffered from congenital club foot, was dismissed on grounds of his disability.

Held, by the industrial tribunal, that the applicant had been unlawfully discriminated against. The employer had not taken appropriate steps to make reasonable adjustments by providing specialist seating, when the cost of doing so was not great.

Q   What effect will the requirement to make reasonable adjustments for disabled employees have on the fairness of dismissals for ill health?

Kenny v Hampshire Constabulary (1999) EAT
The employers withdrew a job offer that had been made to the plaintiff on the grounds that they were unable to provide, after some investigation, the necessary degree of support for his needs, which included assistance in urinating.

Held, by the EAT, that the employers had not discriminated against the plaintiff contrary to s 5(2) of the Disability Discrimination Act 1995. The arrangements which were necessary to enable the applicant to take up employment with the employer did not fall within the duty to make a reasonable adjustment under s 6. The adjustments that the employer is under a duty to make refer to 'job related' issues; employers are not under a statutory duty to provide carers to attend to their employees' personal needs, such as assistance in going to the toilet.

Note ———

Also on the issue of reasonable adjustments, see *Morse v Wiltshire County Council* (1998).

Section 7   Exemption for small businesses
(1) Nothing in this Part applies in relation to an employer who has fewer than 20 employees.

(2)–(10) ...

Note

Similarly to the other statutes dealing with race and sex discrimination, the Disability Discrimination Act contains provisions outlawing victimisation and includes a vicarious liability provision (see ss 55–58). In addition, the Disability Rights Commission Act received the Royal Assent on 27 July 1999. It establishes a Disability Rights Commission, which has similar functions to the Equal Opportunities Commission (EOC) and the Commission for Racial Equality (CRE) set up under the Sex Discrimination Act and Race Relations Act respectively. One distinction, however, is that the Act provides for a less formal investigation procedure than is presently in use by the EOC and CRE.

10 Trade Unions and their Members

10.1 Members' rights and the common law doctrines

10.1.1 The 'right to work'

Nagle v Fielden (1966) CA

The plaintiff had been refused a licence as a horse trainer by the Jockey Club merely on the ground of her gender. The Jockey Club had a monopoly of control over flat racing, and so she was unable to practice her chosen profession.

Held, by the Court of Appeal, that the applicant was unlawfully denied a licence. Powerful associations, such as the Jockey Club or trade unions operating a closed shop, with control over the entitlement or 'right to work', must act reasonably when assessing an applicant's membership. *Per* Lord Denning:

> ... the common law ... has for centuries recognised that a man has a right to work at his trade or profession without being unjustly excluded from it. He is not to be shut out from it at the whim of those having governance of it. If they make a rule which enables them to reject his application arbitrarily or capriciously, not reasonably, that rule is bad. It is against public policy.

Edwards v SOGAT (1971) CA

The plaintiff was employed in the printing industry, where a closed shop was in operation. By an oversight, the plaintiff, who was a temporary member, had failed to pay his union fees for six weeks, and was excluded from membership under the rules of the union. His application for re-admission was rejected and he was subsequently dismissed by his employer.

Held, by the Court of Appeal, that such an unfettered and uncontrolled right to withdraw membership, which is a prerequisite for employment, is an interference with a person's implied right to work and, *per* Sachs LJ, 'contrary to public policy for the reasons discussed in *Nagle v Fielden*'.

Note ──

Megarry VC in *McInnes v Onslow Fare* (1978) and Slade J in *Grieg v Insole* (1978) were willing to accept the existence of a modified version of the 'right to work', but the House of Lords in *Cheall v APEX* (1983) criticised Denning's broad formulation of the right, although Lord Diplock thought that it may be applicable in exceptional circumstances of injustice.

Goring v British Actors Equity Association (1987) HC

Pursuant to a referendum of the membership, the union executive council issued an instruction under the union's disciplinary rules, permitting the expulsion of any member who worked in South Africa. The plaintiff took an action in the High Court arguing, *inter alia*, that the instruction under the union rule banning members from working in South Africa interfered with the plaintiff's 'right to work'.

Held, by the High Court, that the 'right to work' does not operate where there is a subsisting contractual relationship between the parties. Where a membership contract exists, the contents of which are contained in the rule book, a union member cannot complain of disciplinary action or expulsion validly carried out under the rules since, by joining the union, the member has agreed to submit to the authority of the union rule book.

R v Jockey Club ex p Ram Racecourses Ltd (1993) HC

The Jockey Club, the body which controls and regulates horse racing, in pursuance of the conclusions of a policy review, excluded the plaintiff's race course from receiving new race fixtures. The plaintiff took an action for a judicial review of the Jockey Club's decision. Counsel for the plaintiff submitted, *inter alia*, that the line of authority deriving from *Nagle v Fielden* provided a remedy, on the basis that the plaintiff had been denied a right to earn a living.

Held, by the Divisional Court (QBD), that if a remedy in private law was clearly inadequate because of the absence of a contractual relationship between the parties, then the grant of a public law remedy, such as a judicial review of a decision to deny entry, was justified. *Per* Simon Brown J:

> Cases like [*Nagle v Fielden, Breen v AEU* and *McInnes v Onslow Fare*] had they arisen today and not some years ago, would have found a natural home in judicial review proceedings. As it was, considerations of public policy forced the courts to devise a new private law creature ... I, for my part, would judge it preferable to develop these principles in future in a public law context than by further distorting private law principles. *Nagle v Fielden* was never, in my judgment, a restraint of trade case properly so called; rather, it brought into play clear considerations of public law.

Note ——————————————————————————————————————

This decision may have been an attempt to resurrect Denning's notion of the 'right to work' in the guise of a public law remedy. However, not only is it debatable whether trade unions are bodies that are susceptible to judicial review but, in any event, the extensive statutory rights developed since 1979 (see below) have made this doctrine essentially redundant.

10.1.2 The bylaw theory

Edwards v SOGAT (1971) CA
For the facts, see 10.1.1, above.

Held, by Lord Denning in the Court of Appeal, that: (I) union rules were not mutually agreed contractual obligations, but were imposed by the union, and so were in the nature of a legislative code analogous to statutory bylaws; (II) rules can therefore be controlled in the same way as statutory bylaws; struck down as unenforceable if they are 'unreasonable'; (III) a rule which destroys or gratuitously interferes with the right to earn a living is unreasonable and invalid.

Note ——————————————————————————————————————

The House of Lords in *Cheall v APEX* (1983) rejected Denning's bylaw thesis on the basis that it could not be invoked where rights against the union are regulated by the contract contained in the rules. Considering the level of judicial criticism directed at this doctrine, it is unlikely to be revived in the future.

10.2 Members' rights and the rule book

10.2.1 Rule book as enforceable contract between union and member

Bonsor v Musicians' Union (1956) HL
Bonsor had failed to pay his subscriptions to the union for a year. The relevant rule specified that, if a member was more than six weeks in arrears, the relevant branch committee could resolve to expel the member. The branch secretary, contrary to the rules, decided personally to inform the plaintiff that he was expelled. The plaintiff submitted that the rule book was a contractual document entered into by the union with all members and, as the rules had not been followed faithfully, the expulsion was unlawful.

It was argued by the union defendants that the union rule book could not be enforced against the union, as s 4 of the Trade Union Act 1871 specifically excluded the courts from entertaining any legal proceedings that had the aim of directly enforcing terms in the rule book relating, *inter alia*, to payment of penalties or subscriptions imposed by the union.

Held, by the House of Lords (following *Taff Vale Railway Co v ASRS* (1901)), that: (I) a union registered under the Trade Union Act 1871 has the capacity to make contracts, and as a quasi-corporation, distinct from its membership, a member could sue the union as a legal entity in its own right; (II) s 4 could not be pleaded as a defence where a member wished to enforce their individual rights under the contract of association; consequently, the full array of civil remedies, including damages, were available to union members in order to protect these rights.

Note ——————————————————————————

The 1871 Act was repealed by the Industrial Relations Act 1971. This Act gave unions full corporate status, including the right to make contracts and to sue and be sued under them. The 1971 Act was subsequently repealed and replaced by the 1974 Trade Union and Labour Relations Act. Unions were not now to be treated as corporate bodies, but were granted many of the attributes of incorporation, including being able to make contracts and to be sued in their own name (now found in s 10(1) of the Trade Union and Labour Relations (Consolidation) Act 1992).

10.2.2 Enforcement of the rule book and disciplinary action

Blackall v National Union of Foundary Workers (1923) HC
Blackall was expelled for being 19 weeks in arrears with his subscriptions. The relevant rule permitted expulsions only where a member was 20 weeks in arrears.

Held, by the High Court, that the terms of the rule book had not been strictly followed. Consequently, the expulsion was null and void.

Silvester v National Union of Printing, Bookbinding and Paper Workers (1966) HC
The plaintiff was charged with acting to the detriment of the union for refusing to obey an instruction of the union. The plaintiff continued to defy the union, and so, further charges were brought against him. His right to appeal under the rules for the first charge was refused, as an investigation of the other charges had not yet been completed.

Held, by the High Court, that the wrongful denial of the appeal on the first charge invalidated the proceedings and vitiated the decision on all the charges.

MacLelland v NUJ (1975) HC

Under rule 15 of the union, a chapel (branch) of the NUJ had the power to discipline a member where he or she failed to attend a compulsory union meeting. At a monthly meeting of MacLelland's chapel, the committee members designated the meeting as compulsory and instructed the membership to attend. MacLelland only attended one part of the meeting and was subsequently disciplined.

Held, by the High Court, that this rule should be construed in such a way that, even if the meeting had been properly convened, there had been compliance with the rule on attendance. The obligation to attend the mandatory meeting did not impose on MacLelland a duty to remain for the full duration. Consequently, the decision to initiate disciplinary action was null and void.

Note

These cases concern the construction and application of express rules. Only in exceptional circumstances will the courts imply a power to discipline or expel a member – see *McVitae v Unison* (1996).

Leigh v NUR (1970) HC

The plaintiff had been nominated as a candidate in the election for president of the union. The general secretary of the union refused to approve his candidature. The plaintiff immediately took action in the courts to overturn this decision. The union contended that the plaintiff was not entitled to legal relief, as he had not first used the domestic remedies as provided in the rule book.

Held, by the High Court, *per* Goff J:

> ... where there is an express provision in the rules that the plaintiff must first exhaust his domestic remedies, the court is not absolutely bound by that because its jurisdiction cannot be ousted, but the plaintiff will have to show just cause why it should interfere with the contractual position.

Note

It is well established that any formal attempt to oust the jurisdiction of the court in matters of law by a provision in the rule book to this effect will be unsuccessful. This rule will be struck down as void and unenforceable as contrary to public policy – see *Lee v Showmen's Guild* (1952), applying *Scott v Avery* (1856). In the case above, an attempt at partial ouster – to enforce domestic procedures first before recourse to the law – Goff J suggested there may be limited circumstances where the courts should recognise a rule that enforces domestic remedies first, such as where procedures can be executed speedily and without bias or prejudice. However, now see s 63 of the Trade Union and Labour Relations (Consolidation) Act 1992. This provides a specific right for members to have access to the courts to pursue a grievance against their union, notwithstanding any contrary rule in the rule book.

Radford v NATSOPA (1972) HC

The plaintiff was charged under the rules with the offence of taking 'wilful action against the union' for consulting a solicitor during a previous dispute with the union. The union argued that the domestic disciplinary body had sole jurisdiction to interpret the meaning of the offence and to take appropriate action unfettered by judicial interference.

Held, by the High Court, that: (I) the courts are fully entitled to consider the true construction of the rules and to examine the sufficiency of evidence presented to the internal tribunal; (II) on the admitted facts, it could not be reasonably construed that consulting a solicitor satisfied the test of 'wilful action against the union'.

Q   If unions phrased their disciplinary rules in very subjective terms – that is, by having rules that permit the domestic tribunal to assess whether, in its 'opinion', the offence has been committed – would it preserve the jurisdiction of the domestic tribunal and avoid judicial intervention?

Esterman v NALGO (1974) HC

During a dispute between NALGO and certain local authorities (and after a ballot which showed 49% of the membership in favour of industrial action), the union, under the rules, instructed the membership not to co-operate with the holding of local government elections. Esterman defied the instruction and was invited to attend a disciplinary branch meeting, which was to consider whether her conduct merited expulsion from the union. The relevant rule stated that members could be expelled for actions 'that render him [*sic*] unfit for membership in the opinion of the executive committee'. She applied to the High Court for an injunction to restrain the disciplinary action.

Held, by the High Court (*per* Templeman J), that the failure of the NALGO executive to obtain a majority vote entitled the applicant to doubt whether the union had the power under the rules to instruct members to take action. The consequence of this misuse of union power to call industrial action was that the applicant's actions in defying the unlawful instructions could not be interpreted as conduct that 'renders him unfit for membership' in the eyes of any reasonable tribunal acting in good faith. Thus, the applicant was entitled to an interlocutory injunction to stop the disciplinary proceedings.

This decision was somewhat controversial, as the injunction was
granted prior to the disciplinary hearing, therefore preventing the
domestic tribunal from hearing the substance of the charges, and so
precluding the settlement of the dispute internally. Although the
approach of the court in *Esterman* was followed in *Porter v NUJ* (1980)
and in *Partington v NALGO* (1981), in more recent cases (see *Longley v
NUJ* (1987), below), the Court of Appeal has attempted to limit the
grant of injunctions prior to internal disciplinary hearings.

Longley v NUJ (1987) CA
A shop steward defied the national executive committee of the NUJ by
working at the Wapping headquarters of News International. He was
expelled for 'conduct detrimental to the interests of the union', which was
defined in the rules as, *inter alia*, 'failure, without reasonable cause, to
comply with an instruction of the NEC'. Longley applied for an
interlocutory injunction to stop the action, arguing he had reasonable
cause to defy the call for a strike, as it was unsupported by a ballot as
required by law.

Held, by the Court of Appeal, that: (I) intervention in advance of the
hearing could be countenanced if it was clear that there were such
exceptional circumstances that no reasonable tribunal acting *bona fide*
could possibly find against the plaintiff; (II) 'exceptional circumstances'
should be given a narrow interpretation. What is required is clear evidence
of bias or that the issues would be prejudged or proper procedures
ignored; (III) the failure to follow ballot procedures was not on its own
sufficient to pass this test.

Taylor v NUM (Derbyshire Area) (No 1) (1984) HC
During the 1984–85 strike, working miners were suspended by the
Derbyshire Area union for failing to abide by strike instructions issued by
the national and area union. The plaintiffs applied for a declaration that
the strike was called in breach of the rule book, as rule 43 required a
national ballot before a strike, which had not been held.

Held, by the High Court, that the strike call was in contravention of the
rules, and so unlawful. As the action was 'unofficial', the plaintiffs were
not breaking union rules in refusing to go on strike and could lawfully
disregard union instructions. As the power to suspend only applied to a
lawful strike, an injunction was also granted to prohibit further
disciplinary action.

In *Taylor v NUM (Derbyshire Area) (No 3)* (1985), the union, applying the
rule in *Foss v Harbottle* (1843), contended that the failure to ballot was a

mere irregularity, which could be condoned by a subsequent decision of the majority of union members through a special delegate conference. Therefore, all action taken under the rule book in support of the strike was not unlawful. Vinelott J rejected this argument; noting that the rule in *Foss v Harbottle* did not apply where action taken was *prima facie ultra vires* the rules, or where the personal rights of members were infringed.

Clarke v Chadburn (1984) HC

During a dispute between dissident members of the NUM, who refused to go on strike, and NUM officials, an extraordinary delegate conference of the NUM was called in July 1984 to add a new r 51, allowing for the disqualification of members, branches and areas and the removal of officers who had ignored strike instructions. The plaintiffs, who were members of the NUM Nottinghamshire Area, applied to the court for a declaration that the resolutions of the conference which altered the rules were void, and for an injunction restraining the NUM President from enforcing the void rule changes.

Held, by the High Court, that both applications would be granted, as the way the changes had been conducted were in breach of the rules. There had been no meeting of the Nottinghamshire Area and no consultation on the rule changes as is necessary under the rules. *Per* Megarry VC:

> ... as long as (the NUM) disregards its own rules and the democratic process for which the rules provide, it must not be surprised if it finds any changes of the rules made by these means are struck down with invalidity.

Note

Also on invalid rule changes, see *Taylor and Foulstone v NUM (Yorkshire Area)* (1984) and *Hopkins v NUS* (1985).

10.2.3 The rule book and the rules of natural justice

White v Kuzych (1951) CA

The applicant was disciplined for his opposition to union policy on the closed shop. He objected to one member of the disciplinary panel, who was known to be particularly hostile to his point of view.

Held, by the Court of Appeal, that this hostility did not automatically vitiate the decision of the disciplinary tribunal. Where questions of bias were raised, what was required of the members of a tribunal was, *per* Viscount Simon:

> ... a will to reach a honest conclusion ... and a resolve not to make up their minds beforehand on his personal guilt, however firmly held their

convictions as to union policy and however strongly they had joined in previous adverse criticism of the respondent's conduct.

Q   If the rule against bias was applied stringently, would trade unions ever be able to discipline their members for actions contrary to union policy?

Taylor v National Union of Seamen (1967) CA

The union general secretary had dismissed an official for insubordination and had presided over his appeal to the executive committee of the union. During the deliberations of the committee, the general secretary made prejudicial comments and allegations irrelevant to the charge.

Held, by the Court of Appeal, that the executive committee was required to consider in a judicial manner whether the decision to dismiss was well founded. The presence and behaviour of the general secretary was clear evidence of bias, which may well have had a material effect on these judicial deliberations.

Roebuck v NUM (Yorkshire Area) (No 2) (1978) HC

Roebuck had been disciplined because of his support of a newspaper, the Sheffield Star, which was being sued for libel by Arthur Scargill, the Yorkshire President at the time. Scargill initiated the disciplinary action, alleging that Roebuck's actions had been 'detrimental to the interests of the union' under rule 42. He sat as chair of the area executive committee which charged the plaintiff and as chair of the disciplinary committee which heard the charge.

Held, by the High Court, that the test of bias which should be applied to determine whether a decision of a disciplinary tribunal should be quashed, was not just whether the tribunal was actually biased against the plaintiff, but whether, *per* Templeman J:

... there is a likelihood of bias in the eyes of the reasonable person who knew nothing of the actual deliberations of the tribunal.

As Scargill acted as the prosecutor and as a judge in his own cause, the 'appearance of bias was inevitable; the exercise of bias conscious or unconscious was probable'.

Radford v NATSOPA (1972) HC

Radford's branch committee had decided to take disciplinary action under the rules against Radford, due to his refusal to follow a redundancy agreement negotiated between the union and his employer. Before the hearing, the disciplinary committee became aware that Radford had instructed solicitors to act on his behalf. When Radford refused to disclose the nature of his discussions with his solicitor, the committee concluded, without hearing from Radford, that he had 'taken action ... wilfully against the union', and expelled him forthwith.

Held, by the High Court, quashing the decision of the domestic tribunal, that, in order to comply with the basic rules of natural justice, a defendant is entitled to notice of charges and to a hearing, so that he or she is given the opportunity to be heard in their own defence.

Q   Is it contrary to natural justice for the rule book of a union to ban legal representation before an internal tribunal? Can a fair and unbiased appeal remedy bias or unfair procedure at the first instance hearing?

10.3 Members' rights and statutory control over discipline

10.3.1 The right not to be 'unjustifiably disciplined'

Section 64

(1) An individual who is or has been a member of a trade union has the right not to be unjustifiably disciplined by the union.

(2) For this purpose, an individual is 'disciplined' by a trade union if a determination is made, or purportedly made, under the rules of the union or by an official of the union or a number of persons including an official that:

(a) he should be expelled from the union or a branch or section of the union;

(b) he should pay a sum to the union, to a branch or section of the union or to any other persons;

(c) ...

(d) he should be deprived to any extent of, or of access to, any benefits, services or facilities which would otherwise be provided or made available to him by virtue of his membership of the union, or a branch or section of the union;

(e) another trade union, or a branch or section of it, should be encouraged or advised not to accept him as a member; or

(f) he should be subjected to some other detriment;

and whether an individual is 'unjustifiably disciplined' shall be determined in accordance with s 65.

(3)–(5) ...

Section 65   Meaning of 'unjustifiably disciplined'

(1) An individual is unjustifiably disciplined if the actual or supposed conduct which constitutes the reason, or one of the reasons, for disciplining him is:

(a) conduct to which this section applies; or

(b) something which is believed by the union to amount to such conduct, but subject to sub-s (6) (cases of bad faith in relation to assertion of wrongdoing).

(2) This section applies to conduct which consists in:

(a) failing to participate in or support a strike or other industrial action or indicating opposition to or a lack of support for such action;

(b) failing to contravene, for a purpose connected with such a strike or other industrial action, a requirement imposed on him by or under a contract of employment;

(c) asserting (whether by bringing proceedings or otherwise) that the union, any official or representative of it or a trustee of its property has contravened, or is proposing to contravene, a requirement which is, or is thought to be, imposed by or under the rules of the union or any other agreement or by any other enactment or any rule of law;

(d) ...

(e) ...

(f) failing to agree, or withdrawing agreement, to the making from his wages (in accordance with arrangements between his employer and the union) of deductions, representing payments to the union in respect of his membership;

(g) resigning or proposing to resign from the union, or from another union, becoming or proposing to become a member of another union, refusing to become a member of another union, or being a member of another union;

(h) working with, or proposing to work with, individuals who are not members of the union or who are or are not members of another union;

(i) working for, or proposing to work for, an employer who employs or who has employed individuals who are not members of the union or who are or are not members of another union;

(j) ...

(3)–(7) ...

TGWU v Webber (1990) EAT

Due to a dispute with the secretary of his branch, Webber had been suspended by his branch, pending expulsion. The Regional Council then recommended his expulsion. Before he had been formally expelled, Webber complained to the tribunal that he had been 'unjustifiably disciplined'.

Held, by the EAT, that: (I) a 'determination' to expel under s 64(2) meant final disposal of the case; (II) as the proceedings here had not finished, this was not a valid determination for the purposes of the section, and the action brought by Webber was dismissed.

NALGO v Killorn (1990) EAT

During an industrial dispute, the applicants had refused to take strike action and had crossed a picket line. The union responded by suspending them from membership and by advertising their names in a union circular sent to all branch members, causing the applicants acute embarrassment.

Held, by the EAT, that: (I) to deny even temporary access to the benefits, services or facilities which derive from membership is a deprivation under the Act; (II) advertising the applicants' names, so that they are held up to ridicule, is 'some other detriment', as it can be defined as 'some disadvantage of whatever nature'.

Medhurst v NALGO (1990) EAT

Medhurst had secretly tape recorded a branch executive meeting. He had refused to deliver up the tape when discovered and was subsequently suspended from membership.

Held, by the EAT, that he had not suffered 'unjustifiable' disciplinary action, as the reason for the suspension of membership did not come under any of the heads listed in s 65.

Bradley v NALGO (1991) EAT

After a ballot on industrial action had been taken, which resulted in a majority in favour of action, NALGO called out members for one day strike action. The applicants refused to take action and crossed picket lines to go to work. All were expelled from the union, contrary to s 64.

Held, by the EAT, that, under the compensation provisions contained in s 67, an award for loss of earnings could not be made. The applicants had not been disadvantaged in the labour market, as union membership was not a necessity to obtain employment. However, in principle, compensation for distress or injury to feelings was permissible. The appropriate award was the statutory minimum; at that time £2,520 (now £5,000).

Q   If a member is disciplined for committing several offences for which only one is 'unjustifiable', is the union entitled to proceed on the other charges?

Q   To what extent does this right weaken union collective responsibility and solidarity?

10.3.2 The right not to be excluded or expelled from a union

Section 174

(1) An individual shall not be excluded or expelled from a trade union, unless the exclusion or expulsion is permitted by this section.

(2) The exclusion or expulsion of an individual from a trade union is permitted by this section if (and only if):

   (a) he does not satisfy, or no longer satisfies, an enforceable membership requirement contained in the rules of the union;

   (b) he does not qualify, or no longer qualifies, for membership of the union by reason of the union operating only in a particular part or particular parts of Great Britain;

   (c) ...

   (d) the exclusion or expulsion is entirely attributable to his conduct.

(3) A requirement in relation to membership of a union is enforceable for the purposes of sub-s (2)(a), if it restricts membership solely by reference to one or more of the following criteria:

   (a) employment in specified trade, industry or profession;

   (b) occupational description (including grade, level or category of appointment);

   (c) possession of specified trade, industrial or professional qualifications or work experience.

(4) For the purposes of sub-s (2)(d), 'conduct', in relation to an individual, does not include:

   (a) his being or ceasing to be, or having been or ceased to be;

      (i)   a member of another trade union;

      (ii) employed by a particular employer or at a particular place;

      (iii) a member of a particular party; or

   (b) conduct to which s 65 ... applies ...

(5) An individual who claims that he has been excluded or expelled from a trade union in contravention of this section may present a complaint to an industrial tribunal.

NACODS v Gluchowski (1996) EAT

The plaintiff was disciplined for failing to support industrial action and was suspended from the union. He claimed this was contrary to s 174.

Held, by the EAT, that 'exclusion', for the purposes of liability under s 174, must be construed strictly. A temporary suspension of membership did not amount to exclusion from the union.

Q   If an individual is expelled, there may well be a claim for unjustifiable discipline under s 64 and for improper expulsion under s 174. In such a case, can the individual make dual applications and obtain damages on both claims?

11 Industrial Action

11.1 Civil liability – the economic torts

The following may come under this heading of liability: inducing breach of contract; interference with contract trade or business; intimidation; conspiracy; inducing breach of statutory duty; economic duress; and inducing breach of an equitable obligation.

11.2 Inducing breach of contract

DC Thomson & Co Ltd v Deakin (1952) CA

The plaintiff was a printer and publisher of periodicals employing non-union labour. The paper they used was supplied by Bowater Ltd. When the plaintiff dismissed an employee who had joined the printers' union, NATSOPA, officials of the union called on other unions to support action against the plaintiff. Bowater lorry drivers, members of the TGWU, informed their employer that they were now minded to refuse to deliver paper to the plaintiff. Bowater Ltd, without requiring the drivers to perform their contractual obligations, informed the plaintiff that they would not honour the contract for the supply of paper. The plaintiff thus alleged that officials of NATSOPA had unlawfully induced a breach of the commercial contract of supply between themselves and Bowater Ltd.

Held, by Jenkins LJ, in the Court of Appeal, that the tort of inducing breach of contract was confined to cases where:

> ... first, that the person charged ... knew of the existence of the contract and intended to procure its breach; secondly, that the person so charged did definitely and unequivocally persuade, induce or procure the employees concerned to break their contracts of employment with the intent I have mentioned; thirdly, that the employees so persuaded, induced or procured did in fact break their contracts of employment; and, fourthly, that breach of the (commercial) contract forming the alleged subject of interference ensued as a necessary consequence ...

On the facts submitted, Jenkins LJ held that the tort of indirectly inducing breach of contract was not made out. The evidence did not establish that a breach of an employment contract by any of the Bowater employees had actually occurred, as the advice by the trade union officials was not acted upon; Bowater had decided independently to refuse to deliver paper to the plaintiff.

11.2.1 Knowledge of the contract

Emerald Construction Co Ltd v Lowthian (1966) CA

The defendants were officers of the building workers union, who objected, on health and safety grounds, to the subcontracting out of labour on large building projects. Here, the main contractors, in defiance of union wishes, subcontracted out work to the plaintiff. The defendants, having learnt of this, advised union members at the site to take industrial action to force the main contractor to desist from employing the subcontractors. The defendants argued they were not liable for inducing breach of contract, as they did not know that the main contractor could only terminate the contract with the plaintiff by acting in breach.

Held, by Lord Denning in the Court of Appeal, that to satisfy this element of the tort, it was not necessary for the union organisers to have knowledge of the precise terms of the contract, so long as they had 'the means of knowledge – which they deliberately disregarded ... Like the man who turns a blind eye'. Liability could therefore be imposed here, as the union officials sought to terminate the contract of which they had knowledge, without caring whether this could be done lawfully or not.

Merkur Island Shipping Corp v Laughton (1983) HL

The International Transport Workers' Federation (ITWF) requested the Transport and General Workers Union to boycott a ship in port in Liverpool after complaints of low wages by its crew. Consequently, when the ship was ready to sail, tugmen and lock keepers, acting on instructions from the union, refused to assist her passage. This resulted in a breach of a complex maritime 'time charter' contract. The owners had let the ship to a charterer, who in turn, had subchartered the ship to another company.

Held, by the House of Lords, that, even though the ITWF official was not privy to the complex terms of the contract (and so did not know for certain who the other parties were or that the action would cause a breach of the contract of hire), it could be assumed that such an official was well informed about these types of contracts common in the shipping industry. A form of constructive knowledge was thus imputed to the defendants.

11.2.2 Intention to break the contract

Emerald Construction v Lowthian (1966) CA

For the facts, see above.

Held, by the Court of Appeal, that intention is inexplicably linked to the degree of knowledge the defendant possesses of the contract; a defendant intends to cause a breach where he or she takes deliberate steps, knowing that a breach will be a consequence of that action. However, as in this particular case, intention is also present in circumstances where the defendant does not have knowledge of the actual terms of the contract, but only has actual or constructive knowledge that the contract exists and is then 'recklessly indifferent' to whether a breach occurs or not.

Q   Will the defendant possess the necessary intent where there is an honest, but false, belief that the deliberate action induced (such as a withdrawal of 'goodwill') is not in breach of the contract of employment?

Falconer v ASLEF and NUR (1986)

The plaintiff was a commuter whose journey was interrupted by strike action on the railways. He sued the rail unions for hotel and subsistence expenses for inducing the breach of his contract of travel with British Rail.

Held, by the county court, that, although the industrial action was aimed at British Rail, rather than the plaintiff, the breach of the plaintiff's contract was a foreseeable and unavoidable consequence of the action. Therefore, in these circumstances, where the unions knew of the contract and risk of breach, the defendants were 'reckless to the consequences' to the plaintiff, and so possessed the necessary intention.

Note ————————————————————————————————

The application of the recklessness test in this way has been heavily criticised, as it expands the range of plaintiffs who may take action from the employer, who is directly involved in the dispute, to members of the public who are caused incidental loss as a byproduct of the action.

11.2.3 Inducement to break the contract

Torquay Hotel Co Ltd v Cousins (1969) CA

The plaintiff hotel owners criticised the defendant for initiating recognition disputes with other hotels in the Torquay region. The defendant reacted by telephoning the oil company Esso and advising them directly that any supplies of oil to the plaintiff would be met by a picket line. In response to this, Esso declined to deliver the oil, arguably, in breach of contract. The contract for the supply of oil between the hotel and Esso included a *force majeure* exemption clause, which excluded Esso's liability in circumstances where a failure to supply oil was due to an industrial dispute.

Held, by Winn LJ, in the Court of Appeal, that inducement has to be given a wide interpretation. There may well be circumstances where mere cautionary advice or information amounts to an inducement. In this case, the provision of information regarding a picket line, given in an intimidating manner over the phone, amounted to an inducement to Esso to break their contract of supply.

Square Grip Reinforcement Co Ltd v MacDonald (1968) CA

The union and employer had been negotiating over recognition. On these negotiations breaking down, officials of the union informed their members at the employer's workplace that the employer had been intransigent during the negotiations. The employees immediately voted for strike action. The employer argued that the union officials had induced the strike action (which caused the breach of employment contracts), since they knew that, on hearing this information, their members would react in this way.

Held, by the Court of Appeal, that statements made, or information provided, always had to be construed in the context of the circumstances. As the union knew that the employees were ripe for strike action, the information provided was an active inducement.

Union Traffic Ltd v TGWU (1989) CA

The plaintiff closed down their road transport depot in Liverpool, making a number of drivers redundant. The defendant, who opposed the closure, set up a picket line at another transport depot 13 miles away. When other transport workers became aware that a picket line had been mounted, they refused to deliver to the picketed depot.

Held, by the Court of Appeal, that, even though the pickets were not actively persuading employees to break their employment contracts, their presence at the entrance to the workplace was intended, and was successful, in its object of inducing breaches of contract. This was sufficient to amount to an inducement for the purposes of the common law tort.

11.2.4 Actual breach of contract

DC Thomson & Co v Deakin (1952) CA

For the facts, see 11.2, above.

Held, by the Court of Appeal, that: (I) the breach of contract must be as a 'necessary consequence' of the defendant's action. It must be shown that, by reason of the withdrawal of the services of the employees concerned, the commercial supplier was unable as a matter of practical possibility to perform the contract; (II) although the commercial contract of supply had been broken, the supply of paper could have been provided by alternative means, that is, by hiring alternative transport. As there had been no attempt to get the paper to the plaintiff in any other way, there had not been a breach of the contract of supply as a 'necessary consequence' of the defendant's act.

Contrast this view with the Court of Appeal's interpretation of this element of the tort in *Dimbleby & Sons v NUJ* (1984).

11.2.5 Defence of justification

South Wales Miners' Federation v Glamorgan Coal Co (1903) CA

Coal miners were paid by the plaintiff on a sliding scale, dependent on the selling price of coal. The scarcer coal was, the higher the price of coal and the higher the miners' wages. To increase wages, the trade union persuaded its members to turn up for work intermittently, so as to limit the supply of coal and so force up the price of coal. The union believed this course of action was in the best interests of both their members and the employer. The employer took action against the union for inducing breach of their workers contracts of employment.

Held, by the Court of Appeal, that the defence of justification did not apply. *Per* Romer LJ:

> ... a defendant sued for knowingly procuring a breach is not justified by necessity merely by showing he had no personal animus against the employer or that it was the advantage or interest of both the defendant and the workmen that the contract should be broken.

Brimelow v Casson (1924) HC

The plaintiff was a theatrical manager, who paid chorus girls who worked for him well below the minimum wage fixed by the Actors' Association. As a consequence, some of these employees resorted to prostitution to enhance their wages. The defendant, shocked by their circumstances, successfully prevailed upon certain theatre proprietors to refuse to honour existing contracts with the plaintiff, so that he was denied the use of their theatres.

Held, by the High Court, that, in these circumstances, as the defendant acted in furtherance of a moral duty and in the public interest, the defence of justification to inducing breach of contract was applicable.

Q   Do you think this defence should be restricted to cases where persons act in pursuance of a legal, rather than a moral duty?

11.3 Interference with contract, trade or business

Torquay Hotel Co Ltd v Cousins (1969) CA

For facts, see 11.2.3, above.

Held, by Lord Denning MR, that, although due to the operation of the clause, there was no technical breach of contract, interference short of breach was itself actionable, as:

> ... the time has come when the principle (of inducing breach of contract) should be extended to cover deliberate and direct interference with the execution of a contract.

Liability for interference with the performance of a contract short of breach can be imposed where the:

> ... interference was deliberate, the defendant had knowledge of the contract, or at least, turned a blind eye to its contents; and, if the interference was indirect, unlawful means was present.

Q   Is Lord Denning's view in *Torquay* – that direct interference short of breach unaccompanied by unlawful means is actionable – consistent with the House of Lords decision in *Allen v Flood* (1898), that interference with contract by lawful means is not a tort?

Merkur Island Shipping Corp v Laughton (1983) HL

The International Transport Workers' Federation, in their campaign against low wages, organised the boycotting of a Liberian registered ship in the River Mersey. This resulted in the disruption of a contract of hire between the owners and hirers of the ship. The contract included a clause which provided that cancellation of the contract was permitted, and payment for hire would cease if the ship was boycotted due to an industrial dispute.

Held, by Lord Diplock in the House of Lords, that: (I) the exclusion clause did not affect the liability of the defendants for indirectly inducing breach of contract by unlawful means, as there had been a breach of the primary obligation in the contract of hire, even though the secondary obligation to pay the hire charges or damages for breach had been removed by the exclusion clause; (II) concurring with Lord Denning's opinion in *Torquay Hotel v Cousins*, there also existed the tort of interference with the performance of a contract short of breach as:

> ... parliamentary recognition that the tort of actionable interference with contractual rights is as broad as Lord Denning stated in *Torquay* ... is, in my view, to be found in s 13(1) of the Trade Union and Labour Relations Act 1974, which refers to inducement not only to 'break a contract', but also 'to interfere with its performance'.

Note

This reference to the statutory immunity to these torts to justify an extension of the law was somewhat mischievous. Parliament had extended the scope of the immunity from mere breach to interference short of breach as a response to the Court of Appeal's innovative judgment in *Torquay Hotel v Cousins*.

Hadmor Productions Ltd v Hamilton (1981) CA

The plaintiff (Hadmor Productions Ltd) was an independent TV production company, who were engaged in contractual negotiations with Thames TV concerning the transmission of certain of their programmes. During a dispute with the plaintiff, the defendant trade union threatened to instruct their members at Thames TV to refuse to transmit any programmes the plaintiff produced. As a consequence, Thames TV pulled out of the negotiations, causing loss to the plaintiff.

Held, by Lord Denning MR, that the plaintiff had a reasonable commercial expectation that a contract would be finalised and the programmes would be broadcast. This expectation had been shattered and frustrated by the proposed boycott. Thus, this was an actionable indirect interference with the plaintiff's trade and business by the unlawful means of threatening to induce breach of employment contracts by strike action.

11.4 Intimidation

Rookes v Barnard (1964) HL

The plaintiff was a skilled draughtsman employed by British Overseas Airways Corporation (BOAC), who had resigned his membership of the relevant union – the Association of Engineering and Shipbuilding Draughtsmen. As the union had a 'closed shop' arrangement with the employer, a full time divisional organiser of the union – Silverthorne, and two branch officers who were employed by BOAC, Fistal and Barnard, threatened the employer that strike action would be taken unless the plaintiff was dismissed from his job. As a consequence of this threat, the plaintiff was sacked.

Held, by the House of Lords, that this was an unlawful threat made directly to a third party (the employer) with the intention of causing loss to the plaintiff, and so was sufficient to constitute the tort of intimidation. A threat to break or to induce others to break a contract of employment was as much an illegal threat for the purposes of the tort of intimidation as a threat to commit violence to person or property. *Per* Lord Devlin:

> ... all that matters to the plaintiff is that, metaphorically speaking, a club has been used. It does not matter to the plaintiff what the club is made of – whether it is a physical club or economic club, a tortious club or an otherwise illegal club.

Note ───

This case revolutionised the law on intimidation. Previously, the tort was only actionable where a violent threat against a third party or the plaintiff had been made. In response to this ground breaking decision, the Labour Government passed the Trade Dispute Act 1965 to explicitly bestow an immunity where there is a threat to break or induce a breach of employment contract.

───

11.5 Conspiracy

11.5.1 Conspiracy to injure

Mogul Steamship Co v McGregor, Gow & Co (1898) CA

A number of shipowners formed an exclusive trade association and decided to lower their freight charges, with the express intention of pricing their commercial rivals out of business. The plaintiffs were shipowners excluded from the association, who suffered severe financial loss as a consequence.

Held, by the Court of Appeal, that an actionable conspiracy had not been committed, as the conspirators had acted merely to protect their trading position, which was a justifiable aim of their competitive pricing policy. The real and legitimate purpose of the combination was to advance the commercial interests of the association, not to cause the loss to the plaintiffs.

Quinn v Leathem (1901) HL

The union defendants were members of the Belfast Journeyman Butchers and Assistants Association who wished to enforce a 'closed shop' in the meat and poultry trade. The plaintiff was a meat producer who employed assistants who were not members of this union. On refusing to employ only staff from the union, the defendants prevailed upon other members of the trade to boycott his produce, which resulted in the breach of supply contracts.

Held, by the House of Lords, that this was an actionable conspiracy, as the union had intentionally caused loss to the plaintiff, and their main purpose in doing so was not to further their own legitimate interests in setting up a closed shop, but to injure the plaintiff out of spite for not following their instructions.

Crofter Handwoven Harris Tweed v Veitch (1942) HL

The plaintiff was a producer of tweed cloth on the island of Harris who obtained their yarn (raw material) from mainland mills at a cheaper price than that charged by island suppliers. In order to ensure a steady supply of work for their members employed in local mills, representatives of the TGWU instructed dockers at the port of Stornoway to refuse to handle all yarn imported into the island.

Held, by the House of Lords, that the predominant purpose of the union was the legitimate protection of the interests of their members. So long as a union genuinely took action to secure benefits for their members, whether or not they knew damage to the plaintiff was a consequence of their actions was not relevant. As no criminal or other tortious means were employed, the combination was not acting as an unlawful conspiracy.

Huntley v Thornton (1957) HC

The plaintiff was a fitter and a member of the Amalgamated Engineering Union. During a trade dispute, members of the union called for strike action at the plaintiff's workplace. The plaintiff refused to participate in the strike and was subsequently disciplined by the district committee of the union. The plaintiff's relationship with other members of the union subsequently deteriorated. The plaintiff left his employment and found work elsewhere. Due to continual union pressure, his new employer terminated his contract.

Held, by the High Court, that this amounted to an actionable conspiracy to injure the plaintiff in his trade as, *per* Harman J, the defendants 'were not furthering a trade dispute or other legitimate interest, but a grudge ... or personal matter'.

Q   Once a *bona fide* trade union purpose is established, are the conspirators still protected where they prosecute the strike selfishly or irresponsibly, aiming to punish or harm the employer?

11.5.2 Conspiracy to commit an unlawful act

Rookes v Barnard (1964) HL

For the facts, see 11.4, above.

Held, by the House of Lords, that the full time union official – Silverthorne – had not committed the tort of intimidation, since he was not employed by the plaintiff and so had not threatened to break his contract of employment. However, in organising the threats by the other workers to break their contracts of employment through strike action, he could be sued for conspiring to commit the tort of intimidation.

Lonhro v Fayed (1991) HL

The Secretary of State had referred the plaintiff's proposed takeover of a public company to the Monopolies and Mergers Commission. The plaintiff alleged that a less than flattering report was then produced by the

Commission as a result of the defendant's campaign of denigration and character assassination. The report required the plaintiffs to give an undertaking not to purchase more than 30% of the target company's equity. As such, this deprived the plaintiffs of an opportunity to take over the company and also provided the defendant with an opportunity to purchase shares the plaintiff would have bought. It was claimed the behaviour of the defendant amounted to a wrongful interference with the plaintiff's trade or business, and was actionable as the tort of conspiracy to injure.

Held, by the House of Lords, that: (I) for the tort of conspiring to commit an unlawful act – where the parties were actively engaged in some illegal activity, such as a breach of contract, tort or crime – the predominant purpose of the combiners was irrelevant; (II) consequently, liability would be imposed, even though the predominant purpose of the defendant was to further their own interests, as they were intentionally engaged in an illegal activity to injure the plaintiff.

11.6 Inducing breach of a statutory duty

Cunard Co Ltd v Stacey (1955) CA
The defendants were all seamen who encouraged fellow employees to take strike action. This was contrary to provisions in the Merchant Shipping Act 1894, which criminalised industrial action by merchant seamen.

Held, by the Court of Appeal, that a civil remedy was open to the shipowners against the defendants who induced others to commit offences under the Act.

Gouriet v UPW (1978) HL
In protest against the apartheid regime in South Africa, the Union of Postal Workers instructed its membership to refuse to process mail destined for South Africa. Under the Post Office Act 1953, it was an offence for persons employed by the Post Office to wilfully delay or omit to deliver postal packets or for any person to solicit or endeavour to procure any other person to commit such an offence.

Held, by the House of Lords, that: (I) the Post Office workers had *prima facie* committed criminal offences under the Post Office Act 1953; (II) there was no cause of action in tort against the defendant, because there was no power within the statute for the plaintiff to sue for inducing breach of this statutory duty; (III) a breach of a statutory duty does not on its own give rise to a civil action by a particular plaintiff, unless it can be shown, on the construction of the statute, that a duty is explicitly owed to the plaintiff as a member of an identifiable class.

Associated Newspapers Group Ltd v Wade (1979) CA

The defendant union (NGA) were in dispute with the publishers of local newspapers in the Nottingham area. The union instructed its members to boycott those plaintiff organisations that refused to stop advertising in these newspapers. The plaintiffs took action against the defendant on the grounds that they were unable to perform their legal duty to publish certain notices to the public.

Held, by Lord Denning MR in the Court of Appeal, that the behaviour of the union interfered with the statutory duty of these organisations to publish, which was directly actionable, as:

> ... trade union leaders have no immunity when a public authority is disabled from performing its statutory duties.

Meade v Haringey Borough Council (1979) CA

The parents of children who could not attend school because of a strike by caretaking staff issued writs to force the local authority to perform their statutory duty to provide full time education for their children as required by the 1944 Education Act.

Held, per Lord Denning MR in the Court of Appeal, that:

> ... the trade unions were the dominating influence in requiring the schools to be closed ...

This caused the local authority to break their statutory duty to provide full time education, which arguably supported an action in tort for those injured by the disruptive action.

Note ———

In later non-union cases (*Lonhro Ltd v Shell* (1982); *CBS Songs Ltd v Amstrad Electronics* (1988); and *X (A Minor) v Bedfordshire County Council* (1995)), Lord Denning's broad formulation for inducing breach of statutory duty, which gives third parties automatic rights of action on breach of statute, was rejected. All these cases re-emphasised the strict 'construction' test (applied by the House of Lords in *Gouriet*) for determining when an actionable breach of statutory duty arises. For an application of this test, see the next case.

Barretts and Baird v IPCS (1987)

Fatstock Officers, employed by the Meat and Livestock Commission (which has the statutory function of inspecting and certifying animals for slaughter), took industrial action via a series of one day strikes. This caused substantial loss to the plaintiff, who was a meat producer.

Held, by the High Court, that, on the construction of the duty imposed by statute, the plaintiff did have a cause of action which could amount to the tort of inducing breach of statutory duty. However, on the facts of the case, the one day strikes were not interfering sufficiently with the work of the abattoirs for there to have been an actual breach of statute.

Associated British Ports v TGWU (1989) HL

The defendant trade union objected to proposals to abolish the statutory scheme regulating the supply of dock labour. After negotiations with employers to replace the scheme failed, the defendant initiated strike action. A clause in the original statutory scheme established that employees should 'work for such periods as are reasonable in the circumstances of the case'. The employers argued that, by calling for strike action, the union was inducing breach of this statutory requirement.

Held, by the House of Lords, that the clause imposed a contractual, rather than a statutory, requirement to work; therefore, the issue of breach of statutory duty did not arise.

11.7 Economic duress

Universe Tankships Inc of Monrovia v ITWF (1982) HL

In the pursuit of a campaign against 'flags of convenience', ships members of the National Union of Seamen boycotted a ship owned by the plaintiff on its arrival at the port of Milford Haven. The union only lifted the boycott when the plaintiff complied with the demands of the union which included, *inter alia*, agreement to pay a substantial sum to the union's welfare fund. The plaintiff made a claim for restitution of this sum on the grounds that consent for entry into this special arrangement was vitiated by the industrial pressure imposed by the union on the plaintiff.

Held, by a majority of the House of Lords, that the plaintiff was entitled to restitution of this payment, since the union was in such a strong bargaining position that the plaintiff was coerced into agreeing to the contractual arrangements. Lords Scarman and Diplock noted, however, that, where the duress was applied 'in contemplation or furtherance of a trade dispute' (see 11.9, below), then for reasons of 'public policy', an action for duress would ordinarily fail.

Note
This decision was followed by the Court of Appeal in *Dimskal Shipping Co v ITWF* (1990).

Q   If industrial pressure *per se* constitutes economic duress, does this put into doubt the operation of the collective bargaining system and the 'right to strike'?

11.8 Inducing breach of an equitable obligation

Prudential Assurance Co v Lorenz (1971)
During an industrial dispute, union officials representing insurance agents working for the plaintiff company induced the agents not to submit their collected premiums to the company.

Held, by the High Court (*per* Plowman J), that there was sufficient legal authority for the view that the defendants were not just inducing breach of a contractual obligation, but were also interfering with a general equitable duty 'to account' implied by the general law relating to fiduciary duties.

> Note
>
> The significance of this decision is that there is no trade dispute immunity for this cause of action. However, trade union concern over this case has been reduced by the decision in the non-union case of *Metall und Rohstoff AG v Donaldson Inc* (1989), where the Court of Appeal held that there was no such tort of inducing breach of trust, and that any common law action for breach of an equitable obligation must be restricted solely to the facts in *Prudential*. The reasoning of the Court of Appeal in *Metall* was upheld by Hoffman LJ in *Law Debenture Trust Corp v Ural Caspian Oil Corp Ltd* (1993).

11.9 Trade union immunities – the Trade Union and Labour Relations (Consolidation) Act 1992

11.9.1 In contemplation or furtherance of a trade dispute

Section 219
(1) An act done by a person in contemplation or furtherance of a trade dispute is not actionable in tort on the ground ...:

    (a) that it induces another person to break a contract or interferes or induces another person to interfere with its performance; or

    (b) that it consists in his threatening that a contract (whether one to which he is a party or not) will be broken or its performance interfered with, or that he will induce another person to break a contract or interfere with its performance.

(2) An agreement or combination by two or more persons to do or procure the doing of an act in contemplation or furtherance of a trade dispute is not actionable in tort if the act is one which, if done without any such agreement or combination, would not be actionable in tort.

Note ───
Immunity from legal action is thus provided for the torts of inducing
breach of contract or for interfering with the performance of a contract
and for the torts of intimidation and conspiracy to injure, so long as the
act which is the subject of the legal action is committed *in contemplation
or furtherance of a trade dispute.*

Express Newspapers Ltd v MacShane (1979) HL

During a dispute with local papers in the Bolton area, the National Union
of Journalists (NUJ) called on its members in the Press Association to
refuse to supply news to these local papers. The defendant union also
called on all its members in national newspapers to take action, so as to
raise the morale of those journalists in Bolton who had gone on strike and
to persuade the remaining journalists in Bolton to join them.

Held, by the House of Lords, that: (I) action in 'furtherance' of a dispute
should be examined in the context of what the union subjectively believed.
All that was required was for the union to honestly and genuinely believe
the action they were taking would further union objectives; (II) even
though the call to members working for national newspapers to support
the action in Bolton would objectively have little influence on the dispute,
the union where still 'furthering' it.

Note ───
In response to this decision, the Government, in the 1980 Employment
Act, legislated to withdraw the immunities in circumstances of
secondary sympathetic action which had no tangible effect on the
primary dispute.

11.9.2 Trade dispute

Section 244

(1) In this Part, a 'trade dispute' means a dispute between workers and
their employer which relates wholly or mainly to one or more of the
following:

    (a) terms and conditions of employment, or the physical conditions in
which any workers are required to work;

    (b) engagement or non engagement, or termination or suspension of
employment or the duties of employment, of one or more workers;

    (c) allocation of work or the duties of employment between workers
or groups of workers;

    (d) matters of discipline;

    (e) a worker's membership or non-membership of a trade union;

(f) facilities for officials of trade unions; and

(g) machinery for negotiation or consultation, and other procedures, relating to any of the above matters, including the recognition by employers or employers' associations of the right of a trade union to represent workers in such negotiations or consultation or in the carrying out of such procedures.

Bents Brewery Co Ltd v Hogan (1945) HC

A trade union official sent out a questionnaire to members of his union, who were employed as managers of public houses, requesting information on their takings, wage bills, etc, in order to have this data available for a future wage claim on their behalf. The disclosure of this information was in breach of their contract of employment.

Held, by the High Court, that the questionnaire had simply been used to collect information for future collective bargaining purposes. Thus, there was no current dispute; no difference of opinion 'in being or imminent'. A dispute would only arise if, after the results of the questionnaire had been considered, a claim was submitted and rejected. Consequently, there was no trade dispute defence available to the defendant.

Q   When does a dispute finish? Should the courts apply an objective or subjective test?

BBC v Hearn (1977) CA

In this case, officials of the television technicians union threatened to instruct their members to prevent transmission of the FA Cup Final to South Africa because of the policy of the union to oppose the apartheid regime in that country.

Held, by the Court of Appeal, that this was not a trade dispute, but a straightforward political action, that did not attract the protection of the immunities. Consequently, an injunction to prevent the disruption of transmission of the event was granted.

Q   Counsel for the union submitted that this was a trade dispute; it was a dispute about the failure of the employer to agree to a variation of contracts of employment to allow their employees to opt out of work that involved broadcasting to South Africa. Why do you think this argument was not accepted by the Court of Appeal?

Sherrard v AUEW (1973) CA

A one day strike was called by the Trade Union Congress (TUC) in protest at the Government's counter-inflation policies, which froze pay across industries. The AUEW followed this call by instructing all members to take strike action, some of whom were employed by the Ministry of Defence.

Held, by Lord Denning MR, that, in general terms, a dispute between the TUC and the Government was not a trade dispute. However, those members of unions in Government installations (such as the Ministry of Defence) who were directly affected by the pay freeze were engaged in a trade dispute with the Government as employer, because ministerial authority was required before a pay rise could be authorised.

Note
Section 244(2) of the Trade Union and Labour Relations (Consolidation) Act 1992 specifically provides that a dispute between government and workers shall be treated as a trade dispute if the dispute has been referred to a joint body for resolution on which there is ministerial representation, or if the dispute cannot be settled without ministerial approval.

Express Newspapers Ltd v Keys (1980) HC

Strikes were held by numerous groups of workers in protest against Government economic policies during a collective 'day of action' called by the TUC. In particular, the general secretaries of SOGAT, NATSOPA, NGA and the NUJ issued directions to their members to take action, which resulted in the disruption of the production of the plaintiff's newspaper.

Held, by the High Court, that this was a political protest strike, the outstanding characteristic of which was that the employer was in no position to do anything about the demands of the union. Thus, as this was not a trade dispute, the inducement was not protected by the statutory immunities.

Mercury Communications v Scott-Garner (1983) CA

The plaintiff company was the beneficiary of the Government's liberalisation of the telecommunications industry. The plaintiff as a newly licensed operator planned to establish a digital communications network by using the British Telecom (BT) system. The Post Office Engineering Union was opposed to privatisation, supported BT's monopoly and instructed their members employed by BT not to connect Mercury to the system.

Held, by the Court of Appeal, that this was not a trade dispute, despite the union's arguments that this action was taken to avoid redundancies and protect their members conditions of employment. *Per* Lord Donaldson MR:

I find it impossible to conclude on the present evidence that the risk to jobs was a major part of what the dispute was about ... on the other hand, there is massive evidence that the union was waging a campaign against the political decisions to liberalise the industry and to privatise BT.

Per May LJ:

> ... there is no doubt that the union is and has for some time been conducting a campaign against liberalisation and privatisation ... and that the present action springs from a political and ideological campaign seeking to maintain the concept of public monopoly against private competition.

Associated British Ports v TGWU (1989) HC

In early 1989, the Government announced its intention to abolish the National Dock Labour Scheme, which had, since 1947, provided a degree of guaranteed employment to dock workers at ports covered by the scheme. After negotiations between union and port employers had broken down on the replacement for the scheme, a successful strike ballot was held and strike action was called by union officials.

Held, by Millet J in the High Court, that the true reason for the dispute was the employer's rejection of the union demand for new national conditions to replace the statutory scheme. This was not a politically inspired dispute with the Government over its abolition, as the strike was not directed at the Government *per se*, but concerned the industrial consequences of the political decision to abolish the scheme.

Wandsworth London Borough Council v NAS/UWT (1993) CA

The Education Reform Act 1988 established a national curriculum for school pupils and required teachers to stage additional tests and assessments for their pupils. The defendant union instructed its members, after a valid ballot, to boycott the tests required under the national curriculum.

Held, by the Court of Appeal, that this was not a political dispute with government motivated by opposition to educational policy *per se*; rather, it was a trade dispute, as it concerned the increase in teachers' workloads created by the implementation of policy by the local authority employer.

Note ──

Both the last two cases demonstrate that, where political decision making has a direct effect on terms and conditions of employment (or on other matters included in the definition in s 244(1)), any resulting dispute will be a 'trade' dispute. However, where there are mixed motives for a dispute, the 'trade' issue has to be predominant. In both cases cited above, evidence to this effect was provided by an examination of union campaign literature stressing the trade issues which accompanied the industrial action ballot paper.

Q   Does ill will, malice or personal animosity between union and employer turn a *prima facie* trade dispute into an unprotected personal dispute?

University College London NHS Trust v Unison (1999) CA
The plaintiff hospital trust entered into negotiations with a consortium under the Private Finance Initiative (PFI) for the consortium to build and run a new hospital. The trust refused the union's request to include a term in the contract to the effect that employees transferred to the consortium (and any future employees) would receive equivalent terms and conditions to those employees who remained with the trust. The union subsequently balloted for industrial action.

Held, by the Court of Appeal, that the definition of a trade dispute had not been satisfied, as the dispute was not between existing employees and their current employer as required by s 244. Here, the dispute was about terms and conditions that would apply to workers after their employment had ceased, and about workers not yet identified and not at presently employed by the plaintiff.

Note
The Court of Appeal believed that this was not, however, a dispute with a political objective. The union's action was primarily motivated in order to protect the terms and conditions of employment of their members.

11.10 Loss of immunity – the Trade Union and Labour Relations (Consolidation) Act 1992

Section 226 Requirement of ballot before action by trade union
(1) An act done by a trade union to induce a person to take part, or continue to take part, in industrial action:

(a) is not protected, unless the industrial action has the support of a ballot ...;

(b) ...

(2) Industrial action shall be regarded as having the support of a ballot only if:

(a) the union has held a ballot in respect of the action:

(i) in relation to which the requirements of s 226B so far as applicable before and during the holding of the ballot were satisfied;

(ii) in relation to which the requirements of ss 227 to 231 were satisfied; and

(iii) in which the majority voting in the ballot answered 'Yes' to the question applicable in accordance with s 229(2) to industrial action of the kind to which the act of inducement relates;

(b) ...

(3) ...

(4) ...

Section 226A Notice of ballot and sample voting paper for employers

(1) The trade union must take such steps as are reasonably necessary to ensure that:

(a) not later than the seventh day before the opening day of the ballot, the notice specified in sub-s (2); and

(b) not later than the third day before the opening day of the ballot, the sample voting paper specified in sub-s (3), is received by every person who it is reasonable for the union to believe will be the employer of persons who will be entitled to vote in the ballot.

(2) The notice referred to in para (a) of sub-s (1) is a notice in writing:

(a) stating that the union intends to hold the ballot;

(b) specifying the date which the union reasonably believes will be the opening day of the ballot; and

(c) describing (so that he can readily ascertain them) the employees of the employer who it is reasonable for the union to believe will be entitled to vote in the ballot.

(3) The sample voting paper referred to in para (b) of sub-s (1) is:

(a) a sample of the form of voting paper which is to be sent to the employees who it is reasonable for the trade union to believe will be entitled to vote in the ballot;

(b) ...

(3A) These rules apply for the purposes of para (c) of sub-s (2):

(a) if the union possesses information as to the number, category or workplace of the employees concerned, a notice must contain that information (at least);

(b) if a notice does not name any employees, that fact shall not be a ground for holding that it does not comply with para (c) of sub-s (2).

(4) ...

(5) ...

Section 226B Appointment of scrutineer

(1) The trade union shall, before the ballot in respect of the industrial action is held, appoint a qualified person ('the scrutineer'), whose terms of appointment shall require him to carry out in relation to the ballot the functions of:

   (a) taking such steps as appear to him to be appropriate for the purpose of enabling him to make a report to the trade union (see s 231B); and

   (b) making the report as soon as reasonably practicable after the date of the ballot and, in any event, not later than the end of the period of four weeks beginning with that date.

(2) ...

(3) The trade union shall ensure that the scrutineer duly carries out the functions conferred on him under sub-s (1) and that there is no interference with the carrying out of those functions from the union or any of its members, officials or employees.

(4) The trade union shall comply with all reasonable requests made by the scrutineer for the purposes of, or in connection with, the carrying out of those functions.

Section 226C Exclusion for small ballots

   ...

Section 227 Entitlement to vote in ballot

(1) Entitlement to vote in the ballot must be accorded equally to all the members of the trade union who it is reasonable at the time of the ballot for the union to believe will be induced to take part or, as the case may be, to continue to take part in the industrial action in question, and to no others.

(2) Repealed.

Section 228 Separate workplace ballots

   ...

Section 229 Voting paper

(1) The method of voting in a ballot must be by the marking of a voting paper by the person voting.

(1A)Each voting paper must:

   (a) state the name of the independent scrutineer;

   (b) clearly specify the address to which, and the date by which, it is to be returned;

(c) be given one of a series of consecutive whole numbers every one of which is used in giving a different number in that series to each voting paper printed or otherwise produced for the purposes of the ballot; and

(d) be marked with its number.

(2) The voting paper must contain at least one of the following questions:

(a) a question (however framed) which requires the person answering it to say, by answering 'Yes' or 'No', whether he is prepared to take part or, as the case may be, to continue to take part in a strike;

(b) a question (however framed) which requires the person answering it to say, by answering 'Yes or No', whether he is prepared to take part or, as the case may be, to continue to take part in industrial action short of a strike.

(2A) For the purposes of sub-s (2), an overtime ban and a call out ban constitute industrial action short of a strike.

(3) The voting paper must specify who, in the event of a vote in favour of industrial action, is authorised for the purposes of s 233 to call upon members to take part or continue to take part in the industrial action.

(4) The following statement must (without being qualified or commented upon by anything else on the voting paper) appear on every voting paper:

If you take part in a strike or other industrial action, you may be in breach of your contract of employment. However, if you are dismissed for taking part in strike or other industrial action which is called officially and is otherwise lawful, the dismissal will be unfair if it takes place fewer than eight weeks after you started taking part in the action and, depending on the circumstances, may be unfair if it takes place later.

Section 230 Conduct of ballot

(1) Every person who is entitled to vote in the ballot must:

(a) be allowed to vote without interference from, or constraint imposed by, the union or any of its members, officials or employees; and

(b) so far as is reasonably practicable, be enabled to do so without incurring any direct cost to himself.

(2) ... so far as is reasonably practicable, every person who is entitled to vote in the ballot must:

(a) have a voting paper sent to him by post at this home address ...;

(b) be given a convenient opportunity to vote by post.

(2A)...

(2B)...

(2C)...

(3) Repealed.

(4) A ballot shall be conducted so as to secure that:

(a) so far as reasonably practicable, those voting do so in secret; and

(b) the votes given in the ballot are fairly and accurately counted.

For the purposes of para (b), an inaccuracy in counting shall be disregarded if it is accidental and on a scale which could not affect the result of the ballot.

Section 231   Information as to result of ballot

...

Section 231A   Employers to be informed of ballot result

...

Section 231B   Scrutineer's report

...

Section 233   Calling of industrial action with support of ballot

(1) Industrial action shall not be regarded as having the support of a ballot unless it is called by a specified person and the conditions specified below are satisfied.

(2) A 'specified person' means a person specified or of a description specified in the voting paper for the ballot in accordance with s 229(3).

(3) The conditions are that:

(a) there must have been no call by the trade union to take part or continue to take part in industrial action to which the ballot relates, or any authorisation or endorsement by the union of any industrial action before the date of the ballot;

(b) there must be a call for industrial action by a specified person, and industrial action to which it relates must take place before the ballot ceases to be effective in accordance with s 234.

(4) ...

Section 234   Period after which ballot ceases to be effective

(1) Subject to the following provisions, a ballot ceases to be effective for the purposes of s 233(3)(b) in relation to industrial action by members of a trade union at the end of the period, beginning with the date of the ballot:

(a) of four weeks, or

(b) of such longer duration not exceeding eight weeks as is agreed between the union and the members' employer.

(2)–(6) ...

Section 234A Notice to employers of industrial action

...

London Underground Ltd v NUR (1989) HC

The NUR called a ballot of its members employed by London Underground, asking them whether they were prepared to take strike action over four specific issues. Before members were balloted, three of the issues in dispute were settled by negotiation. The union failed to publicise this to the membership.

Held, by Simon Brown J in the High Court, that, where there are four separate issues in conflict between the parties, there is no need for there to be four separate questions. However, where all the issues are wrapped up into a single question, they must be current live issues of dispute. This ballot was therefore invalid, as members of the union had voted influenced by a belief that all four issues were still matters of dispute.

Q   Was this case correctly decided if, *per* Millet J, in *ABP v TGWU* (1989): '... what matters is that a majority supported the strike [rather than] why they did so?'

Post Office v UCW (1990) CA

During a dispute over the conversion of post offices to 'agency status', the union called for strike action and action short of a strike, and included on the ballot paper a single question referring to both types of action.

Held, by the Court of Appeal, that the form of question asked in the ballot did not satisfy the requirements of s 229(2) (then s 11 of the Trade Union Act 1984). If a union contemplates calling for both strike action and action short of a strike, it must ask a specific question in respect of both causes of action. A 'rolled up' question is not sufficient.

Connex South Eastern Ltd v RMT (1999) CA

The union successfully balloted for 'strike action' and instructed members to ban overtime and rest day working. The employer argued that the ballot was flawed, as this form of action was, in reality, action short of a strike that required a separate question on the ballot paper.

Held, by the Court of Appeal, that a lawful ballot had been held where union members were asked to vote in favour of 'strike action' – even though the action taken included a ban on overtime and rest day working. This type of action was 'strike action' for the purposes of the definition in s 246 (which states that a strike is 'any concerted stoppage of work'). A concerted stoppage for any period of time (as occurred here) was included within this definition.

Note

This decision indicated that only where a union is balloting for action that does not technically require a stoppage of work – such as a 'go-slow' or 'work to rule' will a question on 'action short of a strike' be required. However, now note s 229(2A), introduced by the Employment Relations Act 1999.

British Railways Board v NUR (1989) CA

The question which arose here concerned the validity of a ballot, where a small minority of members out of a total membership of 70,000 who were called upon to take industrial action had not received ballot papers, because of an inadvertent oversight by the union.

Held, by the Court of Appeal, that this was a case of a failure to provide some of the membership with an opportunity to vote. As, under the statute there was no absolute obligation to provide everyone with a ballot paper, and as only a trifling number of voters were affected, which did not affect the result, the omission did not nullify the ballot.

London Underground v RMT (1995) CA

In furtherance of a trade dispute with London Underground over pay and conditions, the RMT union decided to ballot its members for industrial action. Between the date of the successful ballot and the first day of industrial action, several hundred new members had joined the union who had not voted in the ballot, but who were called out on strike. The employer argued that the action could no longer said to be supported by a ballot as required by s 226(1).

Held, by the Court of Appeal, that the campaign of industrial action had still been legitimised by the ballot, as what was solely of concern was whether a majority of those voting at the time the action was called had voted in favour, and so had declared themselves prepared to take part.

Q   If the Court of Appeal had interpreted the provisions in such a way that all those called out on strike had to be balloted, would unions, in practical terms, ever be able to comply?

Newham Borough Council v NALGO (1993) CA

Employees in the finance department of the plaintiff council took action, preceded by a ballot, in protest at redundancies. During the period prior to the ballot, the union campaigned among its membership for a 'Yes' vote in the ballot. The employer argued this rendered the ballot invalid, as the union had breached s 230(1)(a), which states that the electorate must be permitted to vote without interference from, or have any constraint imposed by, the union, its members or officials.

Held, by the Court of Appeal, that a union is permitted to be partisan in its views and to campaign for a 'Yes' vote in the ballot by the provision of information and advice on the issues. What matters is that the union does not induce members to take action before the ballot result is known.

Q   Where do you draw the line between the mere provision of information on the issues and persuasion or inducement?

Monsanto plc v TGWU (1986) CA

Due to a dispute over temporary working, the union organised a valid and successful ballot of their relevant membership and initiated limited industrial action. This was broken off for negotiations with the employer to settle the dispute. On the breakdown of the negotiations, the industrial action was renewed. The employer argued that it was necessary for the union to hold a further ballot to legitimise the resumption of industrial action.

Held, by the Court of Appeal, that the action had only been temporarily suspended for legitimate negotiations. A new ballot was only required where the action had been abandoned.

Post Office v UCW (1990) CA

During the dispute over the privatisation of post offices, the UCW successfully balloted its members for industrial action. Between October and December 1988, the union called a series of selective one day strikes. Between January and April 1989, the union mounted a public relations campaign in opposition to Post Office policy. In response to the failure of the campaign, industrial action resumed in September 1989 and in January 1990. The employer argued the successful ballot in August 1988 did not legitimise action taken in 1989 and 1990.

Held, by the Court of Appeal, that the industrial action ceased in December 1988. The 1989 action was entirely new and so required the support of a fresh ballot. *Per* Lord Donaldson MR:

> It is implicit in the Act that industrial action, once begun, shall continue without substantial interruption if reliance is to continue to be placed upon the verdict of the ballot.

Q   Does this decision mean that unions are in danger of losing their immunities where they undertake a lengthy campaign with short intermittent strikes?

Tanks and Drum Ltd v TGWU (1991) CA

When negotiations over wages broke down, the union balloted its members for industrial action. The ballot paper (as required by s 233) specified that the general secretary of the union had the authority to call for strike action. A large majority in favour of the strike was achieved, but before action was taken, negotiations resumed. When it became clear that the employer was not negotiating in good faith, shop stewards were given authority by the general secretary to call for strike action.

Held, by the Court of Appeal, that, on the construction of the section, a conditional authorisation can be given. However, a blanket authority to local officials could not be permitted, as that would subvert the plain meaning of the statutory provision. A conditional authorisation is only lawful where explicit authority, as here, is given to named or defined officials.

Section 222 Action to enforce trade union membership

(1) An act is not protected if the reason, or one of the reasons, for which it is done is the fact or belief that a particular employer:

  (a) is employing, has employed or might employ a person who is not a member of a trade union; or

  (b) is failing, has failed or might fail to discriminate against such a person.

(2) ...

(3) An act is not protected if it constitutes, or is one of a number of acts which together constitute, an inducement or attempted inducement of a person:

  (a) to incorporate in a contract to which that person is a party, or a proposed contract to which he intends to be a party, a term or condition which is or would be void by virtue of s 144 (union membership requirement in contract for goods or services); or

  (b) to contravene s 145 (refusal to deal with person on grounds relating to union membership).

(4) ...

(5) ...

Section 223 Action taken because of dismissal for taking unofficial action

An act is not protected if the reason, or one of the reasons, for doing it is the fact or belief that an employer has dismissed one or more employees in circumstances such that, by virtue of s 237 [dismissal in connection with unofficial action], they have no right to complain of unfair dismissal.

Section 224 Secondary action

(1) An act is not protected if one of the facts relied on for the purpose of establishing liability is that there has been secondary action ...

(2) There is secondary action in relation to a trade dispute when, and only when, a person:

(a) induces another to break a contract of employment or interferes or induces another to interfere with its performance; or

(b) threatens that a contract of employment under which he or another is employed will be broken or its performance interfered with, or that he will induce another to break a contract of employment or to interfere with its performance, and the employer under the contract of employment is not the employer party to the dispute.

(3) ...

(4) ...

(5) ...

(6) ...

Section 225 Pressure to impose union recognition requirement

(1) An act is not protected if it constitutes, or is one of a number of acts which together constitute, an inducement or attempted inducement of a person:

(a) to incorporate in a contract to which that person is a party, or a proposed contract to which he intends to be a party, a term or condition which is or would be void by virtue of s 186 (recognition requirement in contract for goods or services); or

(b) to contravene s 187 (refusal to deal with person on grounds of union exclusion).

(2) An act is not protected if:

(a) it interferes with the supply (whether or not under a contract) of goods and services, or can reasonably be expected to have that effect; and

(b) ...

(c) the reason, or one of the reasons, for doing the act is the fact or belief that the supplier ... does not, or might not:

(i) recognise one or more trade unions for the purpose of negotiating on behalf of workers, or any class of worker, employed by him; or

(ii) negotiate or consult with, or with an official of, one or more trade unions.

Glossary

1 Employee Status

Carmichael v National Power   Mutual obligations test

Ferguson v John Dawson and
     Partners   Description given by worker

Gascol Conversions v Mercer   Employment particulars

Hall (Inspector of Taxes)
     v Lorimer   'Economic reality' test

Lee v Chung and Shun Sing   Employee status – fact or law?

Loughran and Kelly v N
     Ireland Housing Executive   Solicitor as employee

Market Investigations v
     Minster of Social Security   Economic reality test

McMeechan v Secretary of
     State for Employment   Employee status – fact or law?

Nethermere (St Neots)
     v Taverna and Gardiner   Mutual obligations test

O'Kelly v Trusthouse Forte   Mutual obligations test

Ready Mixed Concrete v
     Minister of Pensions   Multiple test

Stevenson Jordan and Harrison
     v McDonald and Evans   Organisation test

System Floors (UK)
     v Daniel   Employment particulars

Walker v Crystal Palace FC   Control test

2 Terms of the Contract of Employment

Ali v Christian Salvesen	Implied terms
Anderson v Pringle of Scotland Ltd	Selection procedure as term
BCCI v Ali (No 3)	Trust and confidence
Bartholomew v London Borough of Hackney	Reference
Bass Leisure v Thomas	Mobility clause
Breach v Epsylon Industries	Duty to provide work
Cadoux v Central Regional Council	Collective agreements
Collier v Sunday Referee Publishing	Duty to provide work
Courtaulds Northern Spinning v Sibson	Implied terms
Cresswell v Board of Inland Revenue	Duty to adapt
Delaney v Staples	Deduction from wages
Dryden v Greater Glasgow Health Board	Implied terms – work rules
Faccenda Chicken v Fowler	Confidential information
Greer v Sketchley	Width of restraint clause
Hanley v Pease and Partners	Suspension without pay
Herbert Morris v Saxelby	Restraint of trade
Hivac v Park Royal Scientific Instruments	Spare time work
Hussman Manufacturing v Weir	Deduction from wages
Isle of Wight Tourist Board v Coombes	Trust and confidence
Jack Allen (Sales and Service) v Smith	Restraint of trade and injunctions

Johnstone v Bloomsbury HA	Employer's duties – health
Langston v Amalgamated Union of Engineering Workers (No 2)	Duty to provide work
Lister v Romford Ice and Cold Storage	Duties of the employee
Littlewoods v Harris	Width of restraint clause
Malik v BCCI (In Liquidation)	Trust and confidence
Marley v Forward Trust Group	Collective agreements
Mason v Provident Clothing and Supply	Restraint of trade
Miles v Wakefield MDC	Deduction from wages
Morrish v Henlys (Folkestone)	Duty to obey orders
NCB v Galley	Collective agreements
Nordenfelt v Maxim Nordenfelt Guns and Ammunition	Restraint of trade
Ottoman Bank v Chakarian	Duty to obey orders
Post Office v Roberts	Trust and confidence
Reading v Attorney General	Duty to account
Rock Refrigeration v Jones	Restraint of trade – dismissal
Scally v Southern Health and Social Services Board	Employer's duties – information
Schroeder (A) Music Publishing v Macaulay	Exclusive service contracts
Scorer v Seymour-Johns	Doctrine of severance
Scully UK v Lee	Width of restraint clause
Secretary of State for Employment v ASLEF (No 2)	Duty of fidelity
Shirlaw v Southern Foundries	Implied terms
Spring v Guardian Assurance	References

Sybron Corp v Rochem	Duty to disclose misdeeds
Taylor v Secretary of State for Scotland	Policy as contract term
TSC Europe (UK) v Massey	Non-solicitation clause
Waltons and Morse v Dorrington	Safe working environment
Wandsworth LBC v D'Silva	Code of Practice
Wiluszynski v London Borough of Tower Hamlets	Deductions from wages

3 Health and Safety at Work

Barber v RJB Mining (UK)	Working Time Regulations
Bowater v Rowley Regis BC	*Volenti non fit injuria*
Coltman v Bibby Tankers	Meaning of 'equipment'
Edwards v NCB	'Reasonably practicable'
Hudson v Ridge Manufacturing	Practical jokes at work
Latimer v AEC	Standard of care
Pape v Cumbria CC	Duty to warn of risks
Paris v Stepney BC	Higher standard of care
Pickford v ICI	Repetitive strain injury
R v Associated Octel Co	Liability for contractors
R v F Howe & Son (Engineers)	Health and safety – fine
Square D v Cook	Injuries on others' premises
Stapley v Gypsum Mines	Contributory negligence
Walker v Northumberland CC	Stress liability
White v Chief Constable of S Yorkshire Police	Employees – psychiatric injury
Williams and Clyde Coal v English	Duty of care
Withers v Perry Chain	No precautions possible

4 Terminating the Contract

Alcan Extrusions v Yates	Dismissal – unilateral change in terms
Blyth v Scottish Liberal Club	Summary dismissal – wilful and deliberate disobedience
Bracebridge Engineering v Darby	Constructive dismissal – sexual harassment
Brown v Knowsley BC	Termination – by performance
Brown v Merchant Ferries	Constructive dismissal – requirement for repudiatory conduct
Caledonian Mining v Bassett	Resignation – redundancy payment
Condor v Barron Knights	Frustration – illness
Courtaulds v Andrew	Constructive dismissal – breach of implied term
Denco v Joinson	Summary dismissal – use of confidential information
Dixon v BBC	Dismissal – fixed term contract
E Sussex CC v Walker	Resignation – pressure from employer
Egg Stores v Leibovici	Frustration – incapacity – general test
Ely v YKK Fasteners	Resignation – intimation of intention
FC Shepherd v Jerrom	Frustration – imprisonment – fault
Futty v D & D Brekkes	Dismissal – use of language
Greenaway Harrison v Wiles	Constructive dismissal – anticipatory breach
Halfpenny v Ige Medical Systems	Dismissal – maternity leave – revival of contract
Hare v Murphy Brothers	Frustration – imprisonment
Harman v Flexible Lamps	Frustration – avoidance of rights
Haseltine Lake v Dowler	Dismissal – known date for termination
Hellyer Brothers v Atkinson	Unilateral resignation
Hilton Hotels v Protopapa	Constructive dismissal – vicarious liability
Humber and Birch v University of Liverpool	Termination – mutual agreement

Igbo v Johnson Matthey	Imposed automatic termination agreement
J and J Stern v Simpson	Dismissal – use of language
Kwik Fit v Lineham	Resignation – intention
Laws v London Chronicle	Summary dismissal – gross misconduct
Lewis v Motorworld Garages	Constructive dismissal – breach of implied term
Logan Saltan v Durham CC	Termination – mutual agreement
London Transport Executive v Clark	Termination by conduct
Marshall v Harland Woolf	Frustration – incapacity
Martin v MBS Fastening	Inducing resignation
McAlwane v Boughton Estates	Agreed variation of notice
Neary v Dean of Westminster	Summary dismissal – breach of trust
Norris v Southampton CC	Frustration – imprisonment – fault
Notcutt v Universal Equipment	Frustration – existence of the principle
Pepper v Webb	Summary dismissal – refusal to obey orders
Poussard v Spiers	Discharge of the contract by frustration
Sheffield v Oxford Controls	Resignation – mutually acceptable terms
Sinclair v Neighbour	Summary dismissal – gross breach of good faith
Villella v MFI Furniture	Frustration – foreseeability of illness
Weathersfield v Sargent	Constructive dismissal – communication of reason
Western Excavating v Sharp	Constructive dismissal – repudiatory breach
Williams v Watson Coaches	Frustration – strict application of test
Wiltshire CC v NATFHE	Dismissal – fixed term contract

5 Unfair Dismissal

Adams v Derby CC — Establishing the real reason for dismissal

Alboni v Ind Coope Retail before dismissal date — Reasonableness – employer's actions

British Gas v McCarrick — Reason – employee admission

British Home Stores v Burchell — Reasonable belief in the reason

Byrne v BOC — Fairness – natural justice

Capital Foods Retail v Corrigan — Application – out of time

Chubb Fire Security v Harper — Dismissal – failure to agree change in contract – the disadvantage to employee

Clark v Civil Aviation Authority — Fairness – appeal process

Devis (W) v Atkins — Reason – must be established at time of dismissal

E Berkshire HA v Matadeen — Tribunal decision – perversity

E Lindsey DC v Daubney — Incapability – medical history

Eclipse Blinds v Wright — Incapability – consultation requirement

Ferguson v Prestwick Circuits — Redundancy – consultation

Frames Snooker Centre v Boyce — Fairness – dismissal of a group

Haddon v Van Den Bergh — Reasonableness – test of fairness

Heron v Citylink Nottingham — Redundancy – consultation – exceptional circumstances

Hotson v Wisbech Conservative Club — Reason – labelling

Jean Sorelle v Rybak — Application – out of time

London Fire and Civil Defence Authority v Betty — Incapability – employer's fault

London International College v Sen — Application – out of time

Monie v Coral Racing	Reason – reliance on new and subsequent reason
Mugford v Midland Bank	Redundancy – consultation
P v Nottinghamshire CC	Reason – employee admission
Palmer v Southend-on-Sea BC	Application – out of time
Polkey v AE Dayton Services	Redundancy – consultation
Proctor v British Gypsum	Fairness – consistency between employees
Richmond Engineering v Pearce	Dismissal – failure to agree change in contract – the reasonable employer test
RS Components v RE Irwin	Dismissal – failure to agree changes in contract
RSPCA v Croucher	Reason – employee admission
Schultz v Esso Petroleum	Application – out of time
Spencer v Paragon Wallpapers	Incapability – factors to be taken into account
St Basil's Centre v McCrossan	Application – out of time
St John of God (Care Services) v Brooks	Dismissal – failure to agree change in contract – sound business reason
Thomson v Alloa Motor Co	Reason – must be connected to employment issue
Timex Corp v Thomson	Establishing the real reason for dismissal
Tower Hamlets HA v Anthony	Fairness – failure of procedure
United Distillers v Conlin	Fairness – consistency between employees
West Midlands Co-operative Society v Tipton	Reason and the appeal process
Whitbread v Mills	Fairness – appeal process
Williams v Compair Maxam	Redundancy – consultation
Wilson v Ethicon	Reasonableness – test of fairness

6 Redundancy

Chapman v Goonvean and Rostrowrack China Clay	Free transport to work
Clarkes of Hove v Bakers Union	Special circumstances defence
Cowen v Haden	Redundancy – effect of contract
Hindle v Percival Boats	Meaning of redundancy
Johnson v Nottinghamshire Combined Police Authority	Change in hours of work
Johnson v Peabody Trust	Redundancy – scope of contract
Lesney Products v Nolan	Re-organisation of business
Moon v Homeworthy Furniture (Northern)	Meaning of redundancy
Murray v Foyle Meats	Meaning of redundancy
North Riding Garages v Butterwick	Work of a particular kind
O'Brien v Associated Fire Alarms	Redundancy – mobility
Robinson v British Island Airways	Work of a particular kind
Sanders v Ernest Neale	Redundancy – striking employees
Spencer v Gloucestershire CC	Reasonable to refuse offer
Taylor v Kent CC	Reasonable to refuse offer
Thomas Wragg & Sons v Wood	Reasonable to refuse offer
UK Atomic Energy Authority v Claydon	Mobility clause
Vaux and Associated Breweries v Ward	Redundancy – needs of business
Williams v Compair Maxam	Redundancy procedures

7 Continuity of Employment and Transfer of Undertakings

Allen v Amalgamated Construction	TUPE – transfers between subsidiaries
Askew v Governing Body of Clifton Middle School	TUPE – no transfer
Bernadone v Pall Mall Services Group	TUPE – tortious liability
Berriman v Delabole Slate	TUPE – ETO defence
Booth v USA	Continuity – fixed term contracts
Cowell v Quilter Goodison and QC Management Services	TUPE – definition of employee
Credit Suisse First Boston (Europe) v Lister	TUPE – non-solicitation clause
Dines v Initial Health Care Services	TUPE – contracting out
ECM (Vehicle Delivery Service) v Cox	TUPE – contracting out
Fitzgerald v Hall Russell	Temporary cessation of work
Flack v Kodak	Irregular work patterns
Ford v Warwickshire CC	Temporary cessation of work
Francisco Hernandez Vidal v Gomez Perez	TUPE – contracting out
Katsikas v Konstantinidis	TUPE – objection by employee
Lassman v Secretary of State for Trade and Industry	Continuity – redundancy payment
Ledernes Hovedorganisation (acting from Rygaard) v Dansk Arbejdsgiverforening	TUPE – contracting out test
Litster v Forth Dry Dock	TUPE – dismissal before transfer
Michael Peters v Farnfield	TUPE – no relevant transfer
Morris Angel v Hollande	TUPE – restraint of trade

Nokes v Doncaster Amalgamated Colleries	Continuity – common law position
Premier Motors (Medway) v Total Oil Great Britain	TUPE – relevant transfer
Rask and Christensen v ISS Kantineservice A/S	TUPE – contracting out
Redmond (Dr Sophie) Stichting v Bartol	TUPE – non-commercial

Schmidt v Spar- und Leihkasse
    der früheren Ämter
    Bordesholm
	TUPE – contracting out test

Spijkers v Gebroeders Benedik Abbatoir CV	TUPE – economic entity
Sunley Turriff Holdings v Thomson	TUPE – unfair dismissal

Suzen v Zehnacker
    Gebaudereingung GmbH
    Krankenhausservice
	TUPE – contracting out

Whitehouse v Chas A Blatchford	TUPE – ETO defence
Wilson v St Helens BC	TUPE – variation in contract
Woodhouse v Peter Brotherhood	Continuity – change of employer

8 Equal Pay

Barber v Guardian Royal Exchange Assurance	Equal pay – meaning of pay
Barry v Midland Bank	Severance pay
Bilka-Kaufhaus GmbH v Weber von Hartz	Equal pay – occupational pension
British Coal Corp v Smith	Area of comparison
Bromley v H & J Quick	Job evaluation scheme
Calder v Rowntree Mackintosh Confectionery	Genuine material difference

Capper Pass v Lawton	Like work
Clay Cross (Quarry Services) v Fletcher	Market forces defence
Enderby v Frenchay AHA	Equal pay – justification
Evesham v N Hertfordshire HA and Secretary of State for Health	Equal pay – comparison
Handels-OG Kontorfunktionaerernes Foribund i Danmark v Dansk Arbejdsgiverforening	Equal pay – proof
Hayward v Cammell Laird	Equal value claim
Hicking v Basford Group	Equal pay – time limit
Jenkins v Kingsgate (Clothing Productions) (No 2)	Like work – part-time
Lawrence v Regent Office Care	Equal pay – same employment
Leverton v Clwyd CC	Area of comparison
Levez v TH Jennings (Harlow Pools) (No 2)	Equal pay – time limit
Macarthys v Smith	Comparison with previous employee
Pickstone v Freemans	Equal value claim
R v Secretary of State for Employment ex p EOC	Equal pay – indirect discrimination
Rainey v Greater Glasgow Health Board	Equal pay – justification
Ratcliffe v N Yorkshire CC	Equal pay – material factor
Shields v E Coomes Holdings	Like work
Snoxell v Vauxhall Motors	Red-circling
Strathclyde Regional Council v Wallace	Genuine material difference
Thomas v NCB	Like work

9 Discrimination

Baynton v Saurus General Engineering	Disability discrimination – defence of justification
Brown v Rentokill	Dismissal – pregnancy – illness
Burrett v W Birmingham HA	Direct discrimination – uniform requirements
Burton v De Vere Hotels	Race discrimination – liability for third parties
Chapman v Simon	Inference of discrimination – subconscious prejudice
Clark v TDG	Disability discrimination – less favourable treatment
Coker and Osamor v The Lord Chancellor	Indirect discrimination – appointment on the basis of personal knowledge
De Souza v AA	Racial insult – 'other detriment'
Eke v Commissioners of Customs and Excise	Racial harassment – inadequate investigation
Goodwin v The Patent Office	Disability discrimination – definition of 'disabled person'
HM Prison Service v Johnson	Remedies – guidelines on damages
Home Office v Holmes	Indirect discrimination – requirement to work part time
James v Eastleigh BC	Direct discrimination – the 'but for' test
Jones v Tower Boot Co	Race discrimination – vicarious liability
Kenny v Hampshire Constabulary	Disability discrimination – reasonable adjustments – personal needs
King v Great Britain China Centre	Inference of discrimination – guidelines
London Borough of Lambeth v CRE	Race discrimination – genuine occupational qualification

Mandla v Lee — Meaning of 'racial grounds'

Marshall v Southampton and SW Hampshire AHA — Equal treatment directive – discriminatory retirement ages – emanation of the State

Meade-Hill v British Council — Indirect discrimination – mobility clause

O'Neill v Governors of St Thomas More School — Discriminatory motive

Owen and Briggs v James — racial discrimination – Less favourable treatment

P v S and Cornwall CC — Dismissal – gender reassignment – equal treatment directive

Pearse v Bradford Metropolitan Council — Indirect discrimination – pool for comparison

Perera v Civil Service Commission — Race discrimination – age requirement

Porcelli v Strathclyde Regional Council — Direct discrimination – sexual harassment

Price v Civil Service Commission — Indirect discrimination – age requirement

Qureshi v London Borough of Newham — Discrimination – failure to follow equal opportunities policy

R v Birmingham CC ex p EOC — Intention to discriminate – unnecessary condition

R v Ministry of Defence ex p Smith — Sexual orientation – Art 8 of the ECHR – equal treatment directive

R v Secretary of State for Defence ex p Perkins — Sexual orientation – equal treatment directive – ECJ referral

R v Secretary of State for Employment ex p Seymour — Indirect discrimination – justification

Rees v Apollo Watch Repairs — Dismissal – pregnancy – replacement

Sidhu v Aerospace
   Composite Technology   Race discrimination – vicarious liability
                           for conduct outside of employment

Skyrail Oceanic v Coleman   Discriminatory stereotypes

Tarling v Wisdom
   Toothbrushes   Disability discrimination –
                            reasonable adjustments

Tottenham Green Under Fives
   v Marshall   Race discrimination – genuine
                            occupational qualification

Webb v EMO Cargo (UK)   Equal treatment directive – dismissal –
                            pregnancy

West Midlands Transport
   Executive v Singh   Discrimination – use of statistics

10 Trade Unions and their Members

Blackall v National Union of
   Foundry Workers   Rule book – unlawful expulsion

Bonsor v Musicians' Union   Enforcing the rule book

Bradley v NALGO   Expulsion – statutory protection – remedies

Clarke v Chadburn   Rule book alteration – breach of the rule
                            book

Edwards v SOGAT   'Right to work' – closed shop – public
                            policy – union rules – bylaws

Esterman v NALGO   Construction of the rules – unlawful
                            expulsion

Goring v British Actors
   Equity Association   'Right to work' – authority of union rule
                            book

Leigh v NUR   Disciplinary action – failure to use
                            internal remedies

Longley v NUJ   Expulsion – interlocutory injunction

MacLelland v NUJ   Construction of the rule book –
                            disciplinary action

Medhurst v NALGO — Disciplinary action – statutory protection – 'unjustifiable'

NACODS v Gluchowski — Disciplinary action – 'exclusion' from the union

Nagle v Fielden — 'Right to work' – public policy

NALGO v Killorn — Disciplinary action – statutory protection – denial of temporary benefits

R v Jockey Club ex p Ram Racecourses — Exclusion – judicial review

Radford v NATSOPA — Disciplinary action – rules of natural justice – internal disciplinary tribunal – jurisdiction of the courts

Roebuck v NUM (Yorkshire Area) (No 2) — Disciplinary action – bias

Silvester v National Union of Printing, Bookbinding and Paper Workers — Rule book – unlawful expulsion

Taylor v National Union of Seamen — Disciplinary action – bias

Taylor v NUM (Derbyshire Area) (No 1) — Strike call – breach of rule book

TGWU v Webber — Expulsion – statutory protection – a 'determination' to expel

White v Kuzych — Disciplinary action – bias

11 Industrial Action

Associated British Ports v TGWU — Immunities – industrial consequences of political decision making

Inducing breach of statutory duty – breach of contract insufficient

Associated Newspapers Group v Wade — Inducing breach of statutory duty – trade union immunity

Barretts and Baird v IPCS	Inducing breach of statutory duty – requirement for breach of statute
BBC v Hearn	The immunities – 'trade' dispute
Bents Brewery v Hogan	The immunities – a 'dispute'
Brimelow v Casson	Inducing breach of contract – defence of justification
British Railways Board v NUR	Loss of immunity – balloting – 'opportunity to vote'
Connex South Eastern v RMT	Loss of immunity – balloting – definition of 'strike action'
Crofter Handwoven Harris Tweed v Veitch	Conspiracy – predominant purpose
Cunard v Stacey	Inducing breach of statutory duty
Emerald Construction v Lowthian	Inducing breach of contract – knowledge of the contract – intention
Express Newspapers v Keys	The immunities – political dispute
Express Newspapers v MacShane	The immunities – furthering a dispute
Falconer v ASLEF and NUR	Inducing breach of contract – intention
Gouriet v UPW	Inducing breach of statutory duty – construction of the statute
Hadmor Productions v Hamilton	Interference with contract, trade or business – commercial expectations
Huntley v Thornton	Conspiracy – trade union purpose
London Underground v NUR	Loss of immunity – balloting – separate questions
London Underground v RMT	Loss of immunity – balloting – new members
Lonhro v Fayed	Conspiracy – predominant purpose – intention
Meade v Haringey BC	Inducing breach of statutory duty – construction of the statute

Mercury Communications
  v Scott-Garner   The immunities – ideological dispute

Merkur Island Shipping Corp
  v Laughton   Inducing breach of contract – knowledge of the contract – Interference with contract, trade or business – exclusion clause

Mogul Steamship Co
  v McGregor, Gow & Co   Conspiracy – justification

Monsanto v TGWU   Loss of immunity – balloting – suspension of action

Newham BC v NALGO   Loss of immunity – balloting – interference

Post Office v UCW   Loss of immunity – balloting – additional industrial action – specific question

Prudential Assurance
  v Lorenz   Inducing breach of an equitable obligation

Quinn v Leathem   Conspiracy – intention to cause loss

Rookes v Barnard   Conspiracy – organisation of strike action – intimidation – the unlawful threat

Sherrard v AUEW   The immunities – political dispute

South Wales Miners' Federation
  v Glamorgan Coal   Inducing breach of contract – defence of justification

Square Grip Reinforcement
  v MacDonald   Inducing breach of contract – active inducement

Tanks and Drum v TGWU   Loss of immunity – balloting – conditional authorisation for industrial action

Thomson (DC) v Deakin   Inducing breach of contract – the four elements – actual breach

Torquay Hotel v Cousins   Inducing breach of contract – inducement – interference with contract, trade or business – the elements

Union Traffic v TGWU	Inducing breach of contract – presence at the workplace – inducement
Universe Tankships Inc of Monrovia v ITWF	Economic duress – industrial pressure
UCL Hospital NHS Trust v Unison	Immunities – trade dispute and future employees
Wandsworth LBC v NAS/UWT	Immunities – opposition to educational policy – trade dispute

Index

Absenteeism 94–95
ACAS Codes of Practice
  on redundancy 110
Account, duty to 35, 241
Age
  racial discrimination 191
  retirement 203–04
Agency workers 3
Alternative employment,
  offers of 129–31
Armed forces 207, 208
Assaults 197

Ballots
  conduct 249–50
  immunities 246–55
  information on
    result..250
  notice 247
  period of
    effectiveness of 250–51
  sample voting
    papers...247
  scrutineers...........................248, 250
  separate workplace 248
  small, exclusion for 248
  strikes 221–22,
                          246–55
  voting
    entitlement 248
    papers 247, 248–49
Bargaining power...............................46
Breach of statutory
  duty 238–40

Business transfers
  See Transfer of
    undertakings

Capability.....................................96, 97,
                           106–09
Closed shops.....................................24
Codes of Practice
  ACAS 110
  disability
    discrimination...........................210
  implied terms 18–19
  redundancy 110
Collective agreements
  contracts of
    employment 20–22
  equal pay......................................174
  implied terms 19–22
  sex discrimination 174
  written statement
    of particulars..............................14
Compensation
  inventions 35–38
  racial
    discrimination....................201–02
  sex discrimination 202
Conduct
  See Misconduct
Confidential
  information 33–34
Conspiracy
  industrial action 236–38
  injure, to.................................236–38
  unlawful act,
    to commit 237–38

Constructive dismissal 83–88
   conduct 84–86
   implied terms 84–85
   reasons for leaving,
     communication of 88
   re-organisation 86–87
   repudiation 85–88
   trust and confidence,
     breach of duty
     of mutual...............................85–86
   variation...87
Continuity of
   employment 137–43
   arrangements 140–41
   beginning of 138
   change of employer 142–43
   custom 140–41
   fixed term contracts..............139, 141
   presumption of 137–38
   seasonal work 140
   sex discrimination 189
   temporary cessation
     of work..................................139–40
   transfer of
     undertakings.............................145
Contracting out 153–58
Contracts of
   employment
   See, also, Termination
     of contract; Terms
     of contract of
     employment
   collective
     agreements 20–22
   exclusive service
     contracts.....................................46
   inducing breach of 229, 232
   inventions 38–39
   status of employees 1–4
   transfer of
     undertakings........................146–49
   written statement
     of particulars........................11–16

Contributory negligence 58–59
Control test 4
Course of employment 196
Criminal offences
   fines 64
   health and safety 64
Custom 18, 140–41

Deductions
   from wages 48–51
Definition of
   employees 1–4
Disability
   discrimination...........................209–14
   adjustments,
     duty to make.......................212–13
   Code of Practice 210–11
   definitions 209–12
   Disability Rights
     Commission 214
   dismissal 211–13
   job applicants 210, 213
   mental impairment 209
   past disabilities..............................210
   small businesses 213–14
Disciplinary action
   rule books 218–22
   statutory control over 224–28
   trade unions 218–22
Discrimination
   See Racial
     discrimination;
     Sex discrimination
   age 191
   definition 211
   disability 209–14
   sexual orientation....................207–08
Dishonesty 94, 96,
                           99, 102
Dismissal 78–91
   constructive...............................83–88
   disability
     discrimination.....................211–13

express 78–81
fixed term contracts 81–83
industrial action 254–55
maternity leave,
    failure to
    return from 80–81
notice, with
    or without 78–81
pregnancy 207
resignation....................................67–69
summary 88–91
transfer of
    undertakings..............................158
variation in terms............................81
Duress
economic 240
industrial action 240
termination by 72–73
Duty of care
employers' duties....................26–28
health and safety 53–55
negligence 26–27
references....................................27–28
transfer of
    undertakings.............................149

Economic duress 240
Economic reality test 5
Employees
See, also, Status of
    employees
account, duty to 35, 241
adaptation to
    new methods 30
confidentiality...........................33–34
definition 1–4
disclosure of own
    and colleagues'
    misdeeds 31–32
duties 29–39
fidelity, duty of 32–33
health and safety 63
inventions 35–39
orders, duty to obey 29–30

reasonable care,
    duty to exercise 30–31
test 4–11
Employers' duties
closed shops 24
duty of care 26–28
health and safety 59–62
negligence 26–27
references.....................................27–28
rights, bringing
    employees'
    attention to 25–26
terms of contracts
    of employment 22–28
trust and confidence,
    duty of mutual 25
wages 22–23
work, providing 23–24
working time 26–27
Employment agencies 10
Employment contracts
See Contracts of
    employment
Equal pay......................................161–82
areas of comparison...............178–80
associated employers..............178–80
collective bargaining 174
comparators 168, 172–73,
                                    175, 179
emanations of
    the State 164
equal value.............................167–70,
                                    173–74,
                                176, 178–79
equal work 164–65
equality clauses 17, 168,
                                    170, 181
European Union 163–65,
                                    181–82
experts 170
genuine material
    differences 170–78
job evaluation
    schemes 167

20

justification 172–73,
    175–77
like work 165–66, 169
market forces 175–76
maternity pay 181
part time
    employment 171–72
'pay', meaning of 180–81
pensions...................................180–81
procedure 169–70
red-circling 177–78
redundancy
    payments...................................180
remedies 181–82
severance pay 177
sex discrimination 171–77,
    181–82
transparency 172
work rated
    as equivalent......................167, 169
Equal treatment 202–07
Equipment..58
Ethnic groups 186
European Union
equal pay 163–65,
    181–82
equal treatment........................202–07
pensions..181
redundancy 135
sex discrimination 202–07
sexual harassment 184–85
sexual orientation..........................207
status of employees 4
transfer of
    undertakings 144–45,
    147–49,
    154–59
working time 65
Exclusive service
contracts...46
Express terms 17

Fairness of dismissals 97–114
Fidelity, duty of 32–33

Fines 64
Fixed term contracts
continuity of
    employment 139, 141
dismissal 81–83
notice 82
Frustration
illness 73–76
imprisonment 76–78
termination of
    employment 73–78

Gender reassignment..................207–08

Harassment 184–85
Health and safety 53–65
civil liability 64
contributory
    negligence 58–59
criminal offences 64
danger, power to
    deal with imminent 64
duty of care 53–55
employees
    charges levied
        against 63
    duties 63
employers' duties......................59–62
equipment 58
fines 64
improvement
    notices 63
independent
    contractors..............................61–62
interference or
    misuse of property.....................63
manufacturers.................................62
misconduct 54
negligence 53–59
practical jokes 54
prohibition notices 63–64
psychiatric harm.......................54–55
reasonably
    practicable 60–61

repetitive strain
  injury 57
safe system of work........................53
self-employment.......................61–62
standard of care 55–58
stress...55
third parties.............................61–62
vicarious liability 59
volenti non fit injuria 59
working time 65
Homosexuals 207–08
Homeworkers...3
Hours of work
See Working time

Illness
  capability 106–09
  frustration 73–76
  pregnancy 205–06
  termination of
    contract 73–76
  time limits 118
  unfair dismissal 106–09
  work causing 76
Immunities of
  trade unions 241–55
  ballots...246–54
  contemplation or
    furtherance of
    trade dispute.......................241–42
  loss of...246–55
  political action 243–46
  recognition 255
  secondary action 242, 255
  trade disputes.........................242–46
Implied terms 17–22
  Codes of Practice 18–19
  collective
    agreements 19–22
  constructive
    dismissal 84–85
  courts, by....................................17–18
  custom, by...18

place of work 120
redundancy....................................120
transfer of
  undertakings.............................149
works rules 18–19
Imprisonment,
  frustration by 76–78
Improvement notices..........................63
Independent contractors
  casual workers 8
  control test...4
  description given
    by worker 8–9
  economic reality test 5
  health and safety 61–62
  multiple test 6
  mutual
    obligations test 7–8
  organisation test............................4–5
  question of
    fact or law 9–11
  status of employees 4–11
Inducing breach
  of contract
  actual breach
    of contract 232–33
  civil liability 229–33
  inducing breach
    of contract 229–33
  industrial action 229–33
  justification 233
  intention to break
    the contract 230–31
  knowledge of
    the contract 230
  recklessness....................................231
Inducing breach of
  an equitable
  obligation...241
Industrial action 229–55
  See, also, Immunities
    of trade unions;
    Strikes

breach of
   statutory duty 238–40
   civil liability 229–33
   conspiracy to injure 236–38
   dismissal 254–55
   economic duress............................240
   economic torts 229–35
   inducing breach
     of contract 229–33
   inducing breach
     of equitable
     obligation...................................241
   interference with
     contract, trade
     or business...........................233–35
   intimidation 235–36
   notice 251–54
   secondary 242, 255
   unofficial 254–55
Inequality of
   bargaining power...........................46
Insolvency 136
Instructions, duty
   to obey 29–30,
              88–90, 99–100
Interference with
   contract, trade
   or business............................233–35
Intimidation 235–36
Inventions 35–39

Job applicants 187, 192,
                210, 213
Jurisdiction of the
   court, ousting the 219–20

Limitation periods
   See Time limits
Lock-outs...142

Manufacturers 62
Marital status 183–84
Maternity leave...........................80–81
Maternity pay 181
Mental impairment 209
Minimum wage 52
Misconduct
   health and safety 54
   reasonable
     suspicion 98
   redundancy...............................128–29
   summary dismissal 90–91
   unfair dismissal 94, 96–106
Mobility clauses 190
Multiple test 6
Mutual obligations
   test 7–8

National Minimum
   Wage.....................................52
Natural justice
   rule books 222–24
   trade unions 222–24
   unfair dismissal 104–06
Negligence
   advice...117
   contributory 58–59
   duty of care 26–27
   employers' duties....................26–27
   health and safety 53–59
   professional 117
   time limits 117
   working time 26–27
Notice
   ballots...247
   dismissal 78–81
   fixed term
     contracts.......................................82
   improvement 63
   industrial action 251–54
   prohibition......................................63
   wages in lieu of 49

Orders, duty to obey....................29–30,
88–90,
99–100
Organisation test 4–5
Ousting the jurisdiction
of the court 219–20

Part time workers
equal pay.................................171–72
sex discrimination 188
Payment
See Equal pay;
Remuneration
Pensions....................................180–81
Practical jokes 54
Pregnancy
dismissal 207
illness 205–06
maternity leave.........................80–81
maternity pay 181
sex discrimination 204–07
Procedural unfairness 104–06
Prohibition notices........................63–64
Psychiatric harm...........................54–55

Racial discrimination 185–87,
192–202
age limits 191
assaults...197
compensation 201–02
course of
employment 196
detriments..............................192, 196
ethnic groups 186–87
exceptions 193–95
genuine occupational
qualifications......................193–95
indirect....................................191, 202
injury to feelings 92
insults...............................192, 195–96
intention 202
job applicants 187, 192
less favourable
treatment 187

personal services 194
procedure 198–200
proof.......................................198–200
racial groups 191
remedies 200–02
terms of contracts.........................182
third parties............................195–97
vicarious liability 195–97
Reasonableness
alternative
employment,
offers of 130
misconduct,
suspicion of.................................98
redundancy............................110, 111,
113–14, 130
time limits 115–16
trade unions 217
unfair dismissal.......................94–95,
99–100,
103–04
Redundancy 119–36
alternative
employment,
offers of 129–31
consultation 109–12,
133–36
continuity of
employment 141
definition 119–27
employees
representatives 133–35
who cannot claim................127–28
equal pay.......................................180
European Union......................135–36
implied terms 120
insolvency 136
misconduct 128–29
need for 119–20
payments,
right to claim........................127–29
place of employment..............120–21
procedure 131–36

guidelines 131–32
individuals,
   in relation to 131
reasonableness 110, 111,
   113–14, 130
re-organisation 110, 112–14,
   124–25
requirements of
   business 121–27
resignation...............................68–69
sex discrimination 173
some other
   substantial reason................112–14
special circumstances
   defence...................................136–37
strikes.......................................128–29
trade unions,
   consultation with 133–36
trial periods.............................130–31
unfair dismissal 109–14
References 27–28
Remuneration
   See Equal pay; Wages
Re-organisation
   constructive
      dismissal 86–87
   redundancy 110, 112–14,
   124–25
Repudiation
   constructive
      dismissal 85–88
   instructions,
      refusal to obey 88–90
   summary dismissal 88–90
Resignation
   constructive..............................70–71
   dismissal 67–69
   intention 69–70
   redundancy................................68–69
   termination of
      employment 67–71

Restraint of trade 42–47
   attempts to prevent
      claims that clauses
      are unlawful 47
   bargaining power,
      inequality of 46
   enforcement 47
   exclusive service
      contracts......................................46
   geographical 44–45
   non-solicitation
      by agreement 45
   restrictive covenants 42
   severance..46
   trade secrets 42
   transfer of
      undertakings.......................150–51
   unlawful 47
Restrictive covenants.........................42
Retirement
   age 203–04
   voluntary...72
Rule books....................................217–24

Safe system of work...........................53
Seasonal work...................................140
Secondary action 242, 255
Self-employment
   employment
      agencies 10
   health and safety 61–62
Severance...................................46, 177
Sex discrimination
   but for test 184, 205
   collective
      agreements 174
   compensation 202
   continuity of
      employment 189
   detriment...........................190, 206
   direct 183–84

disproportionate
  impact 188–90
equal pay 171–77,
  181–82
European Union 202–07
gender reassignment 208
genuine occupational
  qualifications...........................194
harassment 184–85
indirect 171, 174,
  187–90
intention 197
justification 189
less favourable
  treatment 183–85
marital status 183
maternity pay 181
mobility clauses 190
part time
  employment 188
pregnancy 204–07
procedure 197
proof...197
redundancy..................................173
retirement age.........................203–04
stereotyping 185
terms of contracts......................182
unfair dismissal 173
uniforms 185
Sexual harassment 184–85
Sexual orientation 207–08
Sickness
  See Illness
Small businesses.........................213–14
Standard of care 55–58
Statement of
  particulars 11–16
Status of employees....................1–16
  agency workers 3
  contracts of
    employment 1–4
  employees 1–11
  European Union 4
  homeworkers 3

independent
  contractors.............................4–11
statutory definitions 1–4
statutory sick pay.............................2
tests..4–11
'workers' 1–4
written statement
  of particulars 11–16
Statutory sick pay 2
Stereotyping 185
Stress 55
Strikes 221–22,
  246–55
  See, also, Industrial
    action ballots
  continuity of
    employment 142
  inducing.....................................232
  redundancy 128–29
  trade unions 221–22, 226
Summary dismissal 88–91

Termination of contract...............67–91
  See, also, Dismissal;
    Unfair dismissal
  agreement, by 71–73
  dismissal, not
    involving 67–78
  duress...72–73
  frustration
    illness, by...............................73–76
    imprisonment, by.................76–78
  illness 73–76
  imprisonment 76–78
  resignation...............................67–71
  severance 177
  unilateral 69
  unpaid leave 70–72
  voluntary
    retirement 72
Terms of contract
  of employment 17–52
  employees' duties 29–39
  employers' duties....................22–28

equality clauses 17, 168,
170, 181
express terms 17
implied terms 17–22
racial discrimination 182
restraint of trade......................42–47
sex discrimination 182
trust and confidence,
duty of mutual 39–41
variation 47, 81
wages, payment of...................48–52
Time limits
illness 118
incorrect advice........................116–17
negligence 117
presumptions 118
reasonableness 115–16
unfair dismissal 114–18
Trade secrets 42
Trade unions 215–28
See, also, Industrial
action; Immunities of
trade unions
ballots 221–22,
246–55
bias 222–23
bylaw theory...............................217
closed shops 24
common law 215–17
disciplinary action 218–22
statutory control
over 224–28
enforcing
membership of 254
exclusions 227–28
expulsion 216, 217,
226–28
members' rights 215–28
natural justice 222–24
ousting the jurisdiction
of the court 219–20
reasonableness 217
recognition 255

redundancy,
consultation on 133–36
right to work............................215–17
rule books 217–24
disciplinary action 218–22
enforcement of 217–22
natural justice 222–24
strikes................................221–22, 226
transfer of
undertakings..............................159
Transfer of
undertakings............................143–60
common law 143–44
compensation 160
consultation...............................158–60
continuity of
employment 141, 145
contracting out 153–58
contracts of
employment 146–49
dismissal 158
duty of care 149
economic activity 145
economic, technical
or organisational
reason............................147, 151–52
employee
representatives 159
European Union 144–45,
147–49, 154–59
going concern 145
implied terms 149
non-commercial
organisations.............................144
relevant transfers 144–46, 159
restraint of trade....................150–51
time of employment
for application of
regulations............................149–50
trade unions 159
variation..158
Transsexuals 207–08
Trial periods 130–31

Trust and confidence,
mutual duty of
  constructive dismissal 85–86
  employees' duties 39–41
  employers' duties...........................25

Unfair dismissal 79–80,
                             93–118
  absenteeism...............................94–95
  capability 96, 97,
                             106–09
  dishonesty 94, 96,
                           99, 102
  fairness.....................................97–114
  heat of the moment,
    language used in 79–80
  illness 106–09
  misconduct 94, 96–106
  natural justice,
    breach of 104–06
  orders, refusal
    to obey 99–100
  procedural
    unfairness 104–06
  reasonableness........................94–95,
                99–100, 103–04
  reasons for...................................93–97
  redundancy.............................109–14
  sex discrimination 173
  time limits 114–18
  warnings 103–04
Uniforms 185
Unpaid leave.................................70–72

Variation
  constructive
    dismissal 87
  dismissal 81
  terms of contracts
    of employment 47, 81
  transfer of
    undertakings.............................158

unilateral 81
written statement
  of particulars...............................14
Vicarious liability
course of
  employment 196
  health and safety 59
  racial discrimination 195–97
Volenti non fit injuria............................59
Voluntary retirement 72

Wages
See, also, Equal pay
  deductions...................................48–51
  definition 49–50
  employees' duties 48–52
  employers' duties.....................22–23
  itemised pay
    statements 58
  maternity pay 181
National
  Minimum Wage 52
  notice, in lieu of 49
Warnings 103–04
Work, duty to provide.................23–24
Work rules....................................18–19
Workers, definition of 1–4
Working time
  employers' duties.....................26–27
  European Union..............................65
  health and safety 65
  negligence 26–27
Written statement
  of particulars...............................11–16
  collective agreements 14
  enforcement 16
  power to require
    particulars of
    further matters 14–16
  reasonably accessible
    document....................................14
  variation...14